THE
CHINA
BUSINESS
CONUNDRUM

THE
CHINA
BUSINESS
CONUNDRUM

ENSURE THAT "WIN-WIN"
DOESN'T MEAN WESTERN
COMPANIES LOSE TWICE

KENNETH WILCOX

WILEY

Published by John Wiley & Sons, Inc., Hoboken, New Jersey.
Published simultaneously in Canada.

For general information on our other products and services or for technical support, please contact our Customer Care Department within the United States at (800) 762-2974, outside the United States at (317) 572-3993 or fax (317) 572-4002.

Wiley also publishes its books in a variety of electronic formats. Some content that appears in print may not be available in electronic formats. For more information about Wiley products, visit our web site at www.wiley.com.

Library of Congress Cataloging-in-Publication Data

Names: Wilcox, Kenneth (Former chief executive officer of Silicon Valley Bank),
    author.
Title: The China business conundrum : ensure that "win-win" doesn't mean
    western companies lose twice / Kenneth Wilcox.
Description: Hoboken, New Jersey : Wiley, [2025] | Includes bibliographical
    references and index.
Identifiers: LCCN 2024026891 (print) | LCCN 2024026892 (ebook) | ISBN
    9781394294169 (hardback) | ISBN 9781394294176 (adobe pdf) | ISBN
    9781394294183 (epub)
Subjects: LCSH: Silicon Valley Bank. | Banks and banking—China. | Business
    ethics—China.
Classification: LCC HG3334 .W54 2025 (print) | LCC HG3334 (ebook) | DDC
    332.10951—dc23/eng/20240719
LC record available at https://lccn.loc.gov/2024026891
LC ebook record available at https://lccn.loc.gov/2024026892

Cover Design: Jon Boylan
Cover Image: © ishpoka/Shutterstock

SKY10085690_092324

To Ruth Wilcox
Thank you for the adventures so far
and all the ones to come.

CONTENTS

Contents

ACKNOWLEDGMENTS

A writer friend told me that the problem with acknowledgments is that one is sure to forget some member of the throng of individuals who have supported a project like this book, which took almost a decade to create. So it is with great humility that I undertake the happy task of acknowledging people who contributed to this effort, and hope devoutly for the forgiveness of anyone I've inadvertently omitted.

First, of course, I want to acknowledge my wife and companion in adventure, Ruth Wilcox. Without her encouragement and company, there would be no book because we'd never have gone to China. Her patience, intelligence, quick eye, and joy added enormously to my insight and fun.

I also want to thank Ann Leamon, who worked with me to revise the book from its original diary form to a narrative describing the "thrills and chills" of our adventure. I still think she used too many endnotes. And many thanks to Felda Hardymon, venture capitalist and networker extraordinaire, who thought to introduce Ann, a poet, novelist, and former HBS case writer, to me, a banker undergoing his fourth reinvention, this time as an author. Indeed, it was a meeting of minds.

My sincere thanks to three people who provided critical information to revise or enhance my initial suspicions about working in China and who helped with earlier versions of the book. David Barboza of *The Wire*, John Pomfret, and Dana Pomfret, you positioned the document for its liftoff, and I sincerely appreciate all your work.

I send my warmest thanks and gratitude to all my colleagues at SVB and SSVB who have taught me so much, even when we disagreed. Looking at the bank's disintegration in 2023, we're all deeply sad. We never meant for it to end that way.

To all the delightful people I met in China, who shared with me their stories and dreams, my deepest appreciation. I hope I have not hurt your feelings.

And finally, I thank my early readers. Those who read the first version created the chorus that said, "This is great, Ken, but it needs a major rewrite." As with many important pieces of advice, it was what I needed to hear, although not welcome news. Thank you to Pete Hart, Arman Zand, Michael Dunne, Chris Hunt, Coco Kee, Dennis Ziegler, Wes Okumura, Tim Hardin, and Ken Dewoskin for your perceptive feedback and clear insights. My second readers gave me further encouragement to move this project forward—thank you to David Barboza, Felda Hardymon, Jim McGregor, Ken Dewoskin (a second time!), Orville Schell, and Victor Wang. This book is so much better due to your comments.

ABOUT
THE AUTHOR

Ken Wilcox spent 30 years with Silicon Valley Bank (SVB). Between 2001 and 2010, he served as its CEO and then, rather than retiring, moved to Shanghai where he lived for four years establishing SVB's Chinese joint-venture operation (SPD SVB). He concluded his banking career in 2019 holding positions as vice chairman of the joint venture and chairman of SVB.

Along with serving as Chief Credit Officer for Columbia Lake Partners, a UK-based venture debt fund, Ken is now involved with a number of boards and has written several books. His book about leadership, *Leading Through Culture* (Waterside, 2021) and its accompanying workbook, *How About You?* (Waterside, 2023), were well-received. He has given more than 50 speeches, mostly about leadership, for audiences around the world.

Ken's experience includes seven years on the board of the San Francisco branch of the Federal Reserve, which afforded him a front row seat during the global financial crisis of 2008. He has received numerous honors and awards, including the Magnolia Award, Banker of the Year, Entrepreneur of the Year, and Yangpu District Innovation Award.

Prior to his business career, Ken taught German at the college level and wrote several books and articles on aspects of that language. He holds an MBA from Harvard Business School, a PhD in German Studies from Ohio State University, and a BA from Oakland University.

ACRONYMS

CBRC: China Banking Regulatory Commission

CCP: Chinese Communist Party

CSRC: China Securities Regulatory Commission

Fed (the Fed): The Federal Reserve Bank of the United States, the U.S. bank regulator

FTZ: Free Trade Zone

JV: Joint venture

JV Bank: The joint venture bank (SSVB/SPD SVB)

PLA: People's Liberation Army (Chinese national army). Also known as the Red Army.

RMB: Renminbi (also known as Yuan); local Chinese currency

SAFE: State Administration of Foreign Exchange

SOE: State Owned Enterprise

SPDB: Shanghai Pudong Development Bank

SPD SVB: Shanghai Pudong Development Silicon Valley Bank (the JV, name preferred by SPDB)

SSVB: Shanghai Silicon Valley Bank (the JV, name preferred by SVB)

SVB: Silicon Valley Bank

WOFE: Wholly Owned Foreign Enterprise (offshore shells for Chinese companies to allow them to raise foreign currency, usually U.S. dollars)

INTRODUCTION

This is a story about my experience setting up a joint venture bank lending to high-tech start-ups in China. The U.S. bank in the partnership, the bank I'd led for 10 years (to 2011) and was employed by, in total, for 30, was Silicon Valley Bank (SVB)—at the time, the world's largest lender to technology companies. These points would not require elaboration except that as I was wrapping up this volume, SVB collapsed. Its demise stemmed from dynamics set in place long after the events we discuss here and have nothing to do with the Chinese joint venture. On the other hand, you might say this book chronicles SVB's first failure.

This book recounts actual events as truthfully as possible, based on my own records and notes. Some names and details have been changed.

PROLOGUE: THE GREEN HAT AWARD

In 2008, I was invited to attend a celebration in Shanghai at the Crown Royal Hotel. As the CEO of Silicon Valley Bank, the California-based bank that led the world in funding venture capital firms and start-up companies, I was spending a lot of time in China at that point, trying to establish a branch there. We had operations in the other international innovation hotspots—London, Israel, and India—and China's explosive growth in that area was attracting our venture capital clients who wanted one-stop banking services. The invitation came from Lao Ding, the Party Secretary and head of Shanghai's Yangpu District, who was helping us get the necessary banking licenses. Without knowing what to expect, I cleared my schedule and flew the 16 hours from California to China explicitly to attend this event honoring "innovation advisors." Bleary and jet-lagged, I found myself in a ballroom with 300 government officials.

In the middle of the ceremony, a high-ranking government official called me up to the stage. To my astonishment, I learned I'd been nominated as one of the 10 honorees. I racked my brain, trying to figure out what I'd done to be qualified as an innovation advisor at such a lofty level. Finally, with the help of Lao Ding, it became apparent: my staff and I had unintentionally taught his team our business model. During the many months when we had detailed the model with great precision to Lao Ding's team so they could explain it to the government agency that might grant us a license, we'd been involved in a form of inadvertent (at least on our part) "technology transfer."

It was only years later that I understood the whole picture. To see if our business model really worked as described, Lao Ding had transferred his CFO to the Shanghai Rural Commercial Bank where he set up a tech lending team and tested the model in the real world. In essence, I was being honored in front of hundreds of people for (from my point of view) having been snookered. Looking back, I felt like someone had just seduced my wife and then held an awards banquet to compliment me in public for having such good taste to marry her in the first place.

In China, men avoid wearing green hats. Superstition has it that wearing a green hat indicates you've been cuckolded. I firmly believe this award should be called the "Green Hat Prize."

But in my defense, this sort of tech transfer was inevitable. It was how China did things. If we hadn't participated, it's unlikely we would have ever been able to set up an operation in China. Of course, in retrospect, one might wonder if that would have been a bad thing. But at the time, we felt we had no choice.

WHY I WROTE THIS BOOK

In this book, I tell the story of establishing a division of Silicon Valley Bank (SVB)—*my* bank, the bank I ran for 25% of its history—in China, and what went wrong. Because a lot of things went wrong, not least the inadvertent tech transfer that qualified me as an "innovation advisor." Some of the missteps were due to my ineptitude and naiveté, but much came from cultural misunderstandings, even as I had four of the most amazing, informative, joyous, and challenging years of my life. I'd like to spare my readers the pain of my misunderstandings and missteps while allowing them the joy and discovery of those four years of cultural immersion.

This story primarily occurs between 2011 and 2015, predating the failure of the entire bank in 2023. In the Epilogue, I describe my perspective about the bank's collapse. I remain committed to SVB's original vision and to the work it did to support innovation. Its demise grieves me deeply. But that's not the story I'm telling here.

Countless Westerners have had experiences in China like those I describe in this book. Unsatisfying, confusing, and frustrating experiences. But they seldom admit it. They're afraid of disappointing their boards and engendering retaliation from the Chinese Communist Party (CCP). If they're critical, they worry that the CCP will find some way to punish the company they went there to build (assuming it still exists). Possibly, their egos won't let them admit that they've been taken for a ride. And perhaps, in some cases, China is still milking them for knowledge, and for that reason treats them well. Their time will come.

This reluctance to share our failures makes it difficult for Westerners to learn from others' mistakes. As a result, everybody must reinvent the wheel. Western companies as a group could perform better, I believe, if they were more inclined to talk with others about what worked well in China—and what didn't. Collectively, we could make more progress more quickly.

As an example, I have kept careful note of the roughly 150 books I've read that would have been useful in my China journey—and as of late 2022, found only six with this type of unvarnished assessment of business experience.[1] Discussions of this sort, sharing mistakes and successes and refining strategy, definitely take place in China, due to a higher level of cooperation among executives. As a result, Chinese businesses know a lot more about succeeding in America than Americans know about how to succeed in China. I'm hoping this book will help boost some of my colleagues up the learning curve.

Everyone, especially lately, has an opinion about China. Some people seem like "China-bashers" and some people seem like "panda-huggers." Cynics and romantics. Of course, in my own mind, I am neither, but a realist—smack-dab in the middle.

I believe that the West needs to move to the middle of the spectrum in terms of interacting with China. *Now* is the time for realism. Enough of the gratuitous China-bashing, enough of the sentimental panda-hugging. It's time for the West to face the facts objectively and to learn how to deal with them. "Seek truth from facts," said Chinese leader Deng Xiaoping 40 years ago. Today, in the 2020s, we should do so as well.

Since Deng "opened up" China to Western business in the early 1980s, thousands of American companies, enticed by the prospect of gaining a putative billion customers, have sought to establish operations there. Many have failed and many others are in the long, slow process of eventually failing. Many who will eventually fail are not yet even aware of the fact that over the long haul, they cannot win. The obstacles are formidable. Chinese culture is completely foreign to Westerners, resulting in chasms that are difficult to bridge. Chinese business practices are opaque and, to the extent that we come to understand them, it is hard for us to adapt. The Chinese economy is structured differently from that of almost any other country, making it often impossible to replicate our business models there. Largely due to the CCP's incessant propaganda, many Chinese people are highly nationalistic, to the extent that they don't really want foreign companies playing a role in their economy. The current level of nationalistic fervor has been created and is being manipulated by the CCP for its own ends. The CCP only wants you to come, teach China everything you know, and then leave again, never to return.

Today, fewer Western companies go to China than was true 10 years ago, because the relationship between our respective governments has soured.

Even if it improves over the next few years, Western companies that consider entering China should still be wary. The way that the Chinese government treats Western companies is not likely to change, due both to the CCP's overall gameplan and to Chinese culture as it is described here.

In this book, I relate both my experience in setting up a bank focused on lending to technology start-ups in China and what I learned about business and life there. I was both well-prepared, having studied Chinese diligently for the year before, and as ill-prepared as every other Western CEO. I was, however, determined to make a systematic and, to the best of my ability, thorough study of the country and its people.

HOW I STRUCTURED THIS ACCOUNT AND GATHERED MY INFORMATION

A note on the structure of this book: The first half is a narrative account of my four years in China as I tried, in partnership with the CCP, to build a bank that would finance technology companies. The latter half is all about what I learned in that process. The emphasis is on the CCP, the Chinese government, and Chinese culture, and how all three have worked together to create the economic miracle of the past 45 years. In this section, I try to advise those who wish to take their business models to China how to deal successfully with this trio—the CCP, the Chinese government, and Chinese culture—to the extent that it is even possible.

You could, of course, skip the first half and go directly to the second. However, I would not recommend it. Understanding China requires on-the-ground experience and plenty of time. You cannot peel back the myriad layers of the onion in a single day. That effort can take years of trial and error. I think you will get the most out of this book by reading about my four years of trial and error. Vicariously experiencing those four years with me will make it easier to understand the conclusions and recommendations in the latter half of the book. Most books tell you *what* to do, if anything. I think you will benefit from reading what *not* to do as well. China is so complicated and so different that the potential for misinterpretation and misunderstanding is greater than in any other place I have either visited or read about.

In the second half, I'll describe the "theory of China" that I developed through my experience of starting the bank. It is fundamentally composed of two parts:

1. What the 7% of the 1,400,000,000 Chinese residents (roughly 98,000,000 people) who are members of the CCP want to accomplish and how they go about doing that; and
2. How the other 93% see the world and what they believe to be true.

In creating my "theory of China," I did my best to go straight to the source and speak with the largest possible cross-section of Chinese residents I could find. I did a lot of observing, took meticulous notes, and tried to reserve judgment. From time to time, I reviewed my notes and formulated "working hypotheses." Then I would test my hypotheses through further experience on the ground, so to speak, as well as in discussions with both "Old China Hands" (Westerners with extensive experience in China) and Chinese acquaintances of all types.

The time I spent in China, from 2011–2015, was a period of enormous change in that country. Some observers see it as part of the ebb and flow of reform. I see it differently. In keeping with John Garnaut's insightful analysis,[2] I believe my time in China coincided with Xi Jinping's initial moves to implement the Maoist version of Marxism-Stalinism more openly, without concern for how the rest of the world might respond. And I was there as this was first happening.

The most important thing I learned in trying to understand China is the difficulty in shedding preconceived notions, or, colloquially, "jumping over my own shadow." All of us have, in the course of our lives, developed a set of "mental models" that enable us to recognize and interpret things we're experiencing for the first time. By superimposing those mental models on new experiences, we use pattern recognition to understand things more quickly and easily. Otherwise, every time we encountered something new, we'd have to start from scratch.

But suppose those mental models are inadequate and the new things we're experiencing are not just new, but totally different from anything we've ever seen before. Perhaps our previous experience isn't applicable to these new situations. Our mental models may be inadequate precisely because we're applying them to something fundamentally different from anything we've ever encountered. But rather than replace them, we often insist on trying to force our new reality to conform. Which it won't.

For instance, as a young child, a friend moved from Michigan to Florida. Out for a walk, she encountered what she thought was a jump rope—her mental model at work—only to have it slither away, rattling its tail. Clearly, her initial mental model was inadequate! Similarly, one early example of such a disconnect occurred when I learned that the Chinese and U.S. interpretations of the roles of chairman and president differed dramatically. In short, a U.S. chairman manages the board of directors, while the president, often termed CEO, manages the company's strategic direction. In China, the chairman usually plays the role of a president in a U.S. company. Thus, for the first nine months of building the bank, the most senior executive from our joint venture (JV) partner and I—the most senior executive from SVB—both thought we were setting the organization's strategic direction, because he was named chairman and I president. Getting to the bottom of this misunderstanding and then resolving it took the better part of a year.

In China, my wife and I had this experience multiple times. Our mental models were so inapplicable that they had to be held in abeyance. And this is why the Old China Hands, savvy about the ways of the Chinese, often say, "The more time I spend in China, the less I know about it." Welcome to my voyage of discovering—perhaps less about China than about my own ignorance of the place.

NOTES

1. In order of publication: James L. McGregor, *One Billion Customers* (New York: Free Press, 2005); Tim Clissold, *Mr. China* (New York: Harper Collins, 2006); Michael J. Dunn, *American Wheels, Chinese Roads: The Story of General Motors in China* (Hoboken, NJ: Wiley, 2011); Carl E. Walter and Fraser J.T. Howie, *Red Capitalism: The Fragile Financial Foundation of China's Extraordinary Rise* (Hoboken, NJ: John Wiley & Wiley, 2012); Clissold's sequel, *Chinese Rules: Mao's Dog, Deng's Cat, and Five Timeless Lessons from the Front Lines in China* (New York: Harper Collins, 2014); and James Stent, *China's Banking Transformation: The Untold Story* (New York: Oxford University Press, 2017).

2. I discuss Garnaut's perspective at greater length toward the end of the book. For the reader who wishes to skip ahead, I highly recommend his 2017 speech, John Garnaut, "Engineers of the Soul: What Australia Needs to Know About Ideology in Xi Jinping's China" (subsequently reprinted in Bill Bishop's newsletter, *Sinocism*, on January 16, 2019).

PART I

THE LONG LEAD-UP

CHAPTER ONE

SILICON VALLEY BANK GOES TO CHINA

INADVERTENT TECH TRANSFER

I n April 2011, I had just turned 63 and was supposed to retire after a long and successful career at Silicon Valley Bank (SVB), the final decade spent as CEO. Somehow, things turned out a little differently.

The bank was obsessed with succession planning as part of its organizational culture. Shortly after taking the CEO position in April 2001, I'd known that in April 2011 I would say goodbye to my colleagues and start doing the kinds of things people do when they retire: pursue hobbies; get involved with nonprofits; spend more time with my family. But fate had another plan in mind. In April 2011, rather than retiring to tend her garden, my wife, Ruth, and I moved to China. SVB's Board had asked me to found a brand-new bank.

Three questions might arise at this point: Why SVB? Why China? Why me? And a fourth question for me personally: Why did my wife agree?

1.1 WHY SILICON VALLEY BANK? THE BANK FOR INNOVATION

By 2011, when I moved to China, SVB had become known as the Bank for Innovation. It was a uniquely U.S. institution, predicated on funding that uniquely American—but already global—industry, venture capital (VC) firms and the start-ups they backed. As a member of SVB for 30 years, and its leader for a decade, I think of myself as an "SVBer," which is reflected in the language I use. Regardless of its untimely demise, I still feel the same way.

SVB was founded in 1983 by four poker-playing California businessmen who saw the need for a bank to fund start-up companies. At the time, the successes of Tandem Computer, Apple, and Intel had illustrated the possibility of inconceivable success from very humble origins in markets and with products that many people had never imagined.[1] Forty years later, this success is undoubted.

By 2011, SVB had banked such success stories as Amazon, Cisco Systems, Fitbit, and Square. The firm had assets close to $40 billion and offices in six countries, banking 65% of VC-backed technology start-ups globally.[2] Our success was built on our enduring relationships with venture capital firms and our resulting willingness to lend to companies before they had revenue—in contravention to the typical banking model.

SVB's business model was simple to explain but complex to implement. We banked innovation across companies ranging from start-ups through buyouts. We also had a venture capital division, which invested the money it raised from third parties (usually endowments) into private equity funds that we'd worked with for decades. In addition, we offered venture debt to carefully chosen companies, primarily start-ups. While it might seem absurd for a bank to offer debt to a company that might not even have revenues, let alone profits, SVB's approach adjusted for this risk.*

Based on its long history and its ongoing relationships within the VC industry,† SVB had deep knowledge of how the VC firms operated. We made a concerted effort to track the records of their individual partners, focusing on their ability to choose and manage investments. As a result, we could fine-tune the products we provided and the companies we provided them to. This analytical approach reduced our risk, which was critical due to the small margins banks typically earn. SVB bankers developed techniques to assess the creditworthiness of the start-ups we lent to by talking to the venture capitalists and closely monitoring each investee company's spending—easily done, since we typically banked them.[3] The three most important issues were: "Who are the venture capitalists and what are they like?"; "Can we count on the management team to deal with us honorably?"; and "In the event that the company fails, will it have developed intellectual property (IP) that the investors can sell and would those proceeds be enough to pay us back?"

Venture debt has been around for decades and is a helpful instrument for start-ups, their founders, and their venture backers. It's a loan like a regular business loan but its collateral, instead of being the classic "revenues and assets" of typical business lending, is the track record of the

---

* The risk that did in SVB in 2023 was interest rate risk, not the failure of any of its companies.
† Terminology in the VC industry can be confusing. By "venture capital," we mean young, private, fast-growing, and often loss-making companies. We continue to provide banking services to these companies as they go public, but our initial interaction with them stems from a connection made during their venture-backed youth.

company's venture backers and the company's intellectual property. That is, we expected the company to repay us based on the venture funding it received and would raise in the future—thus, to a certain extent, we based the loan on the venture capital firm's record. At worst, if the start-up failed, we had senior rights to its technology, which might be sold to another company to pay back our loan.[4]

As background, a start-up's value increases in discrete jumps as it hits milestones: after years of work, the technology performs as anticipated; the company gets a paying customer or lands an order or surmounts a regulatory hurdle. Achieving such proof points boosts the company's value when it raises more capital.[5] Venture debt extends the business's runway to ensure it reaches a given value-boosting milestone. Raising capital at a higher valuation means the founders and early investors keep a larger share of the company—one share of the company will be worth more than previously. SVB carefully structured the loan to ensure we'd be repaid should the company fail (technically speaking, the bank had seniority), but also took steps to avoid that situation. The company usually received its loan just after it raised capital, which meant it would usually have enough money on hand to pay us back.

Finally, SVB took warrants, the right but not the obligation to buy stock at a set price in the future. In some cases, the warrants would be useless—you don't want to buy the stock of a failed company or even one that's just so-so. Because venture capitalists assume only 30% of their companies (if that many) will succeed, it was inevitable that despite the bank's continuous efforts to hone the model and lend only to the best companies supported by the best VC firms, the portfolio would include some losses.

But when the companies succeeded, the warrants allowed us to buy a certain amount of stock at a discounted price. We then immediately sold the shares. The gains from these transactions generally made up for any losses we suffered in this model. Over its history, Silicon Valley Bank was routinely among the most profitable banks in the United States.

Despite the efforts of other banks to adopt our model, SVB held a leadership position due, in part, to our history. We knew the venture capital landscape and were deeply engaged with many of the best firms, understanding in an intuitive way how they thought about their business. Everything we did, from locating our headquarters in Santa Clara, the heart of Silicon Valley, to our office attire, which was business casual before that became a buzzword, reflected our connection to the innovation industry.

In 2001, when I became the third CEO of SVB, we'd been pursuing the same fundamental strategy since our founding. To our customers, we were "the bank for technology start-ups." Internally, we considered ourselves "the three-legged-stool bank." One-third of our business involved technology start-ups, one-third involved real estate, and one-third involved small businesses. But in our marketing, we emphasized the technology, for two reasons:

- First, serving the needs of tech start-ups made us unique. Virtually all of America's banks finance real estate and small business. But very few of them finance technology start-ups.
- Second, the three elements in combination represented a perfect symbiosis. VC-backed technology start-ups were—on average—cash-rich because they raised money in discrete lumps (termed "rounds") and spent it over two or three years; real estate developers and small business owners were typically cash-poor. In effect, we used the excess cash from the tech start-ups to finance the real estate developers and the small businesses.

As CEO, I wanted to both narrow the focus of the business and expand it. Over the first few years of my tenure, we eliminated all the real estate and small business lending so we could focus on the tech companies. We did this because tech lending was the only part of the market where we could uniquely add value to the customer and leverage the specific advantages of our industry knowledge. Most of the banking industry perceives start-ups as risky, due to their uncertain business prospects. While start-ups *are* risky, our model mitigated this risk, giving us a unique and defensible market position.

The defensibility came from two elements. First, banks that tried to adopt our model usually did it on a small scale. As with any new effort, people would make mistakes and the bank would suffer losses. Given banking's slim margins (according to the Federal Reserve, the industry's average net interest margin between the first quarters of 2009 and 2022 was 2.61%[6]), there was little tolerance for missteps and the project would be quickly shut down.

Second, SVB devoted significant resources to getting to know the individual venture capitalists, both their returns and their character. This deep understanding of the *people* we wanted to work with meant we could anticipate their behavior in challenging situations—and it helped us refine the risk we took. To support the investment in this time-intensive undertaking, we needed to have a big portfolio. In fact, each of our bankers usually served 40 to 50 companies. By comparison, venture capitalists rarely had more than 10 companies in their individual portfolios.

In the mid-2000s, we expanded our tech business in two different ways: We went from dealing only with start-ups to working with tech companies of all sizes. This step itself reduced our risk, because tech companies at different life-stages have very different levels of risk. Consider, for instance, the relative risk of a company developing electric aircraft and Pinterest, a venture-backed company that is now publicly traded. By banking both, we established a much more balanced risk profile.

Then, we expanded our focus from the domestic U.S. market to the entire globe. By 2019, when I fully retired from SVB, it had technology clients of all sizes all over the world. This combination of strategies seemed to work: as of mid-2022, our assets had reached $214.4 billion, putting us into the top 20 banks in the United States in terms of size, and our clients included 50% of U.S.-based VC-backed companies.[7]

Being global is both risky and rare for a bank. Few even make the attempt, but for us it was a necessity, because technology is one of the very few truly global businesses. My philosophy is that you can't be the most cutting-edge business anywhere without being the most cutting-edge everywhere, which is why Apple's iPhone dominates the premium smartphone market. The entire world works off the same global knowledge base, which becomes larger every day as scientists around the planet add to it. And the supply chains that support the manufacture of technology products are both global and highly intertwined.

Our clients, the VC firms that funded innovation, were expanding globally. In the early 2000s, as the VC industry and SVB both reeled from the Nasdaq crash (our stock price fell by 50%), we nonetheless followed our clients who were expanding into India, London, and Israel. In 2005, we followed them to China.

1.2   WHY CHINA?

Early in this millennium, SVB began building its business in Europe and Asia. Our first trips to the People's Republic of China (PRC) were in the year 2000. In fact, I was the featured speaker at the first meetings of both the Shanghai and Beijing chapters of the Chinese Venture Capital Association.

China's innovation industry was hitting the gas. In 2000, China and Hong Kong together were home to a third of all the private equity* capital

---

* A note on terminology: private equity refers to stock that doesn't trade on public markets (that is, the companies are private). Private equity investments range from early-stage technology start-ups, termed venture capital, through medium-sized companies (growth equity) to leveraged buyouts, which are acquisitions of entire companies in transactions that use debt. The term private equity is used, confusingly, to refer both to leveraged buyouts in particular, and to the entire spectrum of investments in private companies (venture capital through buyouts). We use it in its broad meaning here, but most of China's international private equity scene has historically involved early-stage investments, hence the interest of our clients in the region. Leveraged buyouts of large companies would inevitably have shaken up state-owned enterprises, making non-Chinese firms leery of such transactions even if they could get permission, which was extremely unlikely.

under management in Asia ($29.3 billion) and 313 funds, or 22% of the total, most of it in Hong Kong.[8] At that point, China's venture capital industry had raised $2.1 billion and its total private equity pool was $5.2 billion, up 39% from $3.7 billion the year before, due to China's steady 8% growth rate and its accession to the World Trade Organization (WTO). Major investors included corporations (of which a large number were state-owned enterprises, or SOEs), followed by banks and government agencies.

Moreover, the Chinese population, in excess of 1 billion people, was an irresistible lure to any business. Very few nations offer the prospect of building a global company simply by serving domestic demand. China, the United States, the EU, and India come to mind, but few others. And in China, the middle class is the size of the entire U.S. population. Talk to almost any business owner about the Chinese market and they start looking like cartoon characters with dollar signs in their eyes in place of pupils.

Thus, even as the dot-com boom in the United States and Europe imploded, the venture capital industry and our bank were keenly aware of the opportunities across the Pacific. In June 2004, SVB led a six-day trip to China for many of the best-known and most successful venture capital firms in Silicon Valley to give them the lay of the land. The 25 venture capitalists who came represented more than $50 billion under management and participated in 20 meetings with technology companies, regional venture capitalists, private equity firms, local entrepreneurs, and educational and governmental institutions.[9] Virtually every firm represented on that trip established a beachhead in China in the next year or two. In Silicon Valley lore, that trip became legendary.

In December 2005, SVB set up our first Chinese office in Shanghai. Initially, it was difficult to accomplish much. First of all, we had no licenses, so we could only engage in activities that didn't require them, which means . . . almost none. Our Chinese office supported our venture capitalist clients as they invested in Chinese tech start-ups that were owned by off-shore companies (usually located in the Cayman Islands) for the sole purpose of raising money from dollar-denominated funds. These Wholly Owned Foreign Enterprises (WOFEs, pronounced "woof-fees") were a government-sanctioned (or at least ignored) work-around of the ostensible prohibition on domestic Chinese companies receiving U.S. dollar financing.

Before we could move beyond financing WOFEs, we needed a banking license in China. But getting one was not easy. It wasn't like much of the Western world, where as long as you've met the legislative and regulatory requirements and paid the fee, you have a reasonable chance of getting the license. Instead, to get a license to do much of anything in China requires the assistance of one of the myriad government agencies. And these agencies are under no obligation to grant anyone a license to do anything, unless they want to.

And why might they want to? The answer can be summed up in a single word: *guanxi*, which is commonly translated as "mutually beneficial relationship." It's one of those terms that Westerners learn as soon as they arrive in China, and then discourse on *ad nauseum*. But the operational meaning of *guanxi* is actually far more complex than that. Functionally, the term has elements of leverage—that is, mutual obligation—that an outsider would be wise to keep in mind. It involves knowing what your counterparty needs (both personally and professionally, which usually overlap) and advancing their goals with a shared understanding that you will call in the favor at some point. I found that I spent an enormous amount of time building *guanxi* by taking meetings, arranging introductions, and doing other things that appeared to be completely unrelated to the job at hand, but turned out to be essential.

The case of a foreigner trying to get a banking license presented all the challenges of *guanxi*. The benefit to you, the foreigner, is obvious: you want a license. The benefit to the license-granting agency ultimately falls into at least one of three categories—and, at best, into all three:

1. Fundamentally, granting a license to you must be seen as benefiting China, meaning you're bringing something to China that the

country needs. The license grantor may reap some personal gain from their help in getting you the license, but to all appearances, the license must help China succeed.

2. For the specific agency, whatever your license will allow you to do must further the achievement of one of its goals as defined by its key performance indicators (KPIs).

3. And for someone in the agency to take on the task of being your champion in getting the license, your line of business must help *that person* reach their goals as defined in their personal KPIs. Ideally, you'll also be able to help members of your champion's family achieve *their* goals as well. Therefore, you have to develop a "personal" relationship with that individual. This may take several meetings over an extended period. Actually, it may take years.

This is the case of getting a license to do almost anything in China. And this is not what Americans are used to.

In my case, the Chinese government wanted to learn from SVB how to finance the creation and application of technology. That is, the Party wanted us to teach them our secrets for success. And we were willing to do it—to what we hoped would be a minimal extent, just enough that we could get the license.

One may reasonably ask why. There are two answers: one is simple naiveté. We never thought, never even considered, that opening a bank in China would be much different from establishing operations in London, Israel, and Bangalore, all of which we'd done successfully. But the other reason is more fundamental to our business. I believe that even if we *had* known everything that would happen in the process of establishing the bank, we would have still done it. Differently, I'll grant you, but we would have built a bank in China because that's where our customers were going. And if we didn't go with them to China, they'd find someone else to serve them, first in China and then, we feared, in the rest of the world as well.

I call this the "reverse osmosis" theory. When I met the woman who became my wife, I soon learned she loved the symphony. I did not. I feared, though, that if I didn't accompany this beautiful, intelligent woman to the symphony she loved, some other eager young gentleman would fill my place. Therefore, I cultivated an appreciation of music, even if only as a place to take a nap. Similarly, if SVB could not handle the needs of our venture capitalist clients as they expanded into China, they would eventually turn to an organization that could, first in China and then across the globe. If we weren't there, eventually we wouldn't be anywhere.

And as the relationship between SVB and China's government, which we learned later was virtually indistinguishable from the CCP, evolved* we were courted assiduously—with the overblown flattery of a lovestruck swain. Mr. Yu, Party Secretary of Shanghai, whom I met in 2009 as we were still debating whether to build a bank in China, was highly complimentary of SVB. China was building its own innovation space, he told me, and among other things, needed to learn how to finance technology. He— which meant China, a country of 1.3 billion people at the time—had concluded that we, Silicon Valley Bank, *my* bank, was the best in the world at financing technology.

Yu made it very clear that this was no off-the-cuff judgment. His team had searched the globe and determined that we were indeed the best. He even made specific comparisons: we were better than Morgan Stanley or Goldman Sachs, he insisted. He greatly admired us. It would be an honor for China if we would build a bank, especially in Shanghai, the province (city–state) for which he was responsible. He would personally see to it that we'd be welcomed with open arms and that we'd be successful, which, it turned out, was more nuanced than we initially understood. This flattery

---

* Throughout this section of the book, I will refer to the Chinese government as China or the CCP fairly interchangeably. Please be aware that the CCP is not a single or even a consistent actor. It is monolithic with respect to its ideology, but not in terms of the members' immediate goals or how strategy is implemented.

got to the point that it was almost unbelievable—I knew we were good, but we weren't *that* good, although I did enjoy telling Goldman Sachs a few years later that we were deemed better than they.

How could I resist? How could my board resist? Back in Santa Clara, the board decided to commit $100 million to establishing SVB's operations in China. But a fundamental question quickly arose: Who would lead the effort? It needed to be someone with deep knowledge of the SVB model and its culture, someone senior enough to command respect and make decisions, and someone willing to uproot themselves and their family to move to China for a substantial period. In 2010, the board made its decision: it would be me.

1.3   WHY ME?

As I noted earlier, I had long known that I would be retiring in 2011 at the age of 63. I had certainly been looking forward to retirement and the time it offered to immerse myself in subjects I'd been unable to pursue during my career. But in discussions with the board, it became obvious that I was a logical choice to lead SVB into its new beachhead in China.

I was one of the most senior and longest-tenured individuals at a bank known for the long tenures of its staff. Once people settle into SVB, they become absorbed in the multifaceted nature of its business and the constant exposure to innovation. It's a place for people who don't think like stereotypical bankers. Its culture is one of its strengths, and so valuable that I wrote a book about it. Who would be a better standard-bearer of SVB culture than I?

As the soon-to-be-retired CEO of the operation, I possessed both internal knowledge and external prestige. I had spent decades getting things done as the bank survived crises, honed its business model, and expanded internationally. People within the bank and even on the boards of other companies took my calls. My age was an advantage in China, which reveres its seniors. And my title gave me the all-important "face," or standing.

I'd also been the literal face of SVB to China since our initial forays there. I had addressed the inaugural meetings of the Beijing and Shanghai Venture Capital Association meetings. From an organizational perspective, I was the only logical person to lead this effort.

Personally, the project thrilled me. I have always loved reinvention. After earning a PhD in German and landing a tenure track position at University of North Carolina, I had left academia to earn an MBA at Harvard Business School. I had worked at Bank of New England only to reinvent myself as president of SVB's East Coast division. But since moving west, it had been almost a decade since I had reinvented myself. It was time.

But there were other, less lofty reasons for me to lead this effort. I *was* on the verge of retirement. My career prospects would not be resting on the outcome of a risky project, much though I wanted it to succeed. After the China adventure, I could travel, spend time with my family, do all the things I'd planned as I contemplated this next phase of my life. I didn't have to worry about moving a family because both boys were on their own. Ruth, my wife, was as eager for this adventure as I. And I believed in the bank and the critical importance of funding innovation to make the world a better place. In taking this model to China and deploying it to finance Chinese start-ups, I would not only be expanding the bank, but I'd also be supporting innovation, possibly breakthroughs that might save the planet.

Oh, and finally—I was the only person at the bank who wanted to go. Due to spousal obligations or children in school or fear of the unknown, no one else could do it at that time. But Ruth thought it would be a grand adventure. I suppose we had a greater spirit of adventure than the rest of SVB—or maybe the stars were aligned for us in a way that they weren't for anyone else.

A year before we moved, Ruth and I signed up for weekly Mandarin lessons and committed to daily practice sessions. We were to establish SVB in China to bank innovation. Little did we know that it would not be so easy.

Takeaways from the Trenches

- The Chinese market looks tantalizingly attractive, from a distance. But be prepared: even though China's 1.4 billion consumers may want your product, you may need to take a different approach to marketing it in China than you are accustomed to elsewhere.
- You might not even have to look for an entry to China. China may find you before you find it. Researchers in China comb the globe, looking for Western companies that have something China wants. The CCP may come to you with an invitation. This should make you wary.
- The CCP controls China in many ways. Licensing is a primary one. The CCP trades licenses, usually with strings attached, for knowledge. Both possibilities—that China comes to you and that you're allowed into China—are mesmerizing, and both are fraught with risk. You may end up chasing China until it catches you.
- *Guanxi* is all about tit for tat. Usually you will give much more than you will get.

NOTES

1. Felda Hardymon and Ann Leamon, "Silicon Valley Bank," *Harvard Business School Case No. 800-332* (Boston: Harvard Business Press, 2000), 1.
2. Nathaniel Popper, "Silicon Valley Bank Strengthens Its Roots," *New York Times*, April 1, 2015, https://www.nytimes.com/2015/04/02/business/deal book/silicon-valley-bank-strengthens-its-roots.html.
3. Popper, "Silicon Valley Bank Strengthens Its Roots."
4. Hardymon and Leamon, "Silicon Valley Bank," 3.
5. For an accessible source for how venture capital works, see Josh Lerner and Ann Leamon, *Venture Capital, Private Equity, and the Financing of Entrepreneurship*, 2nd ed. (Hoboken, NJ: Wiley, 2023).
6. Federal Reserve Bank of New York, "Quarterly Trends for Consolidated U.S. Banking Organizations First Quarter 2022," https://www.newyorkfed.org/medialibrary/media/research/banking_research/quarterlytrends2022q1.pdf.

7. Silicon Valley Bank, " Facts at a Glance," n.d., https://www.svb.com/newsroom/facts-at-a-glance.

8. AVCA, "The 2002 Guide to Venture Capital in Asia," *Asian Venture Capital Journal* 13th ed., October 2001, 24, as cited in Felda Hardymon, Josh Lerner, and Ann Leamon, "Chengwei Ventures and the hdt* Investment," *Harvard Business School Case No. 802-089* (Boston: Harvard Business Press, 2002), 4.

9. Silicon Valley Bank, "Silicon Valley Bank Leads Delegation of Venture Capitalists on Educational and Networking Trip to Beijing and Shanghai." Press release, June 14, 2004, https://www.svb.com/news/company-news/silicon-valley-bank-leads-delegation-of-venture-capitalists-on-educational-and-networking-trip-to-beijing-and-shanghai.

CHAPTER TWO

IT STARTS WITH *GUANXI*

KISSING FROGS AND FINDING A PRINCE

From the time we set up the Shanghai office in late 2005 until we established the joint venture bank (JV Bank), our predominantly Chinese staff of 12 handled the needs of the WOFEs (Wholly Owned Foreign Enterprises), which were minimal. They also hosted a constant stream of executives from SVB (including myself), who were laying the groundwork to get a license to replicate our bank in China, trying to build relationships with higher-level officials, and courting what appeared to be the most likely joint venture (JV) partner, Shanghai Pudong Development Bank (SPDB).

Indeed, the staff's most consuming project was doing what I called "kissing frogs and looking for the prince." One early interaction that struck me as odd occurred when a member of the staff who had worked with me for years said that a well-connected acquaintance had offered to introduce us to the people who could get us a license—if we paid her $2 million. I declined the offer.

To get our license without such intercession, we first needed enough *guanxi* to interest an agency in working with us. The confusing thing is that it didn't even have to be a financially oriented agency. It could be an agricultural agency as long as someone there had good connections and could get us in front of an appropriate agency. And for that, we needed a sponsor. All of our qualifications and all of our assets couldn't get us a license without that sponsor.

2.1   A PRINCE AT LAST

In 2007, we had our first breakthrough, and it came (of course) through *guanxi*. Our office was in the Shui On Plaza on Huaihai Road (named for the location of one of the decisive battles between the Communist Party and the Nationalist Party in late 1948). Our landlord was Vincent Lo, the Hong Kong real estate developer who'd built the office tower and the surrounding development, known as Xintiandi. In March 2007, Vincent contacted me in California and asked me to join a delegation consisting of himself, Dick Kramlich (co-founder of New Enterprise Associates, or NEA, one of the world's largest and most successful venture capital firms), and a handful of others. Our mission was to tour the Yangtze Delta area, the center of which is Shanghai, to find a cross-border project in which we could all get involved. We would then tout our success, especially to Chinese government officials. The subtext was that Vincent was building his *guanxi* with the CCP, and we had been tapped to assist him.

Vincent, born and raised in Hong Kong, made a lot of money creating novel and extremely attractive real estate developments in China, the best-known of which is Xintiandi. Located at the eastern end of the "former French Concession"[1] in Shanghai, Xintiandi includes retail, gallery, living, office, and green space. Part of the area is done in refurbished, old-style "Shikumen" buildings, the rest in modern, glass-and-steel architecture. As part of the deal, the government gave Vincent an old villa on the edge of Xintiandi, which he converted into a "club." This club was his own private home away from home, where he could hold receptions and dinners for important visitors.

Vincent's accomplishments required immense levels of *guanxi* with the Chinese government. More than once, he invited me to a dinner for government officials in his clubhouse, to be—as I discovered—his foil. At some point in the dinner, Vincent would heap elaborate praise on the one-party system. The denouement to his acclamation was always the same. He would pirouette, point at me, and exclaim: "See, Ken, like I've always said, the one-party system works much better than what you have in the United States." Fortunately, I wasn't expected to respond.

In the course of the 2007 trip around the Yangtze Delta with Vincent and Dick, I met Party Secretary Ding, the head of the Yangpu District of Shanghai. It was "love at first sight" on both sides. He was the most overtly friendly Chinese official I ever met. His first name was not "Lao"—no one goes by their first name in China although some people go by both names—but everyone called him Lao Ding. Lao is an endearment meaning "old." He never greeted me without a big bear hug (very atypical in China; in fact, my Chinese-language textbook included a whole lesson titled "Chinese Don't Like to Hug"). What I didn't know at the time was that the rapidly developing relationship between us was the very definition of *guanxi*, as it was mutually beneficial on multiple dimensions.

First, as we were becoming aware, China was trying to learn how to finance technology ventures and considered our bank the world expert.

Second, one of Lao Ding's KPIs was to turn the Yangpu District, which was a rustbelt of old industry, into a hub of innovation. Not coincidentally, one of Vincent Lo's goals was to build an innovation center in Yangpu. And third, whether I desired it or not, Lao Ding was determined to develop a "personal" relationship with me. Fortunately, he wasn't a heavy drinker, or I might have been subjected to some heavy baijiu sessions to reach the level of *guanxi* he was targeting. (Baijiu is considered China's national drink. It's often made of distilled sorghum, although rice, wheat, barley, or millet can be used, and it has a punishingly high alcohol content. Dan Rather, covering Nixon's trip to China in 1972, described it as "liquid razor blades."[2] The general idea is that if you don't trust someone enough to get stinking drunk with them, you shouldn't be business partners.)

During the next couple of years, our team spent hundreds of hours with Lao Ding and his team helping them understand our business model so that they could do a better job of explaining it to the relevant government officials, whose assistance we would need if we were to obtain a license. Lao Ding needed to be able to explain to them why they should meet with us and how helping us get a banking license could help China. Little did we suspect there might be an ulterior motive.

The relationship with Lao Ding proved fortuitous for SVB. It led to a series of meetings with Vice Mayor Tu, the head of financial services in Shanghai, who later became the head of the China Investment Corporation (CIC), one of the largest sovereign wealth funds in the world. But even more importantly, it led to several meetings with the then-Party Secretary of Shanghai, Yu Zhengsheng,[3] who later became a member of the Standing Committee under PRC President Xi Jinping.

In 2008, a year after I met Lao Ding, one of his lieutenants, the CFO for the Yangpu District, resigned to join the Shanghai Rural Commercial Bank. There he started a technology lending group using the description of our business model we provided Lao Ding's team so they could explain our approach to the government and get us the needed license. The success of this project meant I received the "innovation advisors" award described at the start of this book. We were chagrined, but I doubt SVB would have made any progress in China had we not shared information to that extent. We would have been constrained to working with WOFEs. Yet I'm not sure that would have been the worst thing: the profits from our WOFE operation were not insubstantial. To the extent possible, we tried to pull the WOFEs into the JV bank, but in some cases, it wasn't possible. Like so much else in China, it was complicated.

2.2   REACHING THE KING

For all that I would have preferred *not* to transfer our business model in such a wholesale way, the exchange moved us along our trajectory. In 2009, facilitated by Lao Ding, we had a series of meetings with Party Secretary Yu. We were told that this was a very special honor. Most people did not get to spend time with the Party Secretary. We were special.

And Secretary Yu was going to help us, he promised. Some of the most difficult things for foreigners to deal with in China, he pointed out, were the vast differences in culture between China and the West. It would be easy for a foreign bank to stumble, lose its way, or be taken advantage of by unscrupulous businesspeople. To help us avoid these pitfalls, he recommended (read: *required*) that we have a JV partner. He and his team would find one for us. We needn't worry. He would help.

In my naiveté, I was thrilled. After all these years kissing frogs, we'd finally found a prince (Lao Ding), and he'd led us directly to the king himself (Party Secretary Yu). Obviously, we were pretty good, I mused, or darn lucky . . . or both.

In the following months, under the guidance of Yu, everything began to fall into place. Beijing, the seat of the China Banking Regulatory Commission

(CBRC)—the banking regulator at that time—miraculously began to show interest in granting us a license. Tu Guangshao, the vice mayor in charge of financial services in Shanghai, even traveled to Santa Clara to visit with our management team and increase the *guanxi* between us.

Not long after the vice mayor returned from his trip, we learned that Shanghai Pudong Development Bank (SPDB), Shanghai's largest bank, would be our JV partner. This was the very organization we'd been courting so assiduously. We visited them in China, and in time, they visited us in California. In retrospect, I realized that we had chased them until they caught us. But that understanding was long in the future. We were thrilled to finally be making progress.

While SPDB was the largest bank in Shanghai, it had only started to expand internationally. By the end of 2010, the bank's total assets were RMB 2.19 trillion ($331.7 billion), and its after-tax profit was RMB19.18 billion ($2.9 billion). At the time, it had 36 branches and employed 28,000 people in more than 100 cities across China. It had just opened its first overseas branch, in Hong Kong.[4] Established in 1993, it was originally charged with bankrolling the manufacturing SOEs that sprang up on the eastern side of the Huangpu (literally, Yellow River), across from the financial heart of the city. ("Pudong" literally means "East of the River." One of the small triumphs in my ongoing skirmish with the Chinese language was realizing that the suffix "Dong" meant "east," while "Xi" meant "west." Since the names of many streets and locations employ this directional taxonomy, cracking this linguistic nut helped tremendously to orient myself.)

As Shanghai mirrored China's overall transition from a manufacturing to an innovation economy, SPDB had followed suit. By the mid-2000s, it was focused on funding efforts to attract and support high-tech companies— but only those that the government deemed worthwhile. At the same time, it still funded some of the remaining manufacturing operations in the city-state. In fact, what we failed to fully grasp was right in front of our faces: it was originally *the* bank for developing Shanghai's Pudong district. That is, it was founded solely to support enterprises that would further Pudong's evolution, even though it eventually expanded throughout China.

Note the disconnect: we were Silicon Valley Bank, but even from our founding, we planned to bank organizations beyond Silicon Valley. In China, though, a bank's name defines its original purpose.

Lacking this nuanced understanding, I made a significant blunder as we discussed the name of the bank. I suggested it might be "the Bank for Innovation," and was stunned by the ensuing uproar. I only later realized my gaffe: as the Chinese banking industry was resurrected after Mao destroyed it, specific divisions of the government bank were created to focus on funneling money to different parts of the economy. Along with the Bank of China, there are the Agricultural Bank of China, the China Construction Bank, the Bank of Communications, and the Industrial and Commercial Bank of China. My suggested tag line was interpreted as proposing that we would bank *all* the innovative efforts in the country, a particularly delicate topic since innovation was clearly the next big thing and the Chinese government wanted to decide who banked it. It would be a Chinese bank, of course.

I learned later, from one of China's most experienced senior bankers, that these top five banks—each of which, individually, is bigger than the largest bank in the United States—are in many ways just one bank with five faces. They swap strategies and executives, often at the behest of the Organization Department—a sort of massive, centralized HR department for the CCP, which assigns the millions of Party members to various positions, tracks their progress, and is responsible for a constant revolving door among bureaucrats.

SPDB had other unusual characteristics. It was (to our eyes) vastly overstaffed with individuals who showed no interest in customer service whatsoever. What I soon learned was that this overstaffing was not unique to SPDB—it was the case with all Chinese banks. These high staffing levels led to a lot of "sucking up" among the junior staff who wanted to be promoted. Early in the JV's development, I saw this quality painfully demonstrated at a dinner that included Mr. Luo, SPDB's president, Mr. Xiang, the leader of small business lending at SPDB at the time, and a few of us from the joint venture. About every 10 minutes, Xiang rose from his chair, held up a fresh glass of baijiu, and saluted Luo for his greatness and geniality as the head of SPDB. The compliments were completely over the top: never had there been such a brilliant leader; nor one so handsome or affable. The bizarre interaction continued until Xiang collapsed. Happily, the other guests were not compelled to match him, drink for drink. This was hardly unique to SPDB or to Luo, but completely foreign to us.

Beyond the human resource issue, SPDB's operations were also different from what we were used to. It did very little underwriting. That is, it didn't study a situation and identify the associated risks prior to lending to it. In the Chinese banking world, underwriting is not understood as it is in the West. Fundamentally, banks lend to groups that the government wants them to, which means there is little risk. There is risk management and extensive reporting to the CBRC—on a daily basis, as opposed to the situation in the United States where the Federal Reserve (the Fed) has mandated monthly, quarterly, and annual reports. But the amount of risk taken on by Chinese banks is reflected in their employees' compensation structure. U.S. bank employees are typically compensated through a mix of roughly 80% salary and 20% performance-based bonus. The Fed strenuously objects to a greater bonus share, lest it encourage excessive risk taking. In China, the proportions are reversed. As a result of this incentive scheme, along with the different perspective on risk, Chinese banks take on much more risk than do institutions in the United States. If the banks get into trouble due to bad loans (to the companies the government told them to lend to), the government quietly recapitalizes them. As long as the executives have good *guanxi*, no one goes to jail.

SPDB and our team engaged in long discussions about how we would work together. We both agreed we would think of the new bank as a child, born of the union of the two parents, SPDB and SVB. And as parents, it was our mutual obligation to nourish our child, support it, and provide it with the resources it would need to grow. Above all, neither of us would ever compete against it.

SPDB alleged that it never did and never would engage in servicing tech companies. We'd already been servicing tech companies in China since 2005 through our work with the WOFEs. We agreed to transfer all the business that we legally could from our own offshore business into the new JV bank. Conceptually, SPDB would be getting half of the profits from that offshore business for free, as a sign of our goodwill and commitment.

During these negotiations, we were granted a number of "wins." At the time, I was proudest of our percentage ownership in the new bank. In the past, the CCP had never permitted an American commercial bank to enter into a joint venture with a Chinese commercial bank that involved creating a new commercial bank. In that sense, this was a watershed event.

On occasion, the CCP had allowed American commercial banks to buy into Chinese commercial banks, but their percentage ownership was typically limited to 5%; on rare occasions, 10 or 15%; and the absolute maximum was 20%. We negotiated 50%! We thought we were geniuses.

I came to learn that percentage ownership in China is irrelevant. If you're in China and your joint-venture partner is a Chinese state-owned company, the Chinese government is in control, no matter how much you own.

Unbeknownst to us, a kind of "secret team" (my term, not theirs) had begun to form in Shanghai, operating in the background and coordinating the effort to bring SVB to China. We never saw the team members together; in fact, for a long time we were unaware of the team's existence. We thought we were dealing with random individuals, and that we, ourselves, were the common thread. We thought we were the instigators and were quite proud of ourselves for all we were accomplishing. Later on, the only way to explain certain developments was to assume the existence of the secret team, which had selected us and was ushering us down an ever-narrowing chute—like pigs in a slaughterhouse—to our destiny.

By now it was late 2010 and SVB's board decided we needed to create a true Chinese entity. As described earlier, if we didn't have a viable Chinese presence, someone else, whether a Chinese bank or a Western organization, would be willing to serve our clients, first in China, and then everywhere. And I, with my imminent retirement from the CEO position, my keen interest in the country, and my one year of Mandarin, would lead it. As a result, in April 2011, Ruth and I packed our things and arrived in Shanghai to "birth a bank."

Takeaways from the Trenches

- You will be expected to get rip-roaring drunk to prove that you are trustworthy.
- China is constantly observing and experimenting, to find out if they can replicate what they observe—and what they might be observing (and replicating) is your company's business model. To get a license to do business in China, you may have to describe your business model in great detail, which will facilitate their efforts at replication.
- The CCP will flatter you. Don't believe them. Flattery is manipulation. Subordinates are constantly flattering their superiors. If they tell you that you have cracked the code, you haven't.
- Misrepresentation is an accepted negotiation tool. In negotiations, people will agree to things that they have no intention of doing.
- The percentage ownership in your joint venture that you negotiate is meaningless. It's China. The CCP is in charge.

NOTES

1. A side note about what I mean by "former French Concession": When the Western powers, led by the British, took control of the "treaty ports"—one of which was Shanghai—in the 1840s, they divided the city into a Chinese section, a French section, a British section, and an "international" section, which eventually became the American section. Awareness of these sections has all but disappeared among the local citizenry, except for the French Concession. Locals still refer to the French section as the "French Concession," much to the chagrin of the Shanghai government.

2. Cited in Cici Zhang, "What's Baijiu, and Where Does Its Unique Flavor Come From?" *Chemical and Engineering News*, August 7, 2018, https://cen.acs.org/environment/food-science/What-s-baijiu-and-where-does-its-unique-flavor-come-from/96/i33.

3. I found it interesting that Yu's father had been a former husband of Mao's infamous fourth wife, Jiang Qing, who was a member of the famed Gang of Four; and Yu's brother was one of the highest-ranking defectors in the history of the CCP.

4. Shanghai Pudong Development Bank, "SPDB HK Bank Opens, Marking a Substantial Step Towards the Bank's Go-global Strategy." Press release, June 8, 2011, https://www.acnnewswire.com/press-release/english/6747/spdb-hk-branch-opens,-marking-a-substantial-step-towards-the-bank's-go-global-strategy.

CHAPTER THREE

ORIENTING OURSELVES

THE STAFF, THE TEAMS, AND THE RUNAROUND

Arriving in China is bound to be disorienting for any Westerner. For the first time since, perhaps, first grade, you cannot read. Unlike Russian, where the alphabet has some corresponding letters, written Chinese, like Arabic, is completely incomprehensible to the average American. *Nothing* corresponds. You are illiterate.

And that doesn't change quickly. Ruth and I started our Mandarin lessons a year before we arrived, when we were in our early sixties. We should have started in our teens, at the latest. Mandarin is a very difficult language for most Westerners to learn. Starting the year before we left for China, I studied Mandarin for at least two hours a day, seven days a week, until 2019.

I eventually passed Level 4 of the Chinese government's testing system, the HSK, which determines the language proficiency of foreigners. That meant I had the proficiency level of a 12-year-old. Sort of. I could read and write like a 12-year-old, and I could speak like a 12-year-old—with a severe learning disability. And yet, to this day, I can barely understand what anybody says to me except for my own personal language instructor, with whom I can converse extensively, understanding almost everything.

Even though I'd been to China some 25 times since 2004, often for weeks at a time, actually *living* there was a huge change. After all the excitement of the send-off, I woke up to the realization of what I'd gotten myself into. We weren't going home in a week or two. For a while, we felt like we were all alone in a place that was totally different from what we were familiar with. Which was true. Visiting China and living there are two completely different experiences. Happily, though, we had the staff of the SVB office to help us. And help us they did.

3.1 SETTLING IN: THE LOCAL STAFF

Our initial office was located in a massive glass building in Xintiandi's mixed-use area. This is an extremely vibrant part of the city, near the small amount of "Old Shanghai" that still exists—low, three-story buildings with flat roofs, rather like the row houses of Philadelphia, that share an alley and a small courtyard. Most were a dingy grey. There was a sense of history, accented by the cooking smells as people prepared their meals on charcoal braziers and dried their laundry on long poles stretched from their windows.

Another part of old Shanghai are the lane houses. Ruth became an expert in finding and wandering through these long alleys of tiny dwellings. The lanes ranged in length from one to several city blocks, twisting and turning, with a gate and a guard at either end. Often the kitchen part of the dwelling would be in the alley itself, with the living and sleeping rooms inside.

Our apartment, in a modern, multistory steel-and-glass building, lacked such historic details—probably a good thing, as Ruth and I would have hardly countenanced cooking over charcoal or drying our laundry on poles in the city's progressively more polluted air—but its location, a five-minute walk from Fuxing Park and three blocks from the office, was ideal.

The staff of our local office bent over backwards to welcome us and help us adjust. Due to its allure as a Western bank pursuing an innovative business model, SVB had been able to attract some remarkably talented individuals, including:

- Elwood Dong, the senior employee in charge. A Shanghai native whose parents had brought him to the United States when he was a toddler, he'd gone to Yale and Harvard Business School and worked for years at the Bank of Boston before joining us.
- Ruby and Roger, who came to us from the accounting firm KPMG and handled analytics.
- Serena, our first employee, then the head of client services.
- Kathy, then in client services, eventually head of HR.
- Shirley, in client services.
- Andrea, our "Jill" of all trades (except client services).
- Ming, a Taiwanese woman who'd come to the United States to attend Wellesley. She led our Chinese funds* business at the time.

---

* SVB always had a fund-of-funds business, in which it raised money from investors and invested it in venture capital funds. Because of our long history with these groups, we had access to many top-tier firms from which many other potential investors were excluded. Through Lao Ding, the Yangpu District gave us about $30 million to invest on their behalf in U.S.-based venture funds.

- Michelle, who worked with Ming.
- Daniel, a Chinese American from San Francisco who was doing his best to learn Mandarin and did business development for the WOFEs.
- Oliver, a native of Shanghai and an altogether delightful person. He joined the effort in 2006 and was my all-around support person there, helping me get things done and stay up to date. Once I arrived in 2011, he continued to be invaluable.
- Arman, originally from Iran, a graduate of the Hass Business School at Berkeley, who had worked for us in India, Israel, the UK, and, for the prior three years, in China. His formal title was team leader of banking for start-ups, but in truth, he was one of those amazing people who did whatever needed to be done. He is one of the few people I met who achieved fluency in Mandarin as an adult.
- Tammy, our receptionist.

Of the 13, 12 were Chinese, and most were Shanghainese. At about the same time as I arrived, two other SVBers joined me from California: Tim Hardin, an American who had led both banking and credit for SVB, and Teresa Li. Teresa had been born in Hong Kong but emigrated to Vancouver, Canada, in her teens and ended up at SVB in Silicon Valley. She joined the Shanghai operation to run the banking team that focused on the needs of larger companies.

We also had a driver assigned to us. Our first was Jack, who took us anywhere we wanted to go, and was extremely solicitous. It was rumored that all the drivers were chosen by the government, and their job was to spy on us. While I can neither confirm nor deny this, I can say that we had to fire Jack after a year or so for stopping the car at intersections, getting out and starting fights with other drivers whose driving styles had offended him, as well as for urinating on the side of the street in the middle of the city. These things happened more than once.

Shortly after I arrived, Arman recruited Victor from a global management consulting firm to be my assistant. We really clicked, and I found his advice priceless. Early on, Victor told me that I'd never succeed in China because I tended to say what I meant and mean what I said. This is not the path to success in China, he admonished me. I kept his point in mind, but never could change that aspect of my personality.

Chrystal, my additional assistant, joined a few months after we arrived. A freelance reporter who had focused on Shanghai's entrepreneurial scene, she wanted more stability. Chrystal was an independent thinker and arrived for her interview dressed not to impress but to embody an attitude of fierce independence, along the lines of "Nobody is going to tell me what to wear!" I liked her from the start. She and Victor accompanied me almost everywhere. We were a team. They took turns translating, and afterward they'd join forces to tell me what people really meant. I would recommend this approach to any Westerner, even if they speak Chinese fluently.

While everyone was critical to the success of the operation, the two who most helped Ruth and me get on our feet were Arman and Victor. Not only had Arman recruited Victor and found our apartment, but he'd kept me up-to-date on what was going on in the office and in the market during the weeks leading up to our arrival.

Victor didn't just manage my schedule and translate for me, but he also helped me understand many of the inscrutabilities of doing business in China. An immediate one was my confusion around scheduling meetings with government officials. At SVB, I'd always scheduled meetings—with both employees and people outside the bank—weeks if not months in advance. Now in China, I knew I needed to meet with hosts of government officials and asked Victor to get me on their calendars. I expected a date several weeks, if not months, in the future.

But instead of giving me a date and time, he would tell me that he'd spoken to the official's assistant, who wouldn't be able to even think about scheduling a meeting until the following Monday. The meeting itself, if it took place at all, would be later in the same week. This happened repeatedly. I was baffled and frustrated. "Why?" I asked, exasperated. Victor explained, patiently at first, that everything in China moves from the top down, including calendars, and covers only the next seven days. On Fridays, the highest-level government officials create their calendars for the next week. These calendars are then passed down to the next level, and so on. Each level's calendar determines the parameters of the calendar for the next level down. This chain of information might not reach the level I was targeting until Monday or so. Only then would the person I was targeting know if they could accommodate my request. If they *could*, it would be later in the same week. Otherwise, we'd start the whole process all over again on the following Monday. This scheduling peculiarity added untold weeks and probably months to the process of establishing the bank.

One of the things that astounded me was the amount of paperwork I was expected to do. In my workday, I spent an inordinate amount of time just signing documents. If I had actually read everything I signed, I would have spent all my waking hours reading. Every single circumstance, every single action, required a document, and as the CEO, I had to sign all of them. Even if these documents were signed by the person who personally participated in the situation being documented, I still had to sign them—often in duplicate, sometimes in triplicate. I allocated several hours a week just to signing things I'd only skimmed.

Particularly important documents required "the chops," which are merely stamps with the company's official name. Since antiquity, important documents have required them. The chops used to be made of ivory and still retain semi-sacred status. Accordingly, they were locked in a safe at all times. Only one or two people were allowed to know the combination to the safe, and the chops could only be removed under special circumstances. Victor treated the chops much like a high priest would a sacred relic. I was never even allowed to handle them.

As I waited to get on various functionaries' calendars, I tried to learn as much as I could about this brave new world I'd entered. To that effect, I met with anyone who had an hour for me. In this initial period, I encountered a number of people who were critically important in helping me develop my "hypotheses of China." I discuss some of them, and their contributions, next.

3.2   SETTLING IN: THE LOCAL EXPERTS

The local experts—both Chinese and expats—contributed to our stay in China in two important ways. First, they provided friendship, laughter, and warm, personal engagement. And second, they gave me important material for understanding both the business and cultural environment, contributing greatly to my "theory of China." While this process sounds dangerously close to using my friends as science experiments, nothing could be further from the truth. Virtually everyone I encountered was interesting in their own right. These were the most entertaining years of our lives, filled with joy and discovery and seasoned with a sense of playing for very high stakes in a game where I didn't quite know all the rules. Among these people without whom my experience in China—and our bank's success, such as it was—would have been much diminished were:

> **Mr. Zhang**, who had gotten rich manufacturing consumer goods in low labor-cost areas in western China and selling them to Americans through major retailers like Target. We developed three distinct ties to Zhang.
>
> First, at the recommendation of Lao Ding, we invited him to invest as a limited partner in one of the funds that we created for the Yangpu District. This move had mixed results, we later learned.

Second, we ended up hiring his daughter, Hannah, who became one of our brightest stars.

Third, Zhang took it upon himself to meet with me regularly and give me advice. All his advice fit into one of two categories: how to deal with the CCP, of which he was an active member; and how to comport oneself. The Party, he told me, is like the Mafia, composed of a number of warring families. The first allegiance is to the family, which is viewed very broadly rather like a Scottish clan, and the second is to the CCP.

With respect to comportment, his main point was: "never be vulnerable." Always place yourself either above your enemies (and everybody is a potential enemy) and fake superiority; or place yourself below your enemy and fake deep respect. "However, never mean what you say or say what you mean," he advised me. "If things go well, claim credit, and if they don't, blame others."

James McGregor, the author of *One Billion Customers,* one of the first books on China that I read. The book so fascinated me that I sought Jim out. At the time, he was living in Beijing. Few Westerners have as clear an understanding of how China works as Jim does—in fact, he is one of the most knowledgeable and entertaining of all the Old China Hands I met throughout my journey.

We met for dinner at a terrific restaurant in Beijing known for its classic northern Chinese dishes. This cuisine is somewhat saltier than food in the South and relies more on wheat in the form of dumplings, noodles, buns, and pancakes rather than rice. Afterward, as we walked outside to find our drivers, Jim asked me earnestly, "Who are your friends here in China?"

I paused, thinking about the question. Before I could answer, he stopped me short. "You don't have any friends in China," he said. "Nobody does. Not even Chinese people. Remember that."

His other piece of unforgettable, essential advice was that the CCP responds to only one thing: leverage. At the time, I had no idea how to put this into practice.

Eddie Wang, a member of the board of the only (allegedly) private bank in China, whom I met early in our stay. Eddie was affable and knowledgeable. He advised me for several months until his ethical (or practical, I was never sure) side caused him to resign, citing a "conflict of interest." The most unexpected advice he gave me was: "*xian zhan hou zou*," which means try things out and ask for regulatory permission later (literally, it translates as "execute first and then report to the Emperor" or, with less blood, "act first and ask forgiveness later"). Based on my experiences working with the U.S. Federal Reserve over the years, this advice was entirely unexpected. If you're a commercial bank under the jurisdiction of the Fed, you'd *better* ask for permission first.

Andrew Au, a native of Hong Kong, ran a Western bank in Shanghai. He was kind enough to meet with me almost anytime I asked, providing advice and background. He told me that my driver almost certainly kept track of my conversations and reported them to somebody. Most experienced, knowledgeable Western executives were convinced that they were being watched by somebody—all the time. China has 1.4 billion people, and a propensity for printing money. I accepted this claim as plausible.

Melvin, another of my early acquaintances, ran the Shanghai branch of a Singaporean bank. We spent hours talking about joint ventures between Western and Chinese companies. His theory was that regardless of the details of the agreement between the two parties, neither would relinquish control to the other, so the employees would never be sure in which direction to salute. As a result, things would not get done.

Robert Griffiths, the consul general in Shanghai at the time, predicted in private that our JV bank would be successful, but not tremendously so. Based on his long experience in China, he believed the CCP would like us to succeed for as long as it took them to learn everything they could from us. Thereafter, he forecast, they would reduce their support, and we would gradually lose ground until we gave up.

Tommy Chen, a Hong Kong native, showed up in my life even before we moved to China. Tommy is one of the best-informed and most affable people I've ever met. Over the course of our many conversations, he provided me with extensive information for my long string of working hypotheses on China. Among other things, he explained that the five largest banks in China are really all the same bank, controlled by the Chinese government (and by definition, the CCP). While most have sold some stock to Western entities, they only did so to obtain additional equity without relinquishing control. Fundamentally one bank with five names, they share strategies and swap CEOs at the whim of the Organization Department, the central CCP HR department.

The Xues, friends of Lao Ding. Shortly after our arrival in Shanghai, we met the Xues. Both of their last names were Xue, but each of these two Xues was written with a different character. The fact that they were married to each other is pure coincidence. Mr. Xue was the president of one of the many subsidiaries of China Everbright Bank, a state-owned (all banks in China are state-controlled) financial services conglomerate and Mrs. Xue was a government official who worked in the Shanghai Financial Services Bureau. Her specific job was collecting information on all the companies in Shanghai and compiling a list of "Little Giants" (companies that her office predicted would do well if properly supported by the government) and arranging to provide them the requisite support. Our meeting was no accident. Both had an agenda.

Lao Ding (of course) made the introduction, inviting Ruth and me to lunch at the private Key Club to meet these "good friends" of his. Over time, I, too, became a member of the Key Club. But on that first visit, we arrived 30 minutes late, because Jack, our driver, couldn't find the address—although we could have walked there from our apartment in less than 15 minutes. The Xues had brought their 17-year-old son.

Within 45 minutes, the conversation had become so lively that the Xues commented how "it already feels like we're old friends." Beware of this phrase! It invariably means that the speaker is about to ask for a favor. At the time, I was still unaware of this, though, and they caught me off guard when in the next breath they asked me if I could arrange an internship for their son at our bank. It needn't be for long, they assured me. Three days would be enough. They just needed to put it on his résumé, as he would soon be applying to study in the United States.

Dumbfounded and reluctant to cause animosity, I stammered my agreement. Looking back, I'm not sure he got much out of it.

I also formed two advisory boards in my first year in China. I wanted real advisory boards, not the kind that many companies put together primarily for marketing purposes. Rather, I wanted advisors who would tell me what I was doing wrong so I could improve our chances of success. Accordingly, I set up one in Shanghai to advise us on how we could better build *guanxi* with the Shanghai government. It comprised a young guy, Fred, from a government agency that dealt with foreign commerce; Erica Huang, who ran the portion of the Zhangjiang Hi-Tech Park that dealt with start-ups; and Clayton, a very experienced local banker. (A couple years later, Clayton's wife flew to LA to give birth to their child to ensure it instantaneous American citizenship.)

The second advisory board, based in Beijing, consisted of three world-famous Chinese venture capitalists. They were especially helpful, but they have explicitly asked me to allow them to remain anonymous. I call them my "Secret Advisory Board," although I later learned it was likely they were not secret at all.

3.3 GETTING TO WORK: THE SECRET TEAM

The secret team, as I mentioned earlier, predated our arrival by two years. I'm not sure that they viewed themselves as a team, but they all knew each other and discussed our situation on an ongoing basis. There was nothing sinister about it; it was just the way things work. Once I was actually on the ground, they started to emerge from the background.

To succeed as a foreign bank, I needed to develop a relationship with the government of Shanghai, but it turned out that only 10 or so people—out of the city's population of 24 million—really mattered. I thought I'd discovered them, but in retrospect the situation may be more complex. It took me months before I noticed that this handful of influential people all seemed to know exactly what I'd said to each of the others. At first, I thought they had been appointed by the government, but others have disagreed, suggesting that they came together spontaneously, probably because my project could help them achieve their KPIs if steered correctly. Who knows? I worked closely with them and ended up learning a lot from them. They included:

Chairman Ji, the chairman of the Shanghai International Group, a state-owned enterprise of which our joint venture partner, SPDB, was a subsidiary. He was the chairman of SPDB as well.

Ji was famous in Shanghai for being a world-class drinker. In that arena, he liked holding gladiatorial drinking contests among dinner guests. At one of his smaller dinners, I watched with fascination as he "ordered" two of the guests to "duel" (each "shot" was a round of Baijiu) until one of them either surrendered or passed out. Ji always seemed supportive, helpful, friendly, astute, and fun, and for some reason, probably to prevent me from losing face, never forced me into one of these contests.

President James Luo, the president of SPDB and chairman of our joint venture. Luo (pronounced like "Lore") had been the president of the Bank of Shanghai before coming to SPDB. Since most of the employees at SPDB were lifers, Luo was viewed by many as an interloper. Our relationship got off to a rocky start, but in time I think we both came to respect each other.

Mr. Liu, the head of banking and CFO of SPDB. When Luo retired in 2012, the Organization Department considered promoting Liu to president. Instead, a Mr. Zhu was brought in to replace Luo. Zhu had no experience in commercial banking, and within two years, he was moved aside, partly due to a lack of relevant experience but also due to a lack of internal support.

During Zhu's two-year tenure, Liu was sent to work in a branch of the government that provided oversight to state-owned enterprises (SOEs). His job was to sell off assets the government no longer wanted and to use the proceeds to acquire new ones. After Zhu left SPBD, the Organization Department brought Liu back as president. He was a top-notch banker.

Lao Ding, the Party Secretary of the Yangpu District and my first "best friend" among the government officials in Shanghai. His mission was to transform the local economy from an old-style rustbelt manufacturing enclave to an innovation center showcasing knowledge-based industries. He seemed to be well-liked by everybody I met in the Shanghai government and in Beijing as well, at least to the extent he was known. Sporting his trademark black leather jacket, he greeted everyone with a broad smile and a bear hug.

When he retired as Party Secretary, not long after I got to know him, the Organization Department gave him a series of "plum" positions to reward him for his loyalty and competence. Normally, at retirement (at that time, the age was 60 for men and 55 for women), you went home and engaged in the typical things retired people do, such as caring for grandchildren, joining "old goats" clubs, hanging out at Fuxing Park, and so on. But you're not supposed to work, unless, of course, the Party wants to reward you, as in the case of Lao Ding. In his retirement, he was put in charge of security at the 2010 Shanghai Expo and then later sent to Italy to assist the Italians in preparing for their World Expo in 2015.

Vice Mayor Tu of Shanghai. Mr. Tu was in charge of the finance department for the city, and renowned as a speaker. Communist tradition in China encouraged an oratorical style that might be called sloganeering: short, declarative sentences issued in a staccato-like intonation pattern that a Western ear would associate with commands, so that each line sounds like an admonishment. Couple that with a heavy reliance on numbers—which are of questionable accuracy but reported as incontrovertible—and you will have perfected it. The speaker might yell: "In 2010 we produced 7 million bushels! In 2011 we produced 8 million bushels!" and so on. To Western listeners, it sounds like the speaker is bawling out the audience and we're quickly exhausted. The Chinese members of the audience don't appear to pay any attention; they're usually reading their phones or snoozing.

But Vice Mayor Tu was different. His oratorical style was strikingly Western. I have no idea how that came about, but he was definitely everybody's favorite speaker, Chinese and Westerners alike.

Dr. Fang, head of the financial services office, who reported directly to Tu. Fang was a generation younger than Tu—or maybe not. He had a baby face, so it was hard to know how old he was. He'd studied in the United States and seemed more worldly and knowledgeable than most of the government officials I met. But he was coldly analytical and, I learned, a rising star in the Party.

Zheng Yang, deputy head of the State Administration for Foreign Exchange (SAFE) in Shanghai. Zheng was always friendly and helpful, but sometimes I think he found me puzzling. At the end of one dinner with him, he told me that he was preparing a speech for his boss on the topic of turning Shanghai into an international financial center. Without even pausing to think, I told him that the main prerequisite for becoming an international financial center would be for Shanghai to change its view of the rest of the world. I told him that they should stop viewing foreigners as barbarians[1] and start viewing them as valued customers with whom they could create a true "win-win." I explained that most of the time, when the Chinese government talks about "win-win," they simply mean that China wins twice. He responded with discomfort but did not contest my statement. Zheng eventually became the head of financial services in Shanghai, after Fang was promoted to a much higher position in Beijing.

Mr. Liao, head of the Shanghai office of the Chinese Banking Regulatory Commission (CBRC). Mr. Liao was a favorite of the SVB team. He came to the CBRC after years of working for Liu Mingkang, a well-known and respected economist who'd studied in London. In 2003, the Organization Department had appointed Liu to reform the banking system from Mao's vision of a piggy bank for the CCP into something that approximated the Western system. In this capacity, he created the CBRC and ran it until his retirement in 2011, with Liao as his protégé in the effort. They were both friendly, ethical, and sincere, in my view.

Their challenge was daunting. Under Mao, when an SOE needed money, the government told the Bank of China to transfer the required amount to the company's account. Because no one distinguished between debt and equity, the money being transferred was conceptually a loan, but with no terms and no specific due date.* Furthermore, as the government had already decided to make the "loan," there was no need for underwriting—that is, assessing the company's creditworthiness. Accordingly, the concept of risk and the relationship between risk and pricing had disappeared as well.

In the first few years of the 2000s, when the CCP wanted to become integrated into the world financial system, the old system had to be abandoned or at least disguised. But old habits die hard, and the system, even today, is not as "reformed" as one might think.

---

* The distinction between debt and equity is important. Debt takes the form of a loan (say, $5 million) with a term (say, five years), an interest rate, and a repayment schedule. Equity investment conveys ownership in a company in exchange for a cash injection. An investor might provide $5 million in exchange for 5% ownership in the company. The investor then shares in the gains or losses of the company proportionately to their ownership and, typically, can exit the position in some manner. If the company goes bankrupt, the equity owners lose all their money. China has a mushy combination of equity and debt, where the terms of a loan aren't really spelled out and if the company doesn't repay it, the government often effectively repays the bank by recapitalizing it in secret.

The government keeps promising to complete the reformation while simultaneously "kicking the can down the road," in part because of the upheaval that would result from forcing the SOEs to pay back loans, improve operational efficiency, and, inevitably, let go of thousands of barely functioning workers. (For more on the banking and economy of China, please see Chapter 14.)

Dean Lu, the dean of the Graduate School of Management at Fudan University. Fudan is considered by many to be one of the three best schools in China (after Tsinghua University and Beijing University). I'd become acquainted with Lu years before and had met with him many times as SVB approached China. When we finally got the bank set up and ready to open, the Organization Department chose him to be on our supervisory board. Specifically, he *was* our supervisory board. A supervisory board in China oversees the company's board of directors, which in turn supervises the company and its management team. Because we were a start-up, the Organization Department apparently felt a one-person board of supervisors would be sufficient.

During the first year, Lu gave me more good advice and encouragement than anyone apart from Victor. Without Lu's encouragement and strategic advice, building the bank would have been even more difficult, if not outright impossible. I learned a lot from him, and I'm grateful.

To clarify, Figure 3.1 shows the individuals on the secret team, along with their reporting relationships, if any.

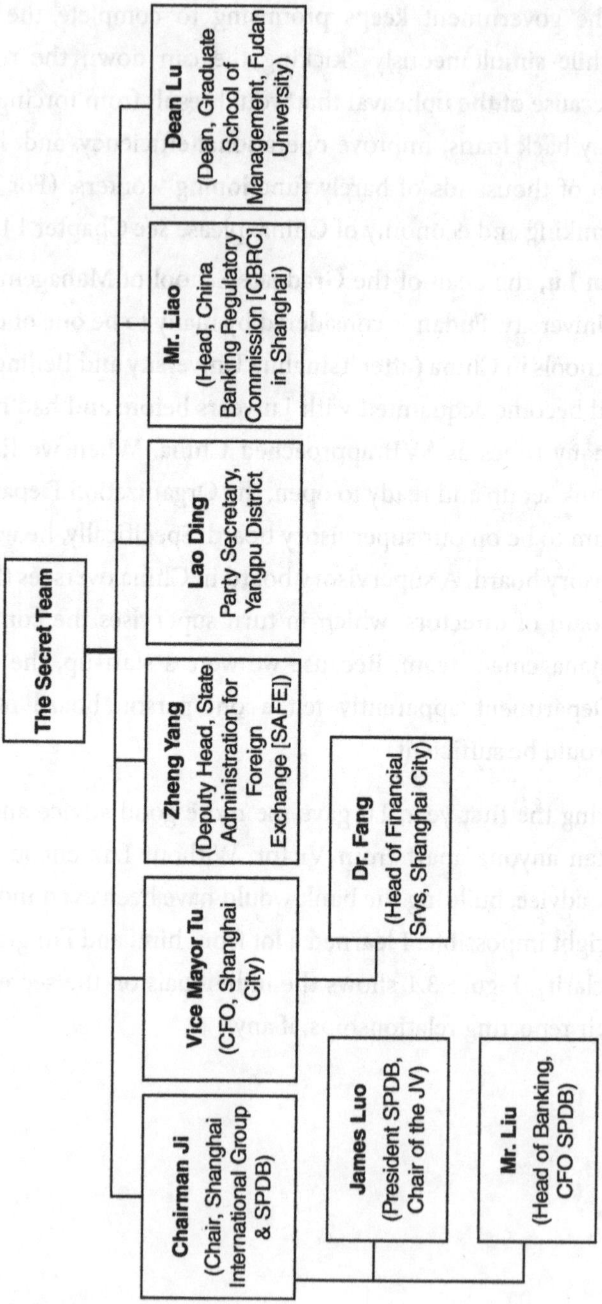

Figure 3.1 Names and reporting relationships among the secret team.

```
                    The Secret Team

Chairman Ji      Vice Mayor Tu    Zheng Yang        Lao Ding         Mr. Liao          Dean Lu
(Chair, Shanghai (CFO, Shanghai   (Deputy Head,     Party Secretary, (Head, China     (Dean, Graduate
International     City)            State             Yangpu District  Banking Regulatory School of
Group            City)            Administration for                 Commission [CBRC] Management, Fudan
& SPDB)                           Foreign                            in Shanghai)      University)
                                  Exchange [SAFE])

James Luo                         Dr. Fang
(President SPDB,                   (Head of Financial
Chair of the JV)                  Srvs, Shanghai City)

Mr. Liu
(Head of Banking,
CFO SPDB)
```

Takeaways from the Trenches

- Learning Mandarin is very difficult, especially if you are a Westerner, and even more so if you are an adult. Still, you will need to learn some Mandarin. People will be nicer to you if you at least try.
- Explore, explore, explore. China is fascinating. Learning about China will help you understand what you are up against.
- It helps to have a driver. No sane Westerner would drive himself in China. If you are doing something meaningful, your driver will likely be a low-level spy.
- Your apartment will be egregiously expensive, and it may well be bugged.
- You will need two interpreters, one to tell you what people said and the other to tell you what they meant.
- You will need to talk with government officials on a regular basis. Appointments may take weeks, or even months, to get.
- As James McGregor said in his book *One Billion Customers*, you will have no friends. Always question the motives of others.
- When someone says to you, "We've only known each other for a short time and yet it already feels like we are old friends," beware! They are about to ask you for a favor, usually so large that you will wish you hadn't met.
- Seek advice always, take it with a grain of salt, add it to your growing body of "knowledge," create working hypotheses, and test them in your interactions with others.

NOTE

1. A deeply held belief among the Chinese (elaborated in Chapter 16) is that foreigners are barbarians.

CHAPTER FOUR

PAINS IN THE NECK

THE NEW BANK'S LOCATION, ORGANIZATION, AND IDENTITY

U pon arriving in Shanghai, I asked Victor to get me on Mr. Luo's calendar. I knew it would take a while to get our banking license, but the government had promised they'd give us one, and thus, I thought, we should get to work right away on making the necessary preparations. To do so, I needed to visit with Luo, my counterpart at SPDB, our JV partner.

It seemed odd, though, that Luo didn't seem to be in any rush to see me.

Nor, when we finally did meet, did he seem to be in any rush to begin our work together. He spoke in vague terms about setting up two groups: a working group and a decision-making group. But for some reason unknown to me, he did not want to get started with either one right away.

With nothing specific to do other than to meet people and try to familiarize myself with my new environment, I decided to at least prepare the people in our office for our upcoming journey. Among the current employees in the Huaihai Road office, I set up two committees: one on operations and one on culture. Both were charged with anticipating potential problems and suggesting ways to address them. I wanted everybody thinking about the issues that JVs, particularly those between U.S. companies and Chinese SOEs, might face. This move also absorbed a lot of nervous energy that the impending "merger" had generated, especially since our new partner had virtually gone radio silent.

In the meantime, I kept after Luo. Victor managed to get me on his calendar every few weeks. Interestingly, he never came to me; he always insisted I come to him. This, at least, gave my driver, Jack, something to do: drive me between our offices, a 30-minute round trip.

SPDB's office was located on the Bund, that historic strip of large, impressive buildings on the banks of the Huangpu River where Western companies, especially banks, had located their headquarters more than a hundred years earlier. SPDB's headquarters had been the Shanghai headquarters of the famous Hong Kong Shanghai Banking Corporation (HSBC) prior to World War II.

Rather than meeting in his office, Luo and I convened in a nearby reception room in the traditional Chinese manner. We sat in large chairs, side by side, turning our heads (his to the right, mine to the left) so that we could see each other, with translators sitting in small chairs just behind us. At the time, I didn't know that this formation indicated the stage of development of our relationship. Strangers sit side-by-side like this, but over time, they will start to sit facing each other. Within a year or so, we began sitting across from each other, signaling that our relationship had progressed to a friendlier level. By then, I'd developed a painful crick in my neck from the first, awkward—in all senses of the word—period.

When Luo announced his intention of forming two groups, I was mystified: Why couldn't the eight-person working group also make the decisions? No, it was clear (to him, at least) that we needed the two groups and that the working group would be composed of more junior people than the decision-making organization. I held my tongue and quickly appointed four representatives to each group from the SVB side. I waited to learn of his appointees, but as spring became humid Shanghai summer and even wore into fall, Luo had no word on the membership from the SPDB side. The semi-established groups waved in the background like flags at half-staff. Every question I raised regarding their composition, mandate, or timeline was either evaded or ignored.

At the time, though, I didn't know that Luo was on the brink of retirement and waging an ultimately fruitless battle with the Organization Department to obtain a waiver that would enable him to stay in his current position for a few years beyond his impending sixtieth birthday. I realized later that he might have been personally inclined to slow-walk our JV's establishment, in hopes of making his involvement seem more important in getting it done.

4.1   THE ORG CHART

The original agreement between SPDB and SVB provided for the following organizational structure:

- SPDB would provide the chair (Luo).
- SVB would provide the president (me).
- SVB would provide the chief credit officer (Tim).
- SPDB would provide the head of IT (Steven).
- SPDB would provide the CFO (Maggie).

- SPDB would provide the head of operations (Yuhu).
- SPDB would provide the head of the general office (Luke).

This arrangement presented a number of complications, the two knottiest of which were:

1. SPDB assumed that the chair would run the company. SVB assumed that the president would run the company and that the chair would be responsible for managing the board, as is the U.S. custom. Even at the end of 2011, we were still debating this.
2. Of the five people whom SPDB seconded (assigned temporarily) to the JV in the list above, none had the appropriate skill sets or work experience. They were incompetent, unprepared, and lacked any desire to work in a joint venture. In their defense, being assigned to the JV raised the real possibility that their career trajectories would be derailed. All but one has since returned to SPDB or moved on.

Ironically, when I learned before my arrival that Luo was to be chairman and I was to be president, I was elated. That's exactly what our team at SVB had been targeting. But these were different mental models at work: I didn't know that in China, the chairman position is functionally the same as the company president in the United States, and a Chinese president is functionally the same as the U.S. chief operating officer, a much more hands-on position involved in execution as opposed to strategy. Luo, I discovered, intended to come to work every day and run the joint venture. Only after half a year of confusion did we recognize this misunderstanding, and resolution took several more months. In the meantime, each of us thought we ran the company, and neither of us could understand why the other one was acting as if he did.

As I fretted about getting the JV operational, Luo's only interest, it seemed, was the organization chart. He wanted me to draw it and bring it back to him for approval. But every time I did this—how hard can it be to draw an org chart, really?—he nixed it. And yet, he couldn't explain exactly what was wrong. It took months of this exasperating back-and-forth before I understood what he was getting at.

From Luo's point of view, my U.S.-style org chart (see Figure 4.1) contained three errors.

First, he wanted me to make it clear that *he* was in charge. Second, he wanted a more vertical, less horizontal arrangement. I anticipated a number of people in the layer below me, but he wanted only one, and that one person was going to be Chinese and appointed by him. Finally, and apparently most importantly, he wanted the chart to include a "general office." (For his vision of the org chart, see Figure 4.2.) In my 30 years of business experience, first at a top-tier business school and then in the working world, I'd never heard of a general office position in an org chart. Yet to Luo, it was a necessity beyond question.

As it turns out, larger organizations in China have enjoyed the "benefits" of a general office for centuries, perhaps even millennia. It's a dynastic tradition. The general office served as a buffer between the emperor and the rest of the world. Nothing arrived on the emperor's desk without being

Figure 4.1   Ken's org chart.
Source: Author.

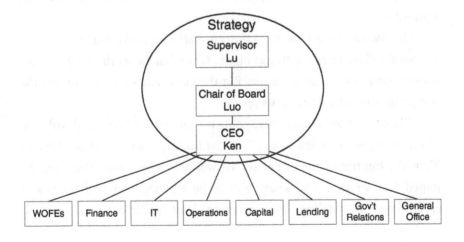

Figure 4.2   Luo's org chart.

Source: Author.

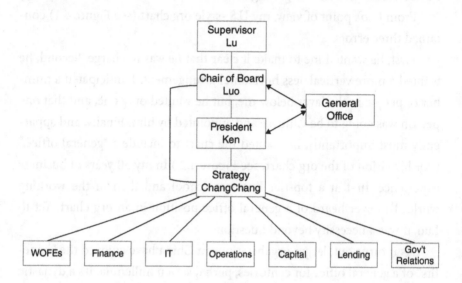

filtered through the general office, and vice versa. When Mao entered Beijing in the spring of 1949, he encamped his troops in the western suburbs known as the "Fragrant Hills" until the fall, at which point he invaded the city proper and subsequently declared the new republic. While still in the Fragrant Hills, he constructed his general office. It was *that high* a priority.

After two months of iterating the org chart, I figured it out and inserted a general office. To move things along, Luo relented on the issue of how many people would report to me. But the last issue—who would run the company—continued to trip us up.

While these discussions were going on, Luo seemed obsessed with discrediting my primary lieutenant, Tim Hardin, the other American slated to be in the top tier of the org chart. I'd worked closely with Tim since he joined SVB in 1995 and knew him to be top-notch in both sales and credit—that is, finding companies to lend to and assessing their creditworthiness, and convincing them to borrow from us. As I envisioned the future, Tim would be in charge of credit, that is, assessing the creditworthiness of potential borrowers. It was clear to me that every other executive in the new bank ought to be Chinese. But we were importing *our* business model to China, and both the president and the head of credit had to be from SVB, not SPDB, for it to work.

For some unknown reason, Luo felt compelled to subject Tim and me to a series of "slogan speeches" about risk management. He acted as if neither of us had ever made a loan before. The process was the following: He would invite us to sit with him in his office, he in the big chair, we on the little chairs. Then he would hold forth on the importance of risk management, which was to be Tim's responsibility, given his position as head of credit. Tim had run global risk management for SVB—and run it well— but one would infer from the tone of Luo's speeches that we were both ignoramuses, especially Tim. Luo's rants were highly repetitive and on the level of advice that you might give to an auditorium full of raw beginners. And they were long! Some of them lasted well over an hour, and a few of them, two. Tim and I routinely left feeling a combination of abashed, irritated, and baffled.

In September, after four months of generally fruitless meetings, I experienced my first breakthrough. One day, in contrast to his usual somewhat condescending demeanor, Luo asked sheepishly if, in the United States, people ever invited their bosses to dinner at their homes. He even seemed to blush. I told him they did, and, to my surprise, he then asked if I would invite him and his wife to dinner at my house. I replied that of course Ruth and I would be delighted to host the two of them for dinner.

I told Ruth as soon as I got home, and she was thrilled—and immediately anxious. "What shall we serve them? We can't make Chinese food; we're no good at it," she lamented. In the end, we decided on Western food, and to make it easier for both of us to join in the conversation, we hired a caterer. We also invited Victor to join us, to translate. We were a little anxious but mentally prepared.

The dinner was a breakthrough. Mr. Luo brought both Mrs. Luo and their daughter, Ke. Both were delightful. The Luos had sent Ke to a high school in the United States, after which she attended both undergraduate (Columbia) and graduate school (Wharton) in the United States. She had then worked for HSBC in Hong Kong before returning to Shanghai.

Mrs. Luo was recently retired from a long career in accounting for an SOE. To all appearances, the three of them really did want to get to know us, and at least Mrs. Luo and Ke wanted us to get to know them as well. Their backgrounds were remarkably different. Mr. Luo and his parents had weathered the Cultural Revolution without incident. Mrs. Luo, however, had not. Her family had been persecuted and, I learned later, her father had been tortured to death because of his class background. She herself had endured some very unpleasant experiences in "the countryside." Like millions of others, she'd been sent to a rural area to learn from the peasants. She told stories of chronic hunger, brutal cold, and being surrounded by menacing-looking wolves one evening. She and her companions had feared for their survival. It was clear her husband would have preferred that she hadn't shared this story, but she was determined to describe her experiences. Following this dinner, my relationship with Luo slowly became more cordial.

But a cordial relationship had its regulatory perils. Shortly after our dinner, Mr. Luo arrived at my office—in itself a mark of rapprochement— with a gift for me: a multicolored glass sculpture of a mythological animal that is part dragon, part lion, and all imagination. It was quite impressive. Ruth and I were certain we'd seen one similar, if not identical, in one of the high-end shops on the edges of Xintiandi. Curious how much Luo had paid for it, we sought it out and discovered it cost $800.

This, I suspected, would be a problem for the audit committee, not the one attached to the Shanghai JV, but at SVB's headquarters in Santa Clara, which maintained strict protocols regarding gifts to bank officers. I was right. The head of audit told me I could either return it to Luo or donate (out of my own money) a like amount to a charity in China and write a memo documenting the event and how I'd handled it. I chose option two to avoid offending the Luos.

This experience brought home the irrelevance of the American Foreign Corrupt Practices Act (AFCPA), or at least the way it was interpreted by our audit committee. There are two issues. First, "corruption"—or extravagant gift giving—is not just rampant in China, it is *foundational*. Everybody in China, at least at that time, sought to cement relationships through giving gifts. And second, the amounts of money involved often—I should say, *regularly*—far exceeded the amount involved here. I believe that the mere existence of the AFCPA suggests the extent to which our lawmakers fail to understand Chinese culture. Returning the gift to Luo would have profoundly insulted him, setting back our nascent relationship. And my gift of $800 to a Chinese charity had no impact whatsoever. Do we want to change Chinese culture, which has existed for 5,000 years, or do we want to succeed in doing business with China? The AFCPA accomplishes neither. And trying to comply with it just layers on administrative annoyances.

I do believe that the AFCPA is important (albeit annoying in a society in which graft is so much a part of daily life). That said, I find it ironic that I had to spend so much of my time proving to our audit committee back in California that I was abiding by the rules, when the biggest threat was not my behavior but the business practices of so many of the people around me.

Comparing notes with other Western CEOs, I discovered many similar experiences. In a number of banks in China, for example, loan officers took kickbacks wherever they could—in exchange for extensions of credit, lower interest rates on loans, or higher interest rates on deposits. Frequently, they would be representing not just the bank that employed them, but also other companies, without their bank's knowledge. For example, they might double as insurance agents, with neither of their employers necessarily aware of the other. And yet, if the Chinese authorities felt like cracking down, the Western CEOs could get into real trouble. Of course, there were often opportunities to avoid trouble by paying off the authority who was threatening the crackdown.

One of my CEO friends told me he regularly paid a "fixer" about $250,000 a year to help him ward off trouble. I suspect that some of that money went to the fixer, while some was used to make threatening authorities just go away. Running a company in China, especially a Western one, can be stressful. There is always the threat of a jail sentence, whether it is deserved or not.

Since Xi Jinping came to power in 2012, the Chinese government has enacted anticorruption measures that preclude gift giving, so my complaints about the AFCPA are, ironically, no longer valid, at least not officially. That said, though, I'm skeptical that Xi really believes he can eliminate gift giving, or that he actually wants to. I believe his war on gift giving actually serves as yet another potential weapon, ready to be used against enemies should he wish.

Over the course of the past dozen years, I've had many dinners with Luo, both one-on-one and in groups, and they've become more and more interesting. At first, they were frustrating, at best, largely due to Luo's propensity to pontificate. In retrospect, I think he adopted this approach to reflect his perception of the proper behavior of the chairman, coupled with a sense of insecurity, as it became more and more evident that the CCP wasn't planning to let him postpone his legally mandated retirement.

For instance, one dinner was held in the official entertainment room at SPDB, with almost 30 people sitting around a very large, round table. While Luo was holding forth, seemingly interminably, Elwood Dong, who'd led our Shanghai office prior to my arrival, was consuming large amounts of Baijiu. At one point, as I turned to whisper something in his ear, I noticed that his eyes had rolled back in his head, to the extent that his pupils were no longer visible. A second later, he fell off his chair and landed on the floor like a sack of flour, nursed back to consciousness by Chen Xiaolei, one of the compliance people at SPDB, while Dong's son frantically called an ambulance. Unconcerned, Luo continued for another quarter hour!

And often, Luo's penchant for pontification had deleterious effects. The night before a major regulatory exam that our entire team, even I, had to take, our management team had a team-building dinner. To give Luo face, I invited him to join us. At 8:30 p.m., I announced my departure, eager for a good night's sleep before the test. In the morning, I learned that Luo had given a monologue on his life and times that lasted until 10:00 p.m. The team felt compelled to stay to the bitter end. Miraculously, we passed the exam.

Toward the end of the first year, in response to stern advice from my secret advisory board in Beijing[1] that I should try harder to improve my relationship with Luo, I consciously changed my behavior. I started inviting him to dinner on a regular basis to talk about history, an interest we shared, accompanied only by Victor and Chrystal, my invaluable assistants.

At these dinners we both got drunk: him on Baijiu, me on bourbon. It was culturally accepted: If you didn't trust someone enough to get drunk with them, how could you possibly do business with them? Victor and Chrystal took turns interpreting. Those dinners were fascinating and extremely informative, primarily because our perspectives were so different. According to Luo, the Americans started the Korean War with an unprovoked attack on North Korea. Furthermore, throughout the 1950s, the United States had been planning a full-scale invasion of China. As a result, Mao had been forced to move almost all industrial production from the coastal cities to more secure spots inland. Luo's version of the Cultural Revolution was far more benign than any other I'd read (or have read since), due perhaps to the fact that his family seems to have done fairly well during that period.

Luo acknowledged that while there were aspects of the Cultural Revolution that were "correct," it might have been a mistake overall. In any case, the Party had acknowledged the mistake and apologized. I told Luo I'd never heard or read that the Party had acknowledged it was wrong in anything, let alone the Cultural Revolution, which cost an estimated 3 million lives and resulted in the persecution of tens to hundreds of millions more.[2] He insisted. I asked him to prove it. A few days later, he gave me a photocopy of a few pages from a book that must have included official records of the Party's notes on various meetings. And there it was! An acknowledgment of error. I was amazed and admitted that he was right. That said, it was one of the most perfunctory acknowledgments of error I've ever read in my life. In my experience, *heartfelt* admissions of error—such as Germany's apology for the Holocaust or Canada's to its Indigenous people—are extremely rare in China. Admitting error is not a Chinese core competency.

These dinners brought us closer together and paved the way for collaboration in other areas later on. I wish I'd started them earlier. Ke told me that Luo loved these dinners as much as I did.

But the improvement in our relationship did not happen linearly. One day early in the fall of 2011, Luo sent word that he wanted to talk with me right away. This time, he even volunteered to come to my office. When he arrived, he was clearly agitated. He began by telling me that he was disappointed in me. He'd trusted me, and I had misled him. SVB had an algorithm, he insisted, and we'd withheld it.

I was startled and skeptical. The accusation sounded a little manipulative. I wondered if someone had put him up to it. It seemed oddly as if he was on a fishing expedition. For starters, Silicon Valley Bank has never had an algorithm, at least not one that determines whom we should and should not lend money to. It would be nice, but to this day, we've never developed one. Our decision-making process involves just plain old hard work. More specifically, it is pattern recognition, honed over an apprenticeship of about 10 years.

But in my opinion, the Chinese tend to be oriented toward engineering-based solutions. Also, although we'd never agreed to turn over our "intellectual property" to SPDB in exchange for market access, it was obvious from their constant expressions of curiosity that the main reason they'd entered this joint venture was to find out how we did what we did. They were certain we had an algorithm, and they wanted us to "share" it.

I volunteered to ask my team to prepare a presentation explaining our model. On the one hand, I resented the mistrust as well as the heavy-handed way in which Luo was attempting to force us to "tell all." On the other hand, it didn't really bother me to give SPDB this presentation. I still believe that it takes years of practice under the watchful eye of a more senior banker, schooled in our business model, to learn to make the decisions that our bankers make. It would be tough for anybody to replicate what we do based on a presentation. Luo was mollified. We set to work, and a week later we made our presentation to a room full of SPDB bankers. By the late afternoon, when we were done, many were dozing in their chairs.

While Luo was my primary SPDB contact, he was not the only one. That first fall, I met a senior SPDBer named Mr. Sun. He managed a group of about 30 analysts who tracked the companies in which SPDB had made investments or collaborated with in joint ventures. I took him to lunch. To me, he seemed ponderous and condescending.

During the lunch, he told me he didn't believe in our business model and thought it was much too risky. (This was not an uncommon response from bankers in any country when they first heard about our model.) He told me that he'd be on the JV's "Party Committee," installed by the Organization Department to make sure that we didn't go too far astray and lose too much money for SPDB. I doubt that we could take this comment literally; I think he was trying to intimidate me.

Although I knew about the Organization Department, I did not yet know what a Party Committee was, and frankly, I still don't have a clear picture. I've received multiple definitions over the years, all of which fit into one of three categories, but no one has been willing to acknowledge that these categories actually exist. Sun then proceeded to tell me what he meant by the phrase Party Committee, and his description fit into the first of these three categories.

As he explained it, there will be a "secret board behind the real board" of our bank and I would never know who's on it. They will all be members of the CCP, and he would be one of them. They will make all the big decisions, which would be implemented through the people representing SPDB on the official board.

The other two categories were much less opaque. In one, the Party Committee was a study group that examined the recent pronouncements of CCP leadership and how they should be applied; and in the other, the Party Committee was nothing more than a social committee that planned the company picnic and holiday celebrations. Since only about 10% of Western companies in China had a Party Committee as of the mid-2010s, but almost 100% have them now, I rather doubt that there has been a sudden interest on the part of the CCP in study groups or party planning. I believe Sun's explanation was correct.

To me, Sun's news was extremely disquieting. Our board in Santa Clara planned to invest well over $100 million in this new bank. If they knew that it would ultimately be run by a bunch of anonymous strangers from the CCP, they would be justifiably upset. I reached out to Luo for an explanation. He met me the very next day at a restaurant on the Bund for lunch, and Liu, SPDB's head of banking, came with him. When I told them what I'd heard, they exchanged knowing glances and then, in concert, sought to brush aside my concerns. They said, "This is all just a product of Sun's imagination. Don't think about it twice. Sun is just silly." Months later, Sun told me that I'd gotten him into a lot of trouble that day. Apparently, it never occurred to him that he'd done it to himself.

Shortly after this episode with Sun, I decided to take the team on a retreat to beautiful Yunnan Province. The "team" at this point consisted solely of the people who'd been in our original office on Huaihai Road, plus four of us from SVB's California headquarters—myself, Tim, Teresa Li, who had just arrived from SVB to lead our large-company banking team, and Mary Dent, the chief counsel for SVB who was here for one of her short visits to help us sort out legal matters. We hadn't yet received our license and Luo hadn't received approval from the SPDB Party Committee to move forward. But we all needed a break, primarily from the anxiety of not knowing why we were stalled.

We convened at the lovely Banyan Tree Resort in Lijiang, surrounded by snowcapped mountains and deep gorges ground out of the earth by mountain streams. We spent our time in deep discussion about what kind of a joint (Eastern–Western) culture we hoped to create and how we would engage our new partners to do so. We were filled with the optimism of novices.

That same first autumn, I heard unpleasant rumors. Some of our local office staff—our bankers—complained to me that SPDB was already competing against us, even before we opened our doors and despite the pact that the "parents" (SVB and SPDB) had sworn to never compete with the "child," our new JV bank. Theoretically, that promise should have been easier for SPDB to keep than for us, because SPDB allegedly had no technology companies as clients, whereas SVB had our offshore business banking WOFEs.

But when I checked into these complaints, they appeared to be true. I brought them up with Luo and Liu. Both insisted that the complaints were unfounded. "We're not competing; *we're letting the customer decide,*" they said. As I later learned, this was not quite the case.

In that same period, SPDB suggested that we let them make a few of the loans that we ourselves would like to make, on our behalf. The regulators still had not granted us our license. Our bankers were chomping at the bit to get started. And SPDB was chomping at the bit to better understand our business model. Accordingly, we decided to accept their "generous" offer of assistance. Our bankers identified a prospective client in Beijing; SPDB's branch in Beijing assigned a banker to implement the loan; and we directed it from the background.

The banker in Beijing set up the loan of $500,000 in RMB, then created an accompanying deposit account for the client and disbursed the loan proceeds into the deposit account. The client now had a half million dollars borrowed from us (the new JV bank), which it held in the new deposit account at SPDB in Beijing. The entire physical side of the relationship was being handled by the SPDB banker in Beijing, but if anything went wrong, the JV bank would be on the hook.

The client was to repay the loan in monthly installments. Every month, the amount of money in the account went down, as the client spent the proceeds, but the loan balance never decreased, as the client wasn't paying it back. We asked the SPDB banker in Beijing to admonish the client. When nothing happened, we talked to the client ourselves. The client insisted that they'd asked the banker in Beijing to take money out of their deposit account every month to pay down the loan, but the banker in Beijing had refused.

It turned out that the banker in Beijing was incentivized *not* to make loans and then manage their repayment, but to maintain as much money as possible in the deposit account. She had no incentive to get the loan paid back! Therefore, she just refused to use any of the money in the deposit account to repay it. In the end, the cash in the deposit account was spent on God knows what. The company ran out of money, the loan was never paid back, the venture capitalists who'd banked the company lost interest and disappeared, and we were poised to report a loss. Not, I thought, an auspicious start.

I brought it up with Luo. It turns out that this arrangement was highly unusual in China, or so I was told. To my surprise, he volunteered to come to my rescue. He called up that banker's supervisor, and apparently, the supervisor bawled her out. In the end, SPDB split the loss with us. Even more surprising, Luo apologized to me for the banker's behavior. Given the incentive systems at SPDB, he said, not every banker would do the right thing ethically, especially if doing so reduced their bonus.

While I had made some progress in building a relationship with Luo, some of my overtures fell flat. Later in that first autumn, Luo invited me to accompany him to a private "wine club." We brought Chrystal along to interpret. The club was located in a beautiful old villa in the former French Concession, accessed via a hidden door that was activated by a hidden button in a nondescript wall.

The club was patronized by so-called red hats, extremely wealthy businessmen who had purchased state assets from the government at bargain-basement prices. It focused on pricey French wine, gourmet Western cooking, and art (kitschy nudes done by the resident painter who lived on the upper floor). I interpreted the invitation as an indication that Luo and I were getting closer. Trying to be a good guest, I offered to introduce the club's manager to some of the cult wineries in Napa Valley (Screaming Eagle, Harlan Estates, and so on) that we banked. "No interest," he said. "We only drink the very best wines in the world, and those are from France." Notwithstanding my association with such "déclassé" libations, the evening was a success.

Late that fall, Luo named his representatives to the working group and the decision-making group he'd mentioned at one of our early meetings. This was a good six months after I'd appointed the people on our side, but it was a big step toward establishing the bank. At last, we could finally get started!

Luo also admitted the cause of the delay. Even as president of SPDB, he didn't have the authority to appoint or hire; rather, he had to wait for the SPDB Party Committee to decide whom to appoint. It's also entirely possible, although not certain, that the SPDB Party Committee may have had to wait for the Organization Department's approval of the appointees. But finally, our groups were constituted.

4.2   ISSUES TO RESOLVE

Once Luo made the appointments, our committees began to meet, and as soon as our committees began to meet, issues arose. The decision-making committee acted as if it was taking the working group's recommendations into account—and both were quickly faced with three major, seemingly intractable disagreements:

1. **Office location:** SPDB wanted our office in Pudong, which was on the east side of the Huangpu River, and was, as recently as 30 years ago, largely swampland and rice paddies. Today it has all the skyscrapers you see in the tourist literature—the famous four huge towers—and more than 400 financial institutions or branches of foreign financial institutions. In fact, SPDB's entire reason for being was as a branch of the Shanghai government that oversaw the government's investment in the SOEs that built Pudong. We at SVB wanted to remain in Luwan, which included the beautiful former French Concession as well as Xintiandi (Vincent Lo's delightful commercial development) on the "Old Shanghai" side on the river. We'd be the only bank there and, besides, it had a "cool," hipster vibe. Young people of all sorts, including budding entrepreneurs, flocked there. It was, we thought, a perfect match.

   Luo's desire to locate our new bank in the Pudong District wasn't surprising. Not only was SPDB historically connected to the area, but in China, businesses tend to locate near other similar businesses. For example, one of my favorite walks in Shanghai led down a street where almost every shop sold musical instruments. On another street, almost every shop sold office supplies. It's no wonder that Pudong houses the headquarters of almost every one of the 400 financial institutions in Shanghai.

2. **Our identity:** This topic covers two sub-issues: the JV's name and its logo. They shared an underlying tension, in that SPDB wanted to emphasize its senior role in the relationship, while SVB wanted to portray the JV as a forward-looking, innovation-centric organization. Specifically, SVB wanted to call the JV SSVB, or Shanghai Silicon Valley Bank. SPDB wanted it to be SPD-SVB, which prioritized SPDB's name and role.

   I wasn't keen on that because, in my view, SPDB didn't bring anything to the party. It was just a bank, located in the Pudong District, known until recently only for rice paddies. SVB was all about Silicon Valley, an internationally recognized concept involving an entrepreneurial state of mind and a problem-solving approach to life.

   The logo discussion fell along the same lines. SPDB wanted our new bank to use its logo to reflect its dominant role. SVB wanted the new bank to have its own logo, to render it distinct and to indicate that it was a bank unto itself and had a different business than either of its parents.

3. **The software backbone:** SPDB wanted the JV to use its home-produced and erratically documented banking software. SVB wanted it to use our own extensively tested, customized, and documented system.

We discussed these three issues for months, and the discussions turned into arguments. Feeling like we were being bulldozed and that the Chinese were operating on the principle of "might makes right," I threw a fit. This was a big mistake.

Liu, the CFO of SPDB, told Elwood Dong that I'd done irreparable damage to the relationship between the organizations. He couldn't have told a more welcoming ear: Elwood was nursing hurt feelings, because my entire role in the project was to supplant him. Liu's comment poured gasoline on the embers of his embarrassment. Now I had, of my own making, tensions not only with our JV partner but also with a member of my senior team.

In time, the relationship stabilized. Elwood became our product manager, which introduced its own set of difficulties. Eventually he retired. And the issues were solved, each in its own way:

1. **Location:** Yangpu (neither won). Unbeknownst to me, Lao Ding had been lobbying the Shanghai government for years to have our new bank located in his district, the Yangpu. Thus, neither SPDB nor SVB was happy. In fact, when the final decision came down, Luo came to me, literally in tears. Thanks to Lao Ding, the government had ordered us to locate in the Yangpu District. Now, at least, Luo and I could unite in our unhappiness.

   I should have seen this coming. Not long before we learned of the government's decision, Lao Ding had secured an apartment for his son, Thomas, who soon came to work for us, about a five-minute walk from the building in which our bank would ultimately reside.

2. **Our identity:** (SPDB won on the name.) The logo was a draw. Officially, the JV's name is SPD-SVB. I kept calling the entity SSVB—as did most people in Shanghai. Every single time I used that name, any SPDBer in the room would correct me, but I didn't stop, and no one threw me in jail.

   As for the logo, Arman cleverly hired a marketing firm from Taiwan for advice. The firm's director, Monika, was completely no-nonsense. She admonished me to throw in the towel. "This is, after all, China," she said. "The CCP *is* in charge." People who operate in China long enough become fatalistic; you try to get what you want but you know you have to roll with the punches.

   In the end, we struck an ingenious compromise. We would still insist on a unique logo, but we asked Luo to design it, with the help of Monika's firm. It worked. Luo did a terrific job, and we're still using that logo today. That said, there was an interim step that stuck in my craw for years. Liu insisted that I come to his office and submit to a two-hour lecture on marketing in general and on logos in particular, delivered by a very condescending young Party official named Ms. Gao. She knew as much about marketing as most American students did—if they'd just bought the textbook for Marketing 101 but hadn't opened it yet. This set the precedent for my future interactions with Ms. Gao.

3. **Banking software:** (SVB won.) In time, everybody concluded that the SPDB banking software, homegrown and largely undocumented, was too much like a bowl of spaghetti for the JV to use. Whew! Sadly, we had to argue for months before we arrived at this happy conclusion.

4.3   THE LETTER AND WHAT I LEARNED

Around this time, Oliver, one of our original and most dependable employees, came to me out of breath and visibly shaken. Sun, the same guy who'd told me about the Party Committee, had given Oliver a "secret letter" and asked him to get it to the SVB board in Santa Clara without my knowledge. The letter announced that SPDB had unilaterally decided to tear up the shareholder agreement both organizations had signed after negotiating for the better part of a year. We would have to negotiate a new one.

SPDB apparently believed it had leverage over us, thinking that SVB had placed all its cards on the table. They wanted to cut a better deal for themselves than the first agreement allowed. When I confronted Sun, he blamed it all on Liu. Liu, in turn, blamed it all on Sun. I'm pretty sure that Sun was lying.

This time, I repressed my inclination to throw a fit. I simply explained to Luo, calmly, that I'd be recommending to the SVB Board that they pull out of the deal. SVB had not yet injected its share of the equity—over $100 million. I couldn't recommend that the bank enter into a joint venture with a company that acted in such bad faith.

It worked.

Within seconds, Sun was again the bad guy. Luo apologized, the letter was retracted, and life went on as if nothing had happened. I never could figure out how the person at SPDB who came up with this ploy forgot we had not yet put our $100 million into the deal.

To me, the lesson was clear: anger weakens your position; leverage strengthens it. I've been operating from this insight ever since, and China has never, so far, proven this "working hypothesis" wrong. Moreover, I was starting to learn what it meant to operate in a country that had not adopted contract law. Essentially, every relationship was up for renegotiation whenever either party felt the balance of power had shifted in their favor. As a result, Chinese companies rely on memos of understanding (MOUs) rather than contracts. These MOUs are always vague and give the parties a huge amount of wiggle room. They lie along a spectrum and sometimes merely serve as a memento to prove to one's boss that you'd had a meeting.

As a Westerner, you should not take an MOU seriously in either direction—things you're obliged to do or things the other organization is committing to do. In my experience, my Chinese counterparties felt no obligation in the wake of an MOU and would change terms at the drop of a hat. Implicit in a contract, on the other hand, is the notion you should live up to whatever is in it. The Chinese, to a great extent, don't think that way.

Teddy Roosevelt, with his adage of "speak softly and carry a big stick," would have dealt so much more effectively with China than did former President Trump.

4.4 ACHIEVING THE IMPOSSIBLE

Finally, in October 2011, we received a license. It was not, however, a license to lend money. In truth, we received a license to start *assembling a bank*. We finally knew how the organization must look before we could receive a license to lend money. We had six months to make it happen, and it was impossible.

At this point, we had about 12 employees—pretty much the number we'd had when I arrived. But if you counted the required positions the license stipulated, we needed to have 62. Much like the Coast Guard refuses to allow a freighter to leave port until all requisite positions are filled, the Chinese regulator wouldn't allow us to open our doors without a full crew, which they deemed to consist of 62 people. We had to go out to the market to hire 50 more people, all with banking experience. Actually, we did receive one person up front: Changchang. Changchang was a mid-level regulator from the China Banking Regulatory Commission (CBRC), which generously donated her to our crew. In our discussions about the org chart, Luo proposed that she would be head of strategy, and as my sole direct report, oversee the whole bank. In other words, she would report to me, and I would report to Luo. I objected on the grounds that she knew nothing about our business model. In the end, I prevailed.

By the end of 2011, we were desperately trying to find qualified people to hire for the JV to fill the positions required by the regulatory authority. Even in this area, two major issues arose:

1. Luo believed that his position as chairman gave him the right to hire a handful of his friends' offspring, none of whom had relevant experience.

2. We also had to hire the offspring of CCP members, because the "best and brightest" of the then-current younger generation were indeed largely CCP members.

I hadn't anticipated the complications that could and did arise from this second issue. The CCP goes out of its way to identify the "best and brightest" high school students and to cajole them into a funnel that will inevitably result in Party membership by the time they graduate from college and enter the workforce. As I've noted, only about 7% of China's 1.4 billion people belong to the CCP. But because they're all hand-selected, on average they're smarter and more capable than their contemporaries. This, in effect, becomes a self-fulfilling prophecy, because the government gives them preferential treatment, which further increases their chances of getting better jobs and more frequent promotions. If you, as a "foreign" company, are recruiting the "best and brightest," you'll likely have a disproportionately high percentage of Party members in your employee base. In our case, more like 25%. Or perhaps even higher. For more on the role of the CCP in the Chinese economy, see Chapter 14.

To give you a sense of where we were in the process of building a bank at this point: Ruth and I arrived in Shanghai early in 2011. Until we were finally granted our license to start assembling the bank in October of 2011, Luo was disinclined to do much; and without Luo, there wasn't much we could do either. It turned out that he couldn't do much until the SPDB Party Committee, possibly with approval from the Organization Department, appointed the people who would represent SPDB on the two committees that were organizing the new bank, and that didn't happen until the fall of 2011.

4.5 DECEMBER 2011

By the end of 2011, Ruth and I had been in Shanghai for eight months. I had spent much of the intervening time trying to schedule meetings, receiving lectures from Luo on various topics of banking on which (I humbly submit) I was as expert as he or more so, trying to learn about the context of Chinese banking, and feeling stymied at many points.

Finally, in December, we were starting to make progress. Our two working groups were operational (one actually working and the other merely "deciding"); we'd begun work on the three big issues (location, identity, and software backbone); and we'd started hiring. Admittedly, we were required to hire far more people than I believed would be optimal, but I was learning the unvarnished truth of Monika's statement: "This is, after all, China. The CCP *is* in charge." And the CCP will be in charge of whatever it's interested in.

And the CCP was making that fact abundantly clear. The CBRC had given us six months to set up the bank, knowing this timeframe would be impossible. We needed at least a year to get the effort fully and operationally staffed, not to just hire the 62 people deemed necessary but also to create policies and manuals covering every facet of our existence and to train those 62 employees on the new policies using the new manuals.

At the same time, the broader context was becoming more fraught with anti-Western sentiment. At the end of December, the government's accusations of cultural hegemony intensified. Hu Jintao (China's president at that time) published an article in a Communist Party magazine, claiming that "... international hostile forces are intensifying the strategic plot of westernizing and dividing China."[3] Chinese leaders have long felt that their culture is globally besieged and belittled, pointing to the country's lack of Nobel prizes in literature and peace. As with so much, though, this complaint is complicated. Individuals born in China have won two Nobels for literature and one for peace, but only one of these, Mo Yan, who won the Nobel Prize for Literature in 2012, is recognized by the CCP. The other two winners were people the CCP doesn't want to acknowledge: dissident writer Gao Xingjian (the 2000 Nobel for Literature) and activist Liu Xiaobo (the 2010 Nobel Peace Prize).[4]

A friend Ruth and I met early in our stay, Huang, was our guide to the modern Shanghai art scene. Educated at Stanford and HBS, he had worked at Intel and then in the Obama administration. He introduced us to scores of gallery owners and artists through the art appreciation society he had founded. Called Xian Dai Ren (modern people), this group met monthly, usually at a studio or a gallery. While Huang claimed that his society had 1,200 members between Shanghai and Beijing, we never saw more than about 50 at a time, albeit seldom the same 50. Through this club, we learned a huge amount about the contemporary Chinese art scene, which, while not always to our taste, was extremely interesting.

But despite Huang's extensive experience in the West, he echoed the sense of Western oppression and regularly warned me that China was sick and tired of being treated like a second-class country by the U.S. government. China was surpassing America, he insisted, and the United States was trying to keep China down.

During our stay thus far, Ruth and I had had a grand time, even if we often felt at sea. Various government officials invited us to dinner to give us "face," or respect, honor, and social standing. In addition, many seemed to delight in goading us into eating things we would never voluntarily consume, including turtle, sea cucumber (also known as sea slug), chicken feet, and other surprises, at least to the Western palate.

More immediately appealing to our Californian palates was wine. In fact, SVB had a small division that focused on banking the California wine industry. Soon after our arrival, we became members of the Bordeaux Society, the brainchild of an enterprising Texan named Andrew Bigby. Many affluent Chinese love wine and believe that the only good wines are either French or Chinese. Members of the Bordeaux Society, as far as we could tell, were almost all Chinese, who met for dinner from time to time in the ballroom of a big hotel. In addition to dinner, the program consisted of drinking French wine; winning French wine through a "lucky draw;"

swearing to never, ever drink anything other than Bordeaux from that day forward; and inducting newcomers into the society. Andrew would call forward the inductees, place a scruffy old red cape over their shoulders, have them take the oath of fidelity to Bordeaux forever, and then place a toy sword on their foreheads, thus anointing them members. Everybody had a great time and went home tipsy.

4.6   WRAPPING UP 2011

As the year wound down, I realized that my understanding of China was becoming more nuanced. A particularly noteworthy insight was supplied by the Chinese wife of an Old China Hand, with whom we had dinner. She explained to us her view of how the government worked: "They are a bunch of thugs," she told us, referring to the CCP. "They control everything in China. They have so much control that the system is in danger of freezing in place—were it not for graft. Graft is like oil. The system is like an engine, and graft is the oil that lubricates the parts and makes it possible for the engine to run. Therefore, graft is not just necessary, it is good."

Another element of Chinese life I was slowly starting to understand was "face." A British executive at a high-end international retailer explained some of the details of the concept, which he claimed most Chinese worry about intensely. He told me that it's illegal for a foreigner to say or do things that "hurt the feelings of the Chinese people." But, he said, most Chinese are not conscious of the fact that foreigners have feelings too. It is never okay, he advised, to show anger, unless you explain that you're angry because of something your Chinese conversation partner has done that "took face away" from you. It's important, he said, to remind Chinese interlocutors that you have face too.

Takeaways from the Trenches

- Looking at the org chart of a Chinese company may be confusing for Westerners. The people who are really in charge may not be on the org chart. They may be on an org chart that you will never see. The same is true of ownership. The names of the real owners of Chinese companies may not appear on the list of shareholders. You may never know who really owns the shares.
- The president of a Chinese company manages day-to-day operations, like a COO in a Western company, while the chairman typically handles more strategic issues, like the CEO in Western organizations.
- Government officials in China have a public speaking style that is different from anything that you have ever experienced. They tend to speak in slogans rather than ideas and use numbers rather than concepts, even though they know the numbers are unreliable.
- Your conversation partners are likely to be answering to people you will never meet. The real decision-makers are often people you have never heard of and never will.
- It is unlikely that you will be invited into the home of your conversation partners.
- Gift giving is expected, ubiquitous, and often borders on bribery. You will receive gifts the value of which will put you in violation of the American Foreign Corrupt Practices Act.
- You will not succeed in building personal relationships and it is almost impossible to build trusting ones. However, you will never succeed if you build acrimonious ones. It is a low-trust commercial culture and, indeed, a low-trust society. Don't expect open friendships but work together to achieve your mutual goals.
- The Chinese tend to think in terms of algorithms or technical solutions. They tend to think as engineers, not lawyers.
- Every organization of any significance has a Party Committee. The Party Committee may make decisions that will influence the course of the business. You may not know who is on the Party Committee.

- You may be given explanations of the behavior of your partners that don't make sense to you. Question everything you are told, but never out loud.
- Nothing is as it seems. People generally don't mean what they say or say what they actually mean. Calling this out will be seen by others as impolite and gratuitously aggressive.
- Party members enjoy privileges that non-Party members do not.
- The CCP has a persecution complex, stemming in part from the "Century of Humiliation" but also from its interpretations of Western actions. In the words of Charlie Brown, they think that "everybody is always picking on them."
- It is extremely important to give people face, but don't expect them to do the same for you.
- Nepotism is common in China.
- If your counterparty feels that they have more leverage than you do on any given day, they may insist that you allow them to renegotiate yesterday's contract. The only way to counteract this is to always have some leverage on your side. Without leverage, you lose.

NOTES

1. My "secret" advisory board in Beijing was probably not really so secret. Although one can never know for sure, I've been advised by many Old China Hands that my whereabouts and the people I spent time with were never very clandestine.
2. This is a very difficult figure to confirm, as such data is regarded as a "state secret." Yongyi Song ("Chronology of Mass Killings During the Chinese Cultural Revolution (1966–1976)," *SciencesPo*, August 25, 2011, https://www.sciencespo.fr/mass-violence-war-massacre-resistance/en/document/chronology-mass-killings-during-chinese-cultural-revolution-1966-1976.html) averaged the results of six studies to arrive at a death toll of 2–3 million. The six cited studies offered estimates ranging from 500,000 to 7.73 million deaths.

3. Quotation from Hu's essay, "Resolutely Follow the Cultural Development Path of Socialism with Chinese Characteristics, Work to Build a Socialist Strong Culture Country," cited in Isaac Stone Fish, "Hu Jintao on China Losing the Culture Wars," *Foreign Policy*, January 3, 2012, https://foreignpolicy.com/2012/01/03/hu-jintao-on-china-losing-the-culture-wars.
4. Fish, "Hu Jintao on China Losing the Culture Wars."

CHAPTER FIVE

SLOGGING ALONG

RESOLVING SOME OF THE MAJOR ISSUES

As 2012 began, the work on the new bank intensified. The "decision-making group" was still debating the three big issues (location, identity, and computer backbone). We were constantly interviewing prospective employees, seeking our requisite 62.

The old SVB crew, together with the people we'd hired since getting our license, moved out of our old office on Huaihai Road and into a vacant wing of SPDB's headquarters on the Bund. This impressive neoclassical building had housed the venerable Hong Kong Shanghai Banking Corporation (HSBC) from 1923 until 1955, six years after the "Liberation." At that point, HSBC moved out of the building and the Shanghai Municipal Government (SMG) moved in. Forty years later, in 1995, the SMG moved out, and the newly formed SPDB took it over. At that point, the main body of the building was renovated, revealing a set of eight mosaic murals on the ceiling of the main dome. They'd been covered over during the Cultural Revolution (1966–1976) to protect them from the Red Guards who would have destroyed them because they were examples of the "four bad olds" (customs, culture, habits, and ideas).

Despite the renovations to the main building, our wing was old, worn, drafty, and depressing. When the heating system was on, it was so hot we had to open the windows, even in the middle of winter, making much of the interior brutally cold. Shanghai winters are usually cold until May, when summer arrives almost overnight, replete with high temperatures and extraordinary humidity. Shanghai skips right over spring without even noticing it.

Within the wing, most of our employees were packed into Room 241, engaged in our ultimately vain efforts to hook up our new bank's software backbone to SPDB's homegrown computer system. When the ordeal was finally abandoned, our employees sported baseball caps inscribed with "We survived Room 241."

For all the progress I thought we'd made in the fall of 2011, Luo still acted like what we would call a CEO and what China would call a chairman—that is, as if he was the highest-ranking decision-making executive. This made my life more difficult than it should have been because he knew virtually nothing about our business model. I not only had to run interference to keep him from leading the whole effort astray, but I had to do it without his knowledge.

In general, Luo seemed to be engaging in a form of harassment—of both Tim and me. He besieged me with an unending litany of complaints, including the following:

1. Our projections were too weak; they did not justify building a bank.

2. Tim, our head of risk management, was also weak and didn't know what he was talking about—despite Tim's long and successful history with SVB in both risk management and sales.

3. We must be hiding the truth behind our success, because what we'd disclosed to him, he claimed, didn't support our contention that we banked more venture-backed technology firms in the United States than any other bank, by an order of magnitude.

4. We didn't know what we were doing. Inadvertently, we behaved in a way that made Luo believe we were either lying or stupid. Elwood Dong, whom I'd charged with developing our initial product set, held regular meetings with product management people from SPDB to understand their existing products. I'm not sure why he was doing this or what he intended to accomplish but it made us look stupid and confused. Finally, I told Elwood that we would do anything *except* what SPDB did. Elwood was a smart guy—degrees from Yale and HBS; 800s on his SATs—and generally well-liked, but widely acknowledged as socially inept.

5. Luo told me that others—for example, Dr. Fang, the head of the financial services office for the city of Shanghai—didn't like our business model either. Fang, on the other hand, told me to avoid making decisions and blame anything that went wrong on Luo.

As a result of Luo's suspicions, we wasted yet more time we didn't have. Tim and I had to endure still more "slogan speeches" from him to ensure that we truly understood risk management, an area in which either of us had vastly more experience than he did, particularly in light of the risk-free way in which Chinese banks had operated ever since Mao reorganized them as government-directed piggy banks for the SOEs.

In addition, I suffered through more slogan speeches from the young Party official, Ms. Gao, who had earlier opined on the logo. Her officiousness was stultifying, and her knowledge of marketing would have been lost in a thimble. I resented not just her imperious attitude and ignorance but the waste of both Victor's and Chrystal's time as they translated for me.

The pressure on me to behave as a subordinate to Luo came from many directions. One of the employees seconded to us from SPDB, also named Luo (no relation), openly challenged my "right" to make decisions without first getting Luo's buy-in, and did so publicly. Even Ke, Luo's daughter, called me and pleaded with me to make all decisions in collaboration with her father.

It may seem arrogant on my part not to have acquiesced and allowed Luo to make all the major decisions. But SVB had committed more than $100 million to this project, and I was the primary steward of that money. In addition, our name and reputation were at stake. If the effort failed, or worse, if it came off half-baked, SVB would look like idiots to our clientele. We'd started this project to serve our global clients in China. It was on me to ensure that we provided the services and standards they expected regardless of our geographic location. Like a copilot when the pilot is losing control of the aircraft, I couldn't let Luo drive the plane into the ground.

Moreover, the context was fiercely contentious. In early 2012, with our location yet to be decided, Luo had leaned on me to visit the Yangpu government and tell them we'd never set up our bank in their district. He was hoping for Pudong, even as I still dreamed of Luwan in Old Shanghai.

In retrospect, Luo was using me to deflect blame from himself in the event that we ended up in Yangpu. By then, he must have known that our chances of getting either of our desired locations were slim and that all signs pointed to Yangpu. Why he wanted to hang me out to dry like that, I didn't know and still don't, unless he still hoped to get his point across while maintaining plausible deniability.

Shortly after our location in Yangpu was announced, officials from the Yangpu District started harassing me. The district government had allocated funds to the JV bank to invest in technology companies based in Yangpu, as part of the effort to build an innovation economy there. In other words, the district government functioned as a limited partner providing capital, and we (as the general partner, or GP) invested their funds for them.

Normally, the GP has almost unlimited discretion, but not in China. The Chinese considered this legal construct to be American and saw no reason to adopt it without adding "Chinese characteristics." Of course, these "characteristics" included the expectation that we would place their money in the best funds operating in China, American-based or otherwise. Beyond that, once we'd invested their money in a fund, they wanted that fund to invest only in the Yangpu District. This would be like giving a fund manager your capital but telling it to invest only in my home state of Michigan. There's much to be said for Michigan, but you'll be missing a lot of good opportunities if you restrict your investments within its borders— and no respectable GP in the United States would accept the mandate.

In addition, they wanted to limit our decision-making authority to merely *recommending* investment decisions. I realized they wanted us to convey all our knowledge to them so they could make the investment decisions themselves—regardless of the time, expertise, and hands-on experience necessary to do this well. It was tantamount to going to a restaurant and refusing to order unless the chef gives you a copy of his recipe book and explicit instructions for making each dish. This relationship was an ongoing source of tension.

Finally, SPDB had temporarily assigned to us five people from its staff (also known as "seconding")—but I couldn't find out what these hires should be paid. The Human Resources Department at SPDB wouldn't tell me, and there truly were no public records on the matter. "State secret," they told us every time we asked.

It may seem impossible that the CEO of a prestigious joint venture wouldn't be able to access the company's payroll records, but it was the truth. Every time I asked, and I did, frequently, I was told to pay these individuals what I felt was reasonable and SPDB would make it right, either boosting pay that was inadequate or reducing it if it was excessive. In time, I discovered that bankers' pay packages really *are* a form of state secret because they are so enormous. In case it's not obvious, the CCP doesn't want the public to know.

5.1 THE BREAKTHROUGH IN THE TEA HOUSE AT THE ZIGZAG BRIDGE

In short, the first half of 2012 was challenging and difficult, and it was unclear whether SPDB—our JV partner, theoretically the coparent of our nascent bank—was friend or foe. But we made small steps forward: a new culture in our baby bank began to poke its head up through the snow, first as feeble shoots, then small blossoms. And by May we were ready to move into our new building in the Yangpu District.

But I was worried. Our October license gave us six months to build the bank. As of the end of April, that time had been exhausted. We couldn't make any money because we didn't have a license, but we couldn't get a license if we didn't hire the necessary 62 people and paying them ensured we weren't going to make money.

Luo was surprisingly sanguine when I brought it up. The China Banking Regulatory Commission (CBRC) extended the provisional license for a second six-month period, until October 2012, and Vice Mayor Tu, the CFO of Shanghai, provided a stipend to cover our expenses—well, 50% of them—until then. Of course, SVB had to support the other 50%, because the only alternative was not to open the bank. What actually happened was that SVB posted a loss on its accounts that reflected its share of our operating costs.

The CBRC coordinated the whole project through Ms. Yang in Beijing. I visited her every month for 90 minutes and she'd spend almost a third of the time roughing me up for not getting things done fast enough. Our relationship could best be described as icy. She treated me like an unwanted foster child.

In retrospect, I understood what was going on. The CCP didn't want us to give up and go home because they wouldn't learn anything more from us. But by giving us impossible deadlines, like starting a bank in six months, we were always on the back foot. The CCP always had the upper hand, and with that leverage, it could keep the pressure on. We wouldn't be allowed to make money, but we'd be kept alive as long as SPDB hadn't learned every-thing there was to know about our model.

And despite our increasingly convivial dinners, the tension at work continued between Luo and me. Until, seemingly out of nowhere, it stopped. Practically between breaths, the power struggle disappeared. I believe this change stemmed from a combination of three things.

First, I think there was an impact from my insistence that Sun's attempted end run with the secret letter to our board in Santa Clara was unacceptable, coupled with my heartfelt threat to advise them to pull out of the deal before we'd contributed our share of the equity. I had leverage.

Second, I received blunt feedback from my anonymous advisory board in Beijing that I would have to behave differently if I wanted to succeed in China. While they agreed with the project's importance and SVB's expertise on the topic of lending to technology companies, they were adamant that my execution to date had been deeply flawed. They insisted on three remedies:

- I needed to show Luo face at every opportunity—invite him to accompany me to important events, introduce him as the genius behind the strategy, and praise him in public.

- I needed to make sure that Luo was highly compensated to stay in the background and let me run the bank.
- And for good measure, I needed to take an interest in Luo's daughter, Ke—her career, her views on life, and her overall welfare.

This advice, issued less as a suggestion and more as a command, proved invaluable. It was easy to implement, and I enjoyed it. Ke proved to be a delightful person—intelligent, interesting, thoughtful, and amusing. And over time, I learned to appreciate Luo too, to truly appreciate him, not just appear to do so.

And third, I found an apparent ally in Dean Lu, who became my main channel to Chairman Ji (head of the Shanghai International Group, of which SPDB was a subsidiary). Lu sensed my frustrations about working with Luo. One day that spring, he suggested we meet for tea. His choice of locations for our rendezvous added an aura of mystery: the nineteenth-century teahouse near the Zigzag Bridge in the Yuyuan Gardens of Shanghai's Old Town.

Zigzag bridges are frequent features of Asian water gardens. The design is structurally efficient, as the offset vertical posts support one another in the muddy bottom. The turns of the walkway—and in some, there are no rails—force the pedestrian to adhere to the tenet of Zen philosophy of being present. If your mind wanders, you'll either stumble into the railing or end up in the drink. Also, Chinese folklore holds that evil spirits can only move in a straight line, so a zigzag bridge confounds them. A building located at the end of one, like the teahouse in question, is uniquely protected.

Perhaps it was the protective aura of the zigzags. During our meeting, Lu reassured me. The secret team was well aware of my frustrations. They were on my side. In particular, Chairman Ji would not let Luo run the new bank and relegate me to a secondary role. After all, the idea was to import the SVB business model. I understood the model; Luo did not. I needed to give Luo face, but I should also run the bank. "Forge on ahead" was Lu's message to me, and Ji would give me cover.

I left the teahouse in a much more cheerful mood than when I'd entered it, fearing that I might be asked to stand down or be put firmly in my place, subordinate to Luo. How I would have reacted in that situation, I didn't know at the time and still don't. I'm just glad I didn't need to find out.

I was slowly learning the protocol: never show anger, but work to create leverage, and learn how and when to exercise it. I understood it but I hadn't perfected it. And I never would.

5.2   A TURNING POINT

On May 25, 2012, we had a party to unveil the new logo in front of all the new bank's employees. It was a bright trio of interlocking triangles that looked a bit like a bird-of-paradise flower. I liked it a lot.

Because Mr. Luo himself had designed it, this was the perfect opportunity for me to praise him in public. I developed an agenda for the event, and I officiated. First, I sang Luo's praises, crediting him as the genius behind our strategy as well as the designer of the logo. Then we had the unveiling. Next on the agenda, Monika, the head of the marketing firm that assisted Luo in the design, was to take the floor and tell all the employees what an amazingly good job Luo had done.

But a disruption emanated from the back of the room. Ms. Gao, SPDB's head of marketing who'd given me the long and condescending speech on Marketing 101 a few months earlier, made her way forward. Thin-lipped, scowling, and wearing an odd outfit of a black suit, white shirt, and tie, she demanded that Luo speak next. She wasn't going to let me continue my agenda.

I stepped down from the podium, ushered her to the door, and told her to leave and never come back. Three months later, after the bank had opened, I found her in our corridors shepherding Chinese reporters around the building. At that time, I took her gently by the arm, led her to the elevator, pressed the button, urged her inside, and reminded her that she wasn't welcome. To the best of my knowledge, she never returned as long as I ran the place.

After Monika's speech, I invited Luo to take the microphone. He spoke for at least 30 minutes. The style of his speech, both in terms of content and delivery, came straight out of an earlier era. Among our employees, who were on average under 30, there was a lot of shuffling of feet and giggling.

The next day I went to see Luo. I told him I was offended by Gao's behavior, and I would not allow her to come into our bank again. To my surprise, Luo told me that he supported me. Her behavior was unacceptable. I deserved face, and she had not given me any.

His next words were even more shocking. He told me that he could empathize with me because he felt the same. The way our employees had treated him had hurt his feelings.[1] He recognized that they'd found his speech boring, and he knew he was out of touch with their generation. I assured him that I supported him, and that I was ashamed our employees hadn't given him face. He seemed genuinely moved by my expressions of empathy. It's not often that a man of Luo's stature in China allows himself to be vulnerable in a conversation with a Westerner, a group historically castigated as "barbarians."

Only a few weeks later, Luo and I were sitting in the conference room where we'd met so often in the past, side by side, facing forward, straining our necks to turn far enough to the side to see each other—just thinking about this flares up that crick in my neck—as we rehashed the org chart issues that had plagued our relationship for almost a year.

And then Luo—suddenly—relented. He told me I would have my way on everything. He shook my hand, rose from his chair, and walked out of the room. He didn't seem angry, only resigned to a new set of circumstances. After he left, Victor stood up and gave me a vigorous high-five, grinning from ear to ear.

What drove Luo's change, I don't know. Two weeks before, yet again, I had gotten fed up and spoken with Lu, our supervisor, who likely took the matter to Chairman Ji who probably called Luo in and told him to cut it out. Maybe Ji had finally lowered the boom. Maybe Luo was tired of the ongoing shadowboxing and the fruitless arguments, or maybe the Organization Department had finally crushed his dream of delayed retirement. I don't know. But that day marked a real turning point in my relationship with Luo.

5.3   PUT IN OUR PLACE

A further example of the difference between running a bank in China and one in the United States occurred in May, at a CBRC meeting with the presidents of the other roughly 100 foreign banks in Shanghai. A study conducted by the Shanghai CBRC had revealed that incidents of fraud were on the rise in Shanghai, but only among the foreign banks. (By "foreign," I mean banks that are based in places other than China, but have entered China in joint ventures, meaning that, for all intents and purposes, they were under the CCP's control.) We received two hours of instruction on the causes of this.

There were three reasons, we were told. First, foreign banks were too trusting of their employees. Chinese banks knew their employees' circumstances to a far greater extent: Did they have financial problems? What were their financial obligations? How well did they get along with their spouses and with the senior members of their extended families? And so on.

For a U.S. bank, U.S. privacy laws precluded getting much of this information. SVB routinely runs credit checks as allowed by law but investigating spousal and familial relationships definitely crossed the line! Yet this was typical of Chinese banks.

As an aside, this wide-ranging knowledge of employees' lives comes about through a social credit system that China started implementing in

2014.[2] It tracks anything the government considers relevant—elements that would typically be included in a credit rating, but also attitudes and behaviors. These might include whether you download the Xi Jinping app and study it daily for 15 minutes, whether you argue with officials, or if you get along with your wife, play too many videogames, break traffic laws, or are reported as making anti-CCP comments. All of this gets into the social credit system, which enforces the concept that "keeping trust is glorious and breaking trust is disgraceful."[3]

The program was expected to be fully operational by 2020,[4] but as of early 2022, participation was still voluntary and piecemeal. Eventually, everyone in China will receive a unique code so they can measure their social credit balances in real time. Even just a few years after introduction, the government started punishing people with low social credit scores by banning them from flights and luxury hotels. Good citizens receive rewards that include discounts on energy bills, expedited travel applications, and better placement on dating apps.[5] As cash disappears in favor of Alipay and WePay, people with low scores may be excluded entirely from payment systems.

Second, the speaker told us that we were more likely to hire substandard employees because foreign banks competed for the same limited pool of potential candidates. We all wanted such attributes as experience overseas, fluency in English, a positive attitude toward the West, and financial competence. How exactly these qualities meant we had substandard candidates puzzled me, as they seemed to indicate intellectual curiosity, breadth of experience, ambition, and ability in a way that a narrower set of abilities— say, functional aptitude alone—did not.

The third reason for fraud, we learned, was that foreign banks underpaid their employees. Of course, it's difficult for foreign banks to know how much they should pay, as the income of Chinese bankers is a state secret and cannot be revealed.

I finally ferreted out parts of the answer about how much Chinese bankers were paid, but never the whole story. The Chinese bank compensation system is completely inverted from the U.S. approach. All Chinese bankers—distinct from janitors or any other nonfinancial positions in banks—start as tellers and work their way up. They're also CCP members. The compensation package is enormous and not just in the typical salary-and-bonus structure, which itself is completely different from the structure in the United States. There, to reduce risk-taking behavior, a performance-related bonus can never exceed 25% of annual salary. In China, the bonus makes up about 75% of the package. Another huge difference from the United States is the staggering number of additional allowances provided to Chinese bankers, covering items such as babysitting, housing, travel, and the like. A Chinese banker is on the gravy train for life. I eventually learned that compensation packages for Chinese bankers are "state secrets" because the CCP simply doesn't want the public to know how much bankers are paid.

We didn't make any changes to our practices as a result of these instructions.

Interestingly, about a year later, Ms. Duan, my favorite person at the CBRC in Beijing (because she neither bullied us nor seemed to want to manipulate us), told me that we risked being defrauded by our Chinese clients (not our staff) to a much greater extent than would be the case if we were culturally Chinese. It took me another year or so to learn that this risk derived from two fundamental Chinese beliefs. First, Westerners "owed" China for the Century of Humiliation, a series of invasions that started with the Opium Wars in 1839. Second, if you hadn't been born Chinese, you would always be an outsider. This attitude extended to companies as well. Even being half-owned by SPDB, 99% staffed by Chinese nationals, and focused on solely banking Chinese start-ups, our bank would never be viewed as Chinese.

In this same timeframe, I was invited to give a speech on financing technology companies. It was a government-sponsored conference, by definition, because all banks except foreign ones are functionally owned by the government, and there's no state-sanctioned freedom of assembly anyway.

I prepared and practiced. On the day in question, Chrystal and I went to the auditorium. At these affairs, the front row was always reserved for the speakers and Chrystal had to sit in the back, translate what the other speakers said, and relay that to me through headphones.

I settled into my seat, put on my headphones, and got comfortable. When I looked up to see who was sitting next to me, I saw—to my surprise—that it was Mr. Ge, one of our board members. Ge was always affable and often a little tipsy.

"What are you doing here?" I asked.

He smiled. "I'm giving a speech on banking technology companies."

I thought that was odd, because SPDB had sworn that it had never banked tech companies and never would, in the spirit of neither parent competing against the child.

Ge's speech immediately preceded mine, and I was shocked to see the slides he was using. They were *my* slides, from the presentation I'd given earlier to SPDB's management in response to Mr. Luo's accusation that I was withholding "the algorithm." When Ge returned to his seat, he jabbed his elbow into my ribs, gave me a huge grin, and like a small boy eager to please, asked me, "How did I do?"

Of course, I had a different set of slides, so it was hardly as if we repeated each other. And Ge was obviously trying to do a good job. Since then, several China experts have said his use of my slides was an indication of admiration. But this interchange emphasizes a fundamental difference between the United States and China. It would never have occurred to him that using my slides was an infraction. In China, copying is viewed as a compliment, not theft, particularly in art. Historically, Chinese artists trained by copying the work of their instructors; a perfect copy meant you were a good artist. Intellectual property protection has been an ongoing issue between China and the West—in 2017, a report from the Commission on the Theft of American Intellectual Property estimated that the United States alone lost between $225 billion and $600 billion due to intellectual property theft by Chinese operators.[6] So IP theft may be a compliment, but it certainly is a profitable one as well.

In June 2012, we were readying the plans for the Yangpu office. The head of our general office, Mr. Shen (who went by "Luke," a name I believe he'd picked up watching old reruns of *Bonanza*) showed me the blueprints for the layout. I was amazed to see the dimensions of my new office (see Figure 5.1). It was identical to Luo's, and together, the two offices comprised 50% of the floor space of one level of the office. (The entire office occupied two floors, so these offices were 25% of the total office space but took up a huge amount of the first floor.) Each office was enormous,

Figure 5.1 Original office layout.

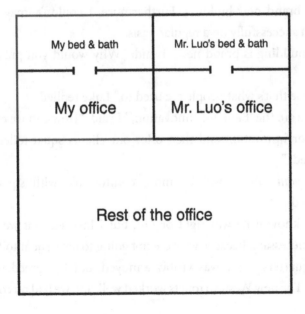

My bed & bath	Mr. Luo's bed & bath
My office	Mr. Luo's office
Rest of the office	

consisting of three separate rooms: a work and meeting space, a bathroom, and a bedroom.

When I asked Luke why we needed so much space, he seemed to be as surprised by my question as I was by the blueprint. He said that every president of a respectable SOE had an office like this. But why the bedroom, I asked. Because, he said, until recently, everybody napped after lunch—the president in his bedroom, and the rest of the employees at their desks. I asked if they still did that. He said not so much anymore, but protocol still required the bedroom. I insisted that we get rid of the bedrooms and the executive bathrooms, leaving more room for expansion if we needed it. Reluctantly, he agreed.

But Luke was less agreeable a few months later when, shortly before our grand opening, he walked me through the new space. I balked at my first sight of the bathrooms for employees and clients. They were all the old-fashioned, squat kind. No seats, just a hole in the center of the floor, and bring your own TP. I'd gotten used to seeing them in older buildings (and always had a bit of tissue in my pocket), but I hadn't expected to find them in a brand-new building. Furthermore, I couldn't imagine myself using them successfully on a regular basis.

"This building is brand new," I said. "Why would you put squat toilets here?"

"Because that's what people are used to," Luke replied.

"But we are the 'Bank for Innovation,'" I said. "How can we claim to be the bank for innovation and then offer our clients squat toilets in their hour of need?"

"Even *your* clients will be more comfortable with squat toilets," Luke insisted.

I don't know if he was right or not, but I insisted that we delay the opening if necessary, because we were not going to have squat toilets in our new headquarters. Luke was visibly annoyed, but he agreed with great reluctance. The new Western toilets worked well, and we had no complaints.

Takeaways from the Trenches

- Memoranda of understanding are preferred over contracts because they reflect the agreement in the moment and are flexible.
- Never admit to making a mistake. Blame anything that goes wrong on others. Take credit for anything that goes well. I received this advice from several people.
- Many things are considered state secrets. Transparency is not encouraged.
- If you have leverage, use it. If your counterparty has leverage, expect him to use it. If you have an opportunity, blacken your competitor's name. Expect him to do the same to you. Business is a blood sport.
- Patronage is the order of the day. Cultivate protectors. Anticipate that your counterparty will as well.
- Never show anger. Your counterparty will interpret anger as weakness.
- Most Chinese do not feel guilt. However, shame is common. Your counterparty will seek to shame you or bully you into renegotiating your contract.
- Copying is considered an expression of admiration, not a crime.

NOTES

1. Lest this comment seem impossibly immature, "the CCP, state media, and various strident nationalists have used the expression 'hurting the feelings of the Chinese people for decades,'" wrote the *Wall Street Journal*. The first usage appeared in 1959, but it has been in common circulation since. (Benjamin Qiu, "China Prepares to Crack Down on 'Hurt Feelings,'" *Wall Steet Journal,* September 25, 2023.) In early September 2023, amendments to China's Public Security Administration Law were proposed that would impose jail time and fines for wearing clothes or symbols that "damage the spirit of the Chinese nation, or that hurt the feelings of the Chinese people." Hsia Hsiao-hwa, "'Hurting the feelings of the Chinese people' could be punished by jail time," *Radio Free Asia,* September 7, 2023, https://www.rfa.org/english/news/china/china-hurt-feelings-09072023123314.html.

2. Katie Canales and Aaron Mok, "China's 'Social Credit' System Ranks Citizens and Punishes Them with Throttled Internet Speeds and Flight Bans if the Communist Party Deems Them Untrustworthy," *Business Insider*, updated November 28, 2022, https://www.businessinsider.com/china-social-credit-system-punishments-and-rewards-explained-2018-4.

3. China Copyright and Media, "Planning Outline for the Construction of a Social Credit System (2014–2020)," April 25, 2015, https://chinacopyrightandmedia .wordpress.com/2014/06/14/planning-outline-for-the-construction-of-a-social-credit-system-2014-2020/, cited in Canales and Mok, "China's 'Social Credit' System Ranks Citizens . . ."

4. Nicole Kobie, "The Complicated Truth About China's Social Credit System," *Wired*, July 6, 2019, https://www.wired.co.uk/article/china-social-credit-system-explained.

5. Canales and Mok, "China's 'Social Credit' System Ranks Citizens. . . ."

6. The National Bureau of Asian Research, "Update to the Report of the Commission on the Theft of American Intellectual Property," February 2017, http://ipcommission.org/report/IP_Commission_Report_Update_2017.pdf.

CHAPTER SIX

THE GRAND OPENING AND YET MORE LICENSES WE DIDN'T HAVE

As we scrambled to meet the deadline for opening the bank, we also worried about finding a date acceptable to the Shanghai government for the grand opening event. We had to open by October, the one-year anniversary of receiving our "getting ready to open the bank" license. The CBRC would not grant another extension, having already doubled the amount of time we'd originally been given. Somehow there was no accommodation made for the first three months while the Party

Committee twiddled its thumbs about appointing members of the working and decision-making groups. That point never came up.

Members of the secret team I spoke with—always individually, never as a group—had been hoping for August 8, as that would be 8-8. The number 8 is considered so auspicious in China that people will often postpone weddings for months just to avail themselves of the good luck that comes to anyone who does anything important on that date.

The challenge was that we all agreed we needed Party Secretary Yu in attendance. This was an astute call, since shortly thereafter, President Xi elevated Yu to the Standing Committee, making him, at least in theory, one of the seven most powerful people in China. But here came the calendar conundrum: he couldn't commit to anything until, at the earliest, one week before, because Yu had to wait for Xi to set his own calendar first, which even *he* did only one week in advance. And once we were on Yu's calendar, it was possible that someone higher up would urgently need a meeting, which would preempt our carefully organized event.

My wife and I and a few of our Chinese friends had been planning a trip to Tibet. Thinking that the grand opening would be on August 8, we booked the trip for later that month. Every day, Victor called his counterpart in Luo's office, who in turn checked almost daily with her counterpart at another office farther up the chain of command, who in turn . . . you get the picture. We had to go through at least four offices, each in turn, to get up to Party Secretary Yu's level. And as August 8 came and went, we realized the date of the Tibet trip was in jeopardy. Finally, we had no choice but to cancel it, which cost us all the money we'd paid in advance. Note to self: pay the surcharge for refundable tickets when dealing with the CCP.

In the end, the opening occurred on August 15. Party Secretary Yu came and spoke briefly. At least 200 government officials attended. I sat next to Vice Mayor Tu, the head of financial services for Shanghai. We talked about the upcoming change in leadership at SPDB. Luo was retiring, to be replaced by Mr. Zhu, who was an old friend of Tu's. Although Zhu had no banking experience, he was well-versed in finance and would do a brilliant job, Tu assured me.

Perhaps foolishly, I put in a good word for Mr. Liu, Luo's second in command. He'd been at SPDB for many years, he'd been practically running the bank himself while reporting to Luo, and we trusted him. Tu laughed nervously.

Shortly after our opening, the Organization Department transferred Liu to another SOE, and Zhu took command of SPDB—and our board. Within two years, Zhu was transferred to some other post, and Liu was brought back to run the show. I never learned what the Organization Department was thinking when it designed this succession plan, although Tu's friendship with Zhu may have gotten the fellow the job, only to have him bungle the execution. I can only say that it baffled me.

6.1   A LICENSE . . . TO WAIT

And so, in August 2012, almost a year and a half after my arrival in Shanghai and 10 months after we'd been granted our first license, the CBRC deemed us ready to open our doors to the public. The grand opening ceremony on August 15 went off without a hitch. The Party Secretary spoke. We were elated. At last, after filling 62 positions, after the battles with Luo, after resolving the issues around the location, the identity, and the IT system, we could finally do what we did best: lend money to innovative start-ups. We couldn't wait.

But we had to.

In the fine print, the license *did* allow us to open the doors to our bank. But we would not be allowed to lend Chinese currency (renminbi, or RMB, literally, "the people's currency") for three years. We could have an office and a staff but we could not make any loans in domestic currency.

This was not a bureaucratic snafu. For decades, by Chinese law, any new bank with any amount of foreign ownership whatsoever had to wait *three years* after opening before it could use Chinese currency. Until those three years were up, it could only use what are called "onshore dollars"—that is, dollars that have passed through the Chinese foreign exchange regulation agency (the State Administration for Foreign Exchange or SAFE) and are *inside* China. Of course, in China, everyone uses RMB because that's the coin of the realm. Employees are paid in RMB, supplies are acquired in RMB, there's no need whatsoever for dollars within China, just as there's very little need for RMB (or Canadian dollars, for that matter) in the United States.

In fact, the Chinese government has established systems to ensure that foreign currency remains with the government rather than with any companies. Companies buying supplies from overseas use the services of an agent or trading company, which is government-controlled or -owned. The companies pay the intermediary in RMB, and it then orders the requested items from overseas vendors and pays in dollars, which the government gets out of the Treasury from its U.S.-dollar denominated trade surplus with the rest of the world. We spent the next three years looking for onshore dollars to lend. They were as scarce as four-leaf clovers.

For the next three years, we had nothing to do apart from teaching the staff how to execute SVB's model in preparation for the day when we'd actually be able to lend RMB. That's right—we'd have to wait for three years after opening (which had already taken almost two years) before we could do business. Worse yet, since the CBRC won't let a bank open without a full staff, we would have to support a full crew of 62 for three years before we could earn any money to pay them.

Now, if you're paying attention, you'll have a number of legitimate questions:

1. Why didn't we know this beforehand? Well, we did. But we didn't believe it. If the CCP wanted us in China to the extent that the Party

Secretary of Shanghai nearly begged us to come, why would they lock us up for five years (two for preparation, and three waiting for permission to use RMB)?

2. What did the CCP expect us to do for the next three years while we waited? That's easy: teach other banks our business model—first and foremost SPDB, but others as well.

3. How did they expect us to sustain ourselves while we waited for permission to use RMB? The Shanghai government graciously provided us with a subsidy that covered about half of our annual loss. SVB covered the rest, not as a subsidy but as a loss on the income statement.

4. Is that legal? Good question! No, not really, or to be specific, both the subsidy and the delay are in violation of the terms that China agreed to when it joined the World Trade Organization (WTO) in 2001.

5. Why did we let this happen to us? First, we were naive and expected the Chinese government to behave in an ethical, logical, and civil manner. Okay, we were stupid. We thought that because we were a 50% JV with SPDB, the government would want us to get moving as soon as we could. Although the restriction on lending RMB was written into the original agreement, we believed it was just for appearances and we'd actually be lending RMB as soon as we got our license. Um, not the case.

Second, there's a story about a frog and a scorpion standing on the bank of a river. The frog is about to cross, and the scorpion, who can't swim, asks the frog if he can hitch a ride on the frog's back. "No," says the frog, "I'm afraid you'll kill me." The scorpion replies, "No I won't, I promise." The frog replies, "Okay, climb aboard." When they reach the other side of the river, the scorpion kills the frog. With his dying breath, the frog asks, "Why did you do that?"

The scorpion replies, "Because I'm a scorpion, stupid." We were the frog.

But wait, there's more! In the United States, if the Fed or the Office of the Comptroller of the Currency gives you a license to set up a bank, you are—from the get-go—allowed to do anything that a chartered bank is permitted to do.

Not so in China. A license, literally, only gives you permission to open your doors, and nothing else. To take deposits requires a separate license. To make a loan requires a separate license. To exchange currencies requires a separate license. To have a website that enables your customers to see their balances requires a separate license. In fact, just to apply for the website license requires you to have been in business for more than one year. Even as of 2021, the SVB JV in China *still* did not have all the licenses that we formally need to execute on our business model. And that has had a material effect on the JV bank's performance. Which, of course, is just the sort of control that the CCP wants.

6.2 THE WORRY OF WARRANTS

One of those prohibited activities for several years was taking warrants. As described earlier, our business model depends on our ability to take warrants, which allow us to buy and then sell stock in successful companies, offsetting losses from unsuccessful companies. The warrants are only a tiny slice of equity (a half percent or so). With this tiny slice of equity, the bank can at least break even and sometimes makes money.

Unfortunately for us, the Chinese went for 27 years under CCP rule (from the "Liberation" in 1949 to the death of Mao in 1976) without differentiating between debt and equity. In fact, to a great extent, China still doesn't fully appreciate this difference. Until we introduced the concept to the Chinese regulators, taking warrants was *functionally* illegal. And it was illegal because *the CBRC hadn't said it was legal.* In the United States, you can generally do something unless the law says you can't. In China, you can't do anything unless the law says you can (regulation by a so-called "positive list"). Only several years after SVB received the initial license, after scores of meetings with regulators, did it become legal for us to take warrants.

That fall of 2012, a very astute financial journalist named Yue Tan interviewed me about our business model at a conference. There were hundreds of people in the audience. Yue said to me: "I've read everything I could about your business model. I believe that you will need to be allowed to take warrants to succeed. Am I right?"

I answered: "Yes, you're right. But I believe that the CBRC will soon allow us to do so." Immediately, a man in the third row stood up and yelled, "I am from the CBRC! Not in my lifetime will you be allowed to take warrants!" I wasn't sure if he was gleeful or mournful. Although he turned out to be wrong, I'm certain he was sincere.

6.3 GROWING ANXIETY

The balance of 2012 was uneventful from a big-picture point of view, but peppered with noteworthy, and in some cases, unsettling, occurrences.

That fall, we began to hear the first "rumblings of impending war." Huang, my young art-appreciating friend, began talking about the likelihood of conflict between China and the United States, which *might*, he insisted, result in a military conflagration. His reasoning was as follows: since the Opium Wars in the 1840s, Western powers had lorded it over China. Now, at long last, China was catching up and would ultimately get ahead of the West, including the United States. America would not be able to tolerate this blow to its supremacy. In the end, Huang thought, it would be the United States that would initiate a military skirmish, probably in response to Xi Jinping's insistence that China control the South China Sea. Interestingly, Huang seemed to identify with China rather than the United States, even though his mother had suffered severely during the Cultural Revolution and he himself had extensive (and apparently positive) experiences in the United States.

The other, complementary rumor was that China and Japan would soon be at war over the Senkaku Islands. Claimed by both China and Japan, these uninhabited islands' value lay in their proximity to shipping lanes, oil reserves, and fishing grounds. They'd been controlled by Japan since the War of 1895, but since the beginning of Xi's gradual rise to power, China's Propaganda Department had gone out of its way to draw attention to them and inflame anti-Japanese sentiment. Even at board lunches with our SPDB counterparts, war with Japan was a regular topic. The SPDB contingent seemed to view it as a certainty.

6.4   REGULATION

Although we had difficulties with some of the SPDB staff, we managed to build an excellent relationship with the CBRC in Shanghai. Mr. Liao, the head (who has since been promoted to personal assistant to Liu He, one of China's vice premiers), treated us fairly and always tried to find constructive solutions to our problems. But he was limited in what he could do, largely by his bosses at the CBRC in Beijing.

We always had trouble with Beijing. In the early years, while Shanghai encouraged us, Beijing was always doing the opposite. Once we'd settled on Shanghai for the SVB joint venture, Beijing took offense and regularly harassed us. The head of financial services for Beijing regularly told us that he was angry we'd chosen Shanghai over Beijing for our first office, and he'd find ways to even the score. Our handlers at the CBRC in Beijing, with one exception, treated us like captured soldiers from an opposing army.

Ms. Yang, the head of the division responsible for us, still treated me like a naughty boy who needed a good bawling out at every meeting. We met monthly while the bank was getting ready to open. Ms. Deng, one of her assistants, complained regularly to Changchang, our head of compliance, that I was a pain in the neck. The bright light in the group was Ms. Duan, Yang's successor as the head of foreign banks. She always spoke to me politely and encouraged me to the extent that she realistically could. Also, she exhibited considerable intellectual curiosity regarding our business model. To her, we were an interesting oddity, and perhaps one that could contribute to China's progress. To the others, we were quite obviously an annoyance.

And then there were those who wanted our business model but weren't willing to pay for it: the Bank of Beijing and Zhongguancun Science Park. Their managers regularly requested meetings to pick our brains and learn as much as they could about how we made loans, but every deal they suggested we do together was 99% in their favor. Sometimes the proposals they made were so extremely one-sided that we could only infer they thought we were stupid or lacked any leverage whatsoever.

In the fall of 2012, the CBRC in Beijing began to complain that the Federal Reserve insisted on examining the activities of our joint venture. Because the JV *was* 50% owned by SVB, a bank that the Fed had chartered, it was their right to regulate us alongside the CBRC. However, that offended the CBRC, presumably out of national pride. Accordingly, the CBRC objected.

There really wasn't a lot we could do to ease the CBRC's concerns. If the Fed says they'll do something, they do it. We just told CBRC that it was a legal issue that had something to do with the fact SVB owned 50% of the joint venture. As a result, the JV was under the Fed's jurisdiction as well as theirs. If SVB had owned a smaller amount, the Fed may have had less interest in what went on with the JV.

The CBRC's issues with the Fed are emblematic of China's issues with conforming to any other country's rules. The CSRC (China Securities Regulatory Commission, the Chinese counterpart to the U.S. Securities and Exchange Commission, or SEC) doesn't allow Chinese companies listed on American exchanges to disclose information to the SEC as required by American law. The reason: "state secret." I believe this is simply to demonstrate sovereignty. In fact, China now has laws prohibiting anyone from sharing information or any form of evidence that might be used in a foreign investigation of a Chinese firm unless approved by the Supreme People's Procuratorate, China's version of a Supreme Court. (In 2020, the U.S. government enacted a law that allowed the SEC to remove Chinese companies from U.S. exchanges if they did not comply with U.S. auditing requirements.[1])

Part of the tension was that the Fed's mission is different from the CBRC's. The Fed's primary mission is to protect depositors from loss, and its secondary mission is to enhance the stability of the banking system. The CBRC is certainly interested in enhancing the banking system's stability, but its primary mission is ensuring that banks provide cheap capital to fund government projects. In fact, until the Chinese real estate laws allowed ordinary citizens to buy and sell apartments, the only place people could put their savings was in banks. That's not necessarily bad, but the ordinary Chinese depositor receives very little interest on their bank deposits. The government benefits because it uses this money to pay for its projects. At the same time, the depositors can be virtually assured they won't lose their money, even if they don't earn anything on it. If their bank fails (that is, if the bank's debts exceed its deposits), the government simply and quietly recapitalizes it.

Ironically, although the Beijing CBRC resisted all efforts by the Fed to regulate the JV, it regularly wanted to send representatives to the San Francisco Fed to learn its techniques. To add insult to injury, they wanted our JV to pay the travel expenses for their delegation. We refused on the grounds that it would be illegal.

Takeaways from the Trenches

- In China, you may only do what you are licensed to do. In the United States, you may do anything that the law does not forbid you to do.
- Every individual activity requires a license. The license is the carrot; pressure and shame are the sticks. No matter how fast you run, you will never catch the carrot, because it is moving faster than you can run.
- China will allow you enough licenses to hold your interest, but not enough to enable you to succeed. You are there so they can learn from you.
- Meter your performance and take small steps to preserve your leverage. If your counterparty promises to do A if you will do B, insist that he do A first, and then never do more than B until after your counterparty fulfills his next commitment.
- Keep your competitor under constant pressure. Expect him to do the same to you.
- Loyalty is considered a more important qualification for an employee than subject matter expertise.
- Don't anticipate good faith. Remain cynical.
- The CCP encourages the Chinese people to believe that the West has humiliated them for 100 years. As a result, we "owe them." They deserve a "hall pass."
- China rewrites history to serve its agenda, on a regular and ongoing basis. See Chapter 15 for additional examples.

NOTE

1. U.S. Securities and Exchange Commission, "Holding Foreign Companies Accountable Act," n.d., accessed February 10, 2022, https://www.sec.gov/hfcaa.

CHAPTER SEVEN

STAFFING

CCP OFFSPRING, PARENTS, AND CULTURAL DIFFERENCES

I mentioned earlier that part of my challenge in setting up the bank was the pressure to hire sons and daughters of well-placed CCP members. While Party members themselves are typically the best and brightest, their offspring may not share their parents' talents. It's no longer a given that the children of Party members will also be in the Party, as membership has become more meritocratic. The Party-member parents, though, possess important connections throughout the economy and often feel it part of their parental duty to advance their children's career paths, regardless of talent. As a matter of course, I steered away from hiring anyone who wasn't qualified, regardless of their lineage, and always adhered to our standard pay grade for compensation. Events in autumn 2012 made me glad of that choice.

7.1 RECRUITING: SONS AND DAUGHTERS OF THE PARTY

In late 2012, rumors started circulating about JPMorgan's Chinese recruitment practices, which were receiving particular attention from the audit committees of American banks doing business in China. These stories had repercussions for us in our little JV in Shanghai.

First, a word on what JPMorgan (JPM) was doing. Between 2006 and 2013, JPM pursued its so-called Sons and Daughters Program.[1] Recognizing that *guanxi* played a much bigger role in China's banking industry than did regulation and law, JPM recruited the offspring of high-level government officials in a very targeted fashion—sometimes these recruits were skilled themselves, but regardless, their parents were in a position to provide JPM with assistance and contacts.

Chinese parents are generally much more active in seeking advantage for their kids than most American parents. While the Varsity Blues scandal showed that wealthy parents in the United States might bribe their kids' way into prestigious colleges, such efforts to smooth the way for one's progeny are much more widespread in China—and far more accepted. If you're a member of the CCP and your children get jobs in a foreign bank, you'll want to help them and their employer succeed. The higher you are in the Chinese government, the more likely it is that you and your connections will be able to help. JPM's offense, from the perspective of the American Foreign Corrupt Practices Act, was not so much that it targeted the sons and daughters of high-level government officials, but that it often paid these recruits several times what their job level was worth in the open market. For this offense, JPM paid fines almost three times the size of the revenues generated through contacts that came from the Sons and Daughters program.

Let me describe to you how that might work in practice with reference to the following examples:

1. **Thomas**

   Thomas was Lao Ding's son. He was a nice enough fellow but not very effective. By the time Lao Ding asked me to hire Thomas, he'd already had a number of previous jobs and apparently had not excelled at any of them. In deference to Lao Ding, we decided to give Thomas a chance. I want to underscore that we paid Thomas exactly what our pay scale suggested, and not a dime more.

   Even so, Lao Ding regularly scheduled meetings with me. Some were to discuss what he could do to help our bank succeed, and others were to discuss why we should promote Thomas and pay him more money. As we did neither, Thomas eventually quit and went elsewhere. To Lao Ding's credit, he never ceased trying to be helpful.

2. **Hannah**

   Hannah was the daughter of Mr. Zhang, whom I mentioned in Chapter 3. Unlike Thomas, Hannah was very effective, and unlike Lao Ding, Zhang did very little to specifically help us. He offered advice but counterbalanced it with annoying complaints. Hannah continued to do well, and her father met with us many times to monitor her progress. He too was always encouraging us to pay Hannah more and to promote her more often.

   To me, Zhang's advice was fascinating. He was the first person I met who referred to the CCP as the Mafia, although some did later, when they got to know me better.[2] Zhang's advice to me was clearly based on *The Art of War*, Sun Tzu's ancient book on warfare that emphasized deception rather than outright conflict. I found it difficult to follow his advice to never admit anything, deny everything, take credit for any successes, and blame all failures on Mr. Luo. I just couldn't do it.

3. Chloe

I met Chloe through an American businessman in Shanghai. One night over drinks, he asked if our JV offered internships, as he had a friend whose daughter who was looking for one. I said that she would be welcome to apply.

We met Chloe, interviewed her, and hired her. She was smart enough, but as we learned in time, immensely entitled and self-centered. Her relationships with her peers were seriously flawed, and she demanded special attention as often as she could.

Within a very short time, her parents reached out and asked if they could visit me. They were high-level officials in the CCP and felt they could help us get traction. Furthermore, they wanted to chart their daughter's progress and find out how long it would take her to become a member of the executive team.

In the summer of 2013, Chloe's parents took me to dinner to tell me that they trusted me and knew I'd never let them down. Translation: advance Chloe's career or be careful.

Happily, within a year, Chloe's attention span had exhausted itself. She felt that she'd learned everything worth knowing about our business model and she moved on. We never asked her parents for help. I felt as if we'd dodged another of China's many bullets.

The relationship of CCP members with their offspring and the organizations who employ those children is strange indeed. I learned this one night when I met with Lao Ding at one of the many private "clubs" in

Shanghai that the CCP had refurbished and allowed its high-ranking members to use. Of course, these clubs are "secret." Somehow, secrecy makes things more exotic in China, and many meetings or minor facts are shrouded in secrecy.

This meeting had all the trappings of a drug deal. Per instructions given in advance by Lao Ding's general office, my driver turned off a main street into a nondescript alley, at the end of which we were intercepted by one of Lao Ding's men, who directed us into another even more nondescript alley, at the end of which was a building that looked like an abandoned warehouse. Inside, however, it had been rendered quite pleasant. As far as I could tell, we were the only people in the entire building. I was concerned, as it seemed like an odd place to meet, and Lao Ding hadn't revealed the agenda beforehand.

As it turned out, Lao Ding wanted to discuss the progress of his son, Thomas, at the bank. We spent two hours talking about ways to increase the slope of his learning curve and thus his career path. The problem with Thomas, and the offspring of many other Party leaders, was that he wasn't highly motivated—to learn our underwriting technique, to create innovative marketing programs, or, in truth, to work hard at anything. He'd been led to believe that having a parent in the Party would be sufficient to ensure his success in life. Such young people are often scorned (or pitied) by their non-Party-affiliated contemporaries.

While many members of the 93% of China's population that are not Party members cherish the CCP due to the aura of Mao's unification of China and the Liberation, young people are starting to show resentment. Older Chinese who are not in the Party say that the nice thing about life under Mao was that everyone was poor and everyone got the same deal. This is not true: CCP members had an easier life, but it was not as obvious because the country was so undeveloped. Now, people in their twenties and thirties realize their Party-member peers get the prestigious internships and better jobs and that, in general, the deck is stacked to their benefit.

The CCP no longer unquestioningly accepts members' children—for instance, Thomas was not a member because he wasn't smart enough. Nonetheless, he got a lot of help from Lao Ding's connections, which bred resentment among his peers who had to work for anything they achieved.

7.2 RETAINING: THE BRAIN DRAIN

That autumn, we lost several SPDB employees who'd been seconded to us at the beginning of the year. They didn't necessarily submit letters of resignation, either. Sometimes they just stopped showing up. This was the case with Yuhu, our head of operations—he just disappeared. When I investigated, I learned that his old boss at SPDB had never really accepted his departure and kept calling him back to meetings in his old department. Yuhu preferred working at SPDB, and only too willingly complied.

Eventually, he came to see me. He wanted to go back to SPDB, he said. Thirty minutes into our conversation, he broke down in tears and *begged* to go back. He didn't feel comfortable in a Western company. And he was worried that the Organization Department would never give him credit for the time he'd spent with us, that he would be sidetracked and forgotten. In effect, he feared his career was over, even though he was only about 40. I was saddened to discover that at least one person wasn't excited and engaged to be part of our business model and the culture we were creating.

On the other hand, I saw this as an opportunity. Yuhu had never struck me as particularly talented, and he certainly was not one to take initiative. He was amusing, to be sure. He'd memorized a great many ancient Chinese poems and enjoyed being called to the podium at our semi-monthly employee meetings to recite them in an impressively dramatic and moving style. But he demonstrated very little respect for me and his other colleagues on our management team. He spent most of his time at our meetings paying no attention whatsoever, texting colleagues back at SPDB, and on occasion even taking calls. I'd told the team several times that we don't use our cell phones during meetings at SVB and that we wouldn't here at our new bank either. But Yuhu paid no attention.

Finally, I did get his attention—for the duration of a single meeting, at least. I worked out a plan with Tim. Per our agreement, Tim brought his cell phone into the meeting, and after a few minutes, he began texting. I walked up to him, grabbed the device out of his hand, bawled him out in front of the whole team, walked to the window, opened it, and told him that the next time he behaved this way, I would throw his phone out the window of our third-floor conference room. The Chinese term is "killing the chicken to frighten the monkey." For at least the remainder of that one meeting, Yuhu behaved.

Steven, the head of IT, another SPDB secondee, also quit for fundamentally the same reasons as Yuhu. Nor did I mourn his loss. While nice enough, he was visibly anxious, passive, lacking in initiative, and hardly a master of his craft. He felt more comfortable being told what to do, something that was anathema in our Western entrepreneurial environment. Like Yuhu, he wept at our meeting where he resigned. Actually, he didn't even formally resign. Instead, he begged permission to go back to the environment in which he was comfortable.

As it turned out, few of our SPDB secondees flourished in our environment. Even some of our direct hires into the JV didn't adapt to the culture. Some—Lynne, the direct-hired head of marketing, and Steven of IT—were rumored to be taking kickbacks. Lynne's alleged bribes came from the personnel of the hotels where we held our events and Steven's from various suppliers. I didn't have to follow up on the rumors because both left by the time I had enough information to pursue the matter. When I left China, everyone from SPDB had returned to their mothership, either under their own steam or with a little encouragement from us.

7.3 DEEPER IN THE JOINT VENTURE

At the same time, we were starting to suspect that not everyone at SPDB fully supported the new bank. Different people within the organization would respond to requests and inquiries from the joint venture in different ways; some with speed and good humor and others reluctantly and with clear distaste. I brought this up with Liu, who hadn't yet left SPDB for his new assignment and seemed to be our most reliable source.

Liu confirmed my suspicions. He told me that there were warring factions at SPDB, particularly with regard to the joint venture. Some thought that SPDB should do as little as it could to help us while learning from us as much as possible to position SPDB for success. Others felt that they should give as much as they could and encourage us as much as possible—in essence, setting the JV up for success. Based on the way things worked out for us over time, I would deduce that the former group held the upper hand.

Also, around that same time, by pure coincidence, I met Fernando Moreira, who'd led the joint venture life insurance company created by China Merchants Bank and Connecticut-based Cigna Insurance. Although his JV was completely different from ours, his perception on JVs in China was very interesting. He believed they almost never work. His reasoning: "one bed, two dreams."

7.3.1 Managing the Lenders

Such a difference was obvious in how SPDB and SVB approached managing our lenders. Tim, our head of credit—one of the very few Americans in our new bank—and Changchang, whom Luo had tried to install as head of strategy but ended up as head of compliance, were debating two distinctly different management approaches. Lenders (bankers) were making decisions all day long: *Is this prospect creditworthy? Is that other client trustworthy?* Whether we would make or lose money depended on whether these lenders had good judgment. Of course, in a way the lenders were conflicted. If they didn't make loans, the bank wouldn't make money. On the other hand, if they made bad loans, the bank would lose money. Tim represented the SVB way of thinking, while Changchang was firmly in favor of the SPDB philosophy.

SVB addressed this tension through training in the mechanics of how to make loans but also, and more importantly, by instilling in the hearts of the lenders an "inner voice," a kind of "lender conscience," that over time told them that a loan would be good or bad, a prospective borrower honest or dishonest. In that way, the lenders eventually became self-governing with minimal monitoring. As a regulated bank in the United States, SVB's lending activity was regularly scrutinized, but we could manage by exception rather than monitoring each individual's specific activities.

The SPDB approach differed dramatically. In China, the banks didn't trust the lenders (their employees!) at all and therefore closely monitored them, all the time. The CBRC didn't really trust the banks either, and required daily (daily!) reporting. Almost every activity had to be reported to one's seniors, which resulted in an avalanche of paperwork that I, as the senior manager of the JV, was expected to read and, in reality, merely skimmed. The adversarial relationship between the lenders and their superiors created a self-fulfilling prophecy. If you don't trust somebody, they will never become trustworthy. And the problem became more entrenched. The more intensely the lenders were monitored, the better they became at fooling their managers. Changchang saw herself as a guard, in effect protecting the lenders from their lesser selves.

Both systems worked, but—in my view—the SVB system was better. I called the SPDB system "cops and robbers," and the SVB system "instilling in lenders the voice of conscience." Another cultural difference, another tension in the relationship.

7.3.2   Assisting Lao Ding

To maintain the JV's relationships with government officials, which generated the *guanxi* necessary to build the bank, was practically another full-
time job. Around this time, Lao Ding, retired from his position as Party
Secretary of the Yangpu District, and having already been thrown two
post-retirement bones by the CCP (one as the head of security for the 2010
Shanghai Expo, and a second as advisor to Italy for their impending Expo),
received a third. He was to lead the development of the largest tech park in
China: not *within* a province, but rather *encompassing* three contiguous
ones: Shanghai, Zhejiang, and Jiangsu.

Lao Ding asked me for help. He wanted me to round up high-level
people from Stanford and Harvard because the CCP intended to involve
them in this project as well. There was just one problem: either Lao Ding
was incapable of envisioning how a tech park that large would actually look
and function, or if he could envision it, he couldn't describe it. It was difficult to recruit people to listen to his presentations, which were always
embarrassing. Despite the amount of time and personal capital the project
consumed, I was relieved when it mysteriously disappeared after a few years.

In time, I came to believe that most of the things China (read, the CCP)
asked me to do to help it initially involved a great deal of fanfare, and yet in
the end died quiet deaths. It was hard for me to motivate myself to go to
extremes to round up the requisite audience—although such is life with
guanxi. My assistance built my relationship and leverage with Lao Ding,
without whose assistance we'd never have made any progress at all.

7.3.3   The Bank That
Didn't Pay Graft

At a dinner with the Luo family at the same time, Mrs. Luo praised me for
introducing Western management practices to China. In her view, SVB

and I were helping her country by showing that it was possible to operate efficiently without paying graft. This was not a universal conclusion. A former SVB employee who had ended up in China doing boutique investment banking work told me our new bank was already widely known in financial circles, largely because we didn't pay graft money. If we did so, he contended, we would develop much more quickly.

Not long thereafter, Sheila, who had joined us in 2005 as our first employee in China, echoed this advice. Over lunch, she told me we were fighting with one hand tied behind our back. We were the only bank in China, foreign or domestic, that didn't pay kickbacks to corporate CFOs for depositing money with us. We *should*, she stated emphatically. We didn't.

Takeaways from the Trenches

- As an institution, the Chinese government sells licenses in exchange for intellectual property. Individually, Party officials sell licenses in exchange for favors, gifts, or bribes.
- If the parents of one of your employees in China are members of the CCP, they will want to meet you and will offer to use their influence to help you. There is always a *quid pro quo*.
- The CCP is composed of warring factions. Be careful to avoid getting injured in the crossfire.
- In general, managers in China micromanage their direct reports. They expect constant praise and loyalty in return.
- Managers tend not to trust their direct reports. Nor do they trust their bosses.
- Party members will regularly ask you to help them accomplish things in the United States, including meeting important people and influencing the course of events.
- In China, it is considered a good practice to "kill the chicken to scare the monkey."

NOTES

1. Antoine Gara, "JPMorgan Agrees to Pay $264 Million Fine for 'Sons and Daughters' Hiring Program in China," *Forbes*, November 17, 2016, https://www.forbes.com/sites/antoinegara/2016/11/17/jpmorgan-agrees-to-pay-264-million-fine-for-sons-and-daughters-hiring-program-in-china/?sh=1459ee8e5688.

2. In his review of Ha Jin's novel *The Woman Back from Moscow*, the noted Sinologist Perry Link quoted the Australian Sinologist Simon Leys as observing "that comparisons of the CCP elite to the mafia are in a sense unfair to the mafia, in which a certain loyalty to 'brothers' does play a part." Perry Link, "A Fallen Artist in Mao's China," *New York Review of Books*, December 7, 2023, 6.

CHAPTER EIGHT

WHERE THE MONEY GOES, FINDING MY SUCCESSOR, AND MORE ABOUT CHINA

On October 26, 2012, David Barboza, a two-time Pulitzer Prize–winning journalist for the *New York Times*, published his seminal article on Chinese Premier Wen Jiaobao, reporting that he had transferred at least $2 billion in state assets to members of his own family.[1] Thereafter, Barboza and his wife were strongly encouraged to leave

China, which they did, and the *New York Times* was banished from the country. There are still *Times* reporters in China, but none of its publications can be found, either in print or online. It was a classic case of killing the messenger.

To the best of my knowledge, the Chinese government launched no investigation of Barboza's story. No one talked about it. There was no outcry. There was no mention of it in the Chinese press. But it was whispered that David and his wife were receiving anonymous death threats. In general, I felt the atmosphere becoming tenser. It was as if we all knew a secret, one that—if disclosed to others—could be explosive.

As 2012 wrapped up, I was becoming aware of how much I had yet to learn, even though I'd already learned a lot. A mountain of challenges still confronted the project, most notably our efforts to use RMB and warrants, protecting our business model from the determined efforts of our JV partner and the rest of the country's banking institutions to steal it, and keeping my employees interested and engaged. In addition, I had to find a successor, a project that I'd been struggling with for almost two years.

8.1 SEEKING A SUCCESSOR

Part of the SVB culture involves developing "bench strength"—every position must have at least one identified successor. This approach extends throughout the organization at every level; it was how I'd known I'd eventually be CEO. In China, identifying my successor was even more important because that person was the keeper of the SVB culture. We had to have that person in place early enough to become immersed in our way of doing things or our ability to move forward after I left would be dramatically impeded.

Thus, we'd started seeking my successor even before I left for China, thinking that we would want a few years of overlap to inculcate the new recruit in our culture and business model. Our top-tier executive search firm had found three candidates (in sequence).

The first of the three candidates was June Luo,[2] whom we found in 2010. She was perfect. She'd worked at the Bank of Nova Scotia for several years, and every interview went better than the one prior. In a matter of weeks, we were professionally in love with June.

And then we popped the question. She sounded pleased and told us that she'd need to discuss our proposal with her boss. We never heard from her again. We sent her pleading emails, asking that she just go to the trouble of telling us no. There was no reply. About six months after Ruth and I arrived in Shanghai, I received an email from her. Could I join her for dinner? Curious, I agreed. The dinner was pleasant. We talked about everything under the sun, except her candidacy. At the end of the dinner, we went our separate ways and have never spoken again.

Our second potential successor was Tina Wang, from the British bank Standard Chartered. She surfaced in 2011, after I was in China. Again, we went through a long and protracted courtship. After many meetings and several dinners, I concluded that she "would do." Again, I popped the question. I asked her how much she was making at Standard Chartered, and I was shocked at the size of the number. She wanted to know our offer, and I told her I would need to consult with my colleagues, as the number she'd given me seemed extremely high, and I knew she would want a raise beyond that.

A few nights later we met again at a restaurant near our old office. She told me she would want an 88% raise over her already very high income. She told me that the number 88 would be fortuitous. I told her this amount would be too rich for us. We parted and have not seen each other since. Later I heard that she'd been hired by East West Bank, and later parted ways with them.

And in fall of 2012, I lost my third potential successor, James Luo (again, no relative to Mr. Luo of SPDB). He never really warmed up to our business model and wanted to change it in ways that rendered it unrecognizable. And, of course, he needed more money—much more, in fact, than we were willing to pay.

In response, my successor as CEO in the United States took over the matter and started looking for someone to replace me himself.

8.2 ENTERTAINMENTS, 2012

As we had found the prior year, despite the frustrating, uncertain, stop-and-start nature of establishing the JV, Ruth and I had some delightful experiences. Many of these were art related. Every month, we attended a chamber music performance at M on the Bund, a gathering place founded by Australian entrepreneur Michelle Garnaut in 1999 as a haven for Western expats. The music was performed by gifted teenaged Chinese music students, and it refreshed our souls.

M on the Bund also hosted a monthly lecture series, which we regularly attended. Particularly memorable was one that spring of 2012 given by the architects of the four towers of Pudong: the Pearl Tower, the Jin Mao Tower, the Shanghai World Financial Center, and the then-still-in-progress Shanghai Tower, which houses the world's highest indoor observation deck. I suppose for some, the details of their construction and their differences relative to other skyscrapers in the world might have been boring; I was fascinated. Perhaps it was the contrast between the country's 5,000 year history and its embrace of cutting-edge building techniques. Perhaps it was the inside look at the building of the CCP's statement that China had come of age. But it was truly one of the most illuminating events of our stay.

In this same time frame, one of our favorite galleries in Shanghai began representing a Taiwanese artist named Zhiyang Huang. Back then, he was featuring a series of sculptures titled "Artwork Landscape: Possessing Numerous Peaks and Ripples" (see Figure 8.1). Because these sculptures were so large, they'd been placed outdoors in the Xintiandi district for Shanghai Art Week. Ruth and I walked past them almost every morning on our way to Fuxing Park, and we were gratified to see so many people stopping to study them.

One morning, Ruth suggested that we should try to buy them and then ask Vincent Lo (the creator and owner of Xintiandi) to put them on

Figure 8.1   Elements of "Artwork Landscape."
Source: Author.

permanent exhibition for the public to enjoy. After he declined, we snuck behind his back and asked his daughter, Stephanie, who was apprenticing to replace her father when he retired. She loved the idea, and we divided up the price among four groups: Vincent and Stephanie, Art Plus (the gallery representing Zhiyang Huang), the artist himself in the form of a discount, and Ruth and me. Stephanie had a bronze plaque made, and we enjoyed seeing it when we walked by. A year or two after Xi came to power, the plaque disappeared. We never knew why but suspect it might be part of the de-Westernization program.

In Autumn 2012, Ruth and I traveled to Beijing to visit the National Museum of History and the famous art district called 798. The museum amazed us—everything in it was larger than life. Under Xi, the museum had reconfigured an entire wing for a new exhibition called "The Road to Rejuvenation."

At the entrance to this exhibition stands the following plaque:

The Chinese nation is a great nation whose people are industrious, courageous, intelligent and peace-loving and have made indelible contributions to the progress of human civilizations. For generations and generations, the Chinese people have been pursuing a dream of national strength and prosperity.

The "Road to Rejuvenation" is a permanent exhibition showcasing the explorations made by the Chinese people from all walks of life who, after being reduced to a semi-colonial, semi-feudal society since the Opium War of 1840, rose in resistance against humiliation and misery, and tried in every way possible to rejuvenate the nation.

The exhibition also highlights the glorious history of China under the leadership of the Communist Party of China (CPC), in which all ethnic groups joined forces to achieve national independence and liberation and strove to build a strong and prosperous country for the well-being of the people. The exhibition therefore clearly demonstrates the historical course of the Chinese people of choosing Marxism, the CPC, the socialist road and the reform and opening-up policy, and China's firm determination in building socialism with Chinese characteristics through adherence to this great banner, this special road and this theoretical system.

Today, the Chinese nation is standing firm in the east, facing a brilliant future of great rejuvenation. The long-cherished dream and aspiration of the Chinese people will surely come to reality.

To, perhaps, our un-surprise, none of the exhibits on the "socialist road and the reform and opening-up policy, and China's firm determination in building socialism with Chinese characteristics" mentioned any of the bumps on that same road, most notably the Tiananmen Square pro-democracy uprising in 1989 and the hundreds or thousands of deaths (and thousands of injuries) resulting from the government's violent response. After our tour, Ruth and I stopped by the gift shop. We looked in the section on Chinese history, thinking it might contain some references to the impact of Tiananmen. Here, we felt righteously indignant—none of the books even mentioned the uprising! It was as if it had never happened!

We decided not to purchase a book at the museum. Looking back, I shake my head at our response. After all, the United States has hardly demonstrated a willingness to accept its less glorious actions. Until recently, would one have found a book on the Tulsa race massacre in that city's bookstore? And that event occurred in 1921.

On a more personal level, we went out practically every night with a variety of acquaintances, Chinese and expats alike. I'm still amazed by the number of interesting people we met. And for my 64th birthday, Luke Shen, the head of our general office, organized a party for me to which he invited all of our employees and a handful of miscellaneous government officials. To our delight, he gave us some tickets to the Shanghai Symphony, a gift that could not have made Ruth happier.

8.2.1 Chinese Medicine

Also that autumn, Diana, the wife of David Wei, a well-known businessman (a one-time member of the Alibaba management team, and later the founder and head of Knight Vision, a well-known venture capital firm), graciously arranged for me to visit a Chinese traditional medicine doctor. There was nothing in particular wrong with me, aside from being old, but for the sake of the cultural experience, I wanted to see a doctor of Chinese medicine.

As in a Western doctor's office, I waited in the reception area until the doctor was ready to see me. Soon, a nurse ushered me into the examination room. Astoundingly, it was devoid of any medical equipment. All it held was a small table with a tiny pillow on it and two chairs, one for the doctor and one for me. The nurse beckoned me to sit down. After a few minutes, the doctor arrived. He asked to look at my tongue and seemed to be studying it intently. Then, he took my hand and placed it on the pillow. He put his fingers on my pulse and held them there for about five whole minutes, apparently in deep thought. At that point, he released my hand and began speaking. He spoke for about 15 minutes, telling me that I was getting older and that some of my subsystems weren't functioning as well as they used to. He mentioned several of them in detail.

Also, he talked about my body in ways that I didn't understand, but presumably would have been easily understood by someone who'd grown up in China and knew this precise vocabulary. Victor provided some translation the next day, but even then, the concepts—hot and cold (*yang* and *yin*) energies and the chi (*qi*), the vital energy that circulates throughout the body—were unfamiliar. Finally, he told me that I was waking up two or sometimes even three times a night to pee. At first, I was amazed. He was right! How could he have known that? This was like visiting a psychic.

Later, in the car on the way home, it suddenly occurred to me that he could have known I was old just by looking at my face. To the best of my knowledge, virtually every man of my age gets up to pee multiple times every night, because we almost all have enlarged prostate glands.

At the end of the visit, the doctor wrote down on a piece of paper at least 50 or 60 characters and handed the paper to a nurse. Two weeks later, a delivery service arrived at our apartment with a large box of capsules, each filled with a mixture of herbs. I tried them for a while but couldn't tell if they made a difference because I didn't think there was anything wrong with me in the first place, and—of course as is always the case when you take medicine—there was no control group. But it sure was interesting.

Nor was this my only experience with Chinese medicine. Halfway through our stay, I woke up one morning with a sharp pain in my left forearm that grew steadily worse. An Australian doctor at a Western clinic in Shanghai took X-rays and diagnosed pinched nerves due to spinal compression. As the weeks rolled by, the pain got worse and worse. I tried epidurals, which worked but only for a week or two. Finally, friends persuaded me to try acupuncture. To my great surprise and relief, it seemed to work. The pain dissipated, and eventually (largely) disappeared.

My first acupuncture treatments were through Chinese doctors at a Western clinic—at $300 per treatment! I decided to try getting acupuncture from Chinese doctors at a Chinese hospital instead.

Victor enrolled me at one near our apartment. From then on, the treatments cost me less than $1 each, and were much more fun. Instead of being treated in a room by myself, I was in a room with about 20 other patients, all of us sitting in a large circle. The doctor, who was well past retirement age, walked around the circle sticking needles in this person and taking them out of that one, all the while making small talk and joking. The room was enveloped in a warm and communal atmosphere. I can't claim that it healed me any faster than the vastly more expensive treatments in the Western clinic, but it certainly made me feel a lot better.

8.3 REFLECTING

In December, Luke, the head of our general office, told me he wanted to go back to SPDB. He had loved helping us build the JV, but he was planning to retire, and he needed to spend his last few months in the environment he'd grown up in. Of course, I gave him my blessing. Sadly, Luke died of cancer less than a year later.

And Oliver, one of our most loyal and beloved employees, quit as well. The process of setting up the bank and the accompanying stress had broken him. He had been closely involved in the most sensitive issues that arose and was perhaps a gentler soul than many of us. He was only about 40 at the time, and I don't believe he's worked since.

8.4 WRAPPING UP 2012

So it was that at the end of 2012, almost two years into the on-the-ground effort to get the bank established and facing an apparently infinite amount of time and complexity before we'd be able to do business, we began to have doubts about our viability in China. We started to feel like we were doomed to fail. This was because of the following:

1. **The regulators.** The CBRC is less than 20 years old, and it has far more regulations than the Fed, which has been in existence for over a century. Furthermore, the CBRC reports to itself, because all Chinese regulators are members of the CCP. The Fed has far less latitude; it reports to Congress and cannot act arbitrarily. The CBRC can. It can apply its regulations when and if it wishes, often to the detriment of non-Chinese entities and the benefit of Chinese operations.[3]

2. **The business model.** Our business model is predicated on a financial system that has a number of unique characteristics, many of which don't exist in the Chinese system: a transparent venture capital community; a distinction between debt and equity; a clear relationship between risk and pricing; a willingness to pay for above-average service; and reliable financial statements. None of these exist in China to the same degree that they do in the United States.

3. **Our foreign status.** The Chinese have a profound sense of being Chinese. More than once, I was invited to speak at the Party School in Beijing about our business model. The first time I spoke there, my audience consisted of about 120 mid-level government officials. They were not only attentive (which is not often the case with similar audiences in China), but utterly enthusiastic. At the end, they told me they "loved" our business model—so much so, in fact, that they wanted one of their own, just like ours. I told them they already had one, and it was our JV. They owned 50% of it, 99% of our employees were PRC citizens, and 100% of our clients were PRC-registered companies. If this wasn't theirs, I didn't know what was, I told them. They all smiled and nodded in apparent agreement. "Yes, yes, we know," they said, "but we want one *of our own.*"

4. **Our partner, SPDB.** As Mr. Liu acknowledged, there were (and are) warring factions at SPDB. Only some of them wanted us to succeed. Those in opposition to the JV generated a plethora of roadblocks. The Party Committee, as seen, waited six months after we arrived in Shanghai to appoint their representatives to the working and decision-making groups, which were essential to building the new entity. The Organization Department seconded to us some of SPDB's least effective employees. The boss of Yuhu, our head of

operations, kept calling him back to SPDB, whispering in his ear that he should return. The HR department refused to tell us how much we should pay those seconded to us and made no effort to convince the secondees that their tenure at the JV would bolster their long-term career opportunities at SPDB. After promising not to, the corporate bankers at SPDB competed openly with the new bank. Accepting their disingenuous excuse ("We're not competing; we're letting the customer decide.") was tantamount to acknowledging that we were both naive and stupid. The management of SPDB had allowed (if not encouraged) Mr. Sun to write the infamous "secret letter," trying to renegotiate our shareholder agreement. Above all, SPDB's culture was so rigid, secretive, and hierarchical that engaging the secondees was not just difficult, it was actually impossible.

Our situation reminded me of a 1970 film I'd seen years before titled *A Man Called Horse*, starring Richard Harris. The premise was this: In 1825, a big-game hunter from England is captured and enslaved by the Sioux Indians. He is forced to labor as a pack animal for an elderly woman in the tribe. He learns their language and eventually proves himself in battle against a neighboring tribe. In time, the chief's daughter falls in love with him, and they want to marry. At first, her father refuses to allow this liaison. In time, the chief relents, but only under the condition that the Englishman submit himself to an initiation rite through which a non-Sioux can become a Sioux. This involves having the skin on his chest slit, leather straps passed through the slits, and then being hoisted up into the air by these leather straps. He agrees. The pain is excruciating, but he survives and becomes a Sioux. His fellow tribesmen lower him and remove the straps. He is allowed to marry the girl and becomes fully integrated into the life of the tribe. Admittedly, the depiction of Native Americans may be biased and antiquated but the story haunted me.

I kept thinking, *maybe this is all a test. Maybe, at some point, just when I think I can no longer tolerate the pain, they'll lower me, remove the straps, some beautiful princess will carry me back to her* hutong [a narrow alley in a traditional residential district of a Chinese city], *and I will have become one of them.*

If you are born Chinese, your fellow Chinese will view you as Chinese forever even if you move to another country. If you weren't, you can never become Chinese. Ever.

And, of course, my dream never came true. It was December 2012. Almost two years had passed. We still could not use Chinese currency. I was still hanging in midair. As if to make tangible the pain of this "man called horse" metaphor, the crick in my neck, due to turning my head sideways in the formal conversations with Luo, reemerged. It was excruciating.

Initially, I'd signed up for two years in China. But the job, as I defined it, wasn't done. I hadn't brought my successor up to speed—in fact, that person hadn't even been identified. And there was *so much more to learn*! I stayed on for two more years. Partly because China fascinated me. Partly because I thrilled at the discovery as we peeled back the layers of the Chinese business onion, weeping as we went. Partly because I was determined to reach President Xi and convince him to let us use Chinese currency, to help the Chinese technology centers join in the global chain of innovation. And partly because we felt like we were making progress, despite the obstacles. I just needed to put my head down and try harder. This sense of optimism, of success just around the corner, is what the Chinese business culture excels at providing to Western companies seeking to enter that market. I was falling into the bear trap.

Takeaways from the Trenches

- The Chinese internet firewall is quite effective. Sometimes major events take place in China or the rest of the world and the majority of China's 1.4 billion people know nothing about them.
- If you want to understand China, read Chinese historians' versions of history. And immerse yourself in Chinese culture. You will find it fascinating, and it will help you understand many things that will otherwise puzzle you.
- If you are to succeed, your company will have to become Chinese. A major step in that direction is appointing a Chinese CEO, preferably a Party member.
- However, don't think that you can become Chinese. That is borderline impossible. Many have tried; almost all have failed. China will never grant you that status, no matter how hard you try.

NOTES

1. David Barboza, "Billions in Hidden Riches for Family of Chinese Leader," *New York Times*, October 25, 2012, https://www.nytimes.com/2012/10/26/business/global/family-of-wen-jiabao-holds-a-hidden-fortune-in-china.html.
2. Again, June was no relation to any of the Luos mentioned thus far. There are only about 100 common last names in China. Each is, in effect, the name of a clan. For example, there are well over 70 million Chens. Even more common are the surnames Li, with 90 million occurrences, and Zhang and Wang, both with 100 million.
3. Although the CBRC merged with the insurance regulator in 2018, forming the China Banking Insurance Regulatory Commission (CBIRC), little has changed.

PART II

AFTER
THE LICENSE

CHAPTER NINE

HASTENING THE TIMELINE

THE FOUR-PRONG STRATEGY AND WHAT "LETTING THE CUSTOMER DECIDE" REALLY MEANS

I started 2013 in a reflective mood. My experience in building the bank had been a very mixed bag. We'd received our license—well, a license—but we couldn't do anything. We'd staffed up as required, but we did nothing but train our employees and field requests from would-be competitors to train their teams. We still had the WOFE business, which had been our sole reason to exist before embarking on the JV. It continued to chug along, but we now shared the profit with our "partner." And the Shanghai government was covering part of our losses due to the regulations that hamstrung our operations—but only part. The fact that we were here, on the ground, making losses stung all the more because we'd known what would happen. We just hadn't believed it would happen to us.

Just before the Spring Festival—the roughly two-week Lunar New Year celebration during which most of China essentially shuts down—Governor Jin of the Yangpu District and his entire staff came to our office to meet with the management team, solely to wish us all a Happy New Year. This gesture conferred great face upon the team and, by extension, the effort.

Every six months, a small episode like this occurred. It made me think that the people I was working with were well-intentioned, and it gave me hope. And hope kept me going—I was constantly hoping for a breakthrough if I just worked harder.

In the quiet of the Spring Festival celebration, with the city practically empty, I sorted through my two years of experiences in China. Building the JV bank was proving to be much more difficult than it had appeared when I'd signed up. But in trying to make sense of the whirlwind, I discerned two major threads:

1. It seemed to me (and still does) that in China under the CCP, people avoid making decisions to the greatest extent possible. Even small issues get pushed upstairs. A minor but indicative example involved Steven, the guy who'd been seconded from SPDB to head our IT. He proved to be incompetent and, evidence strongly suggested, unethical. At the end of 2012, in a spate of tears, he begged to return to the more comfortable culture of SPDB. With little hesitation, I accepted his resignation, assuming he'd be welcomed back to SPDB with open arms.

But that was not the case. Mr. Liu, SPDB's head of banking and CFO at the time, refused to allow Steven to return to his old position. I was aghast that SPDB had seconded to us, their "prize" joint venture, someone so incompetent that he couldn't return to the parent organization. But the process was also a surprise: Liu, second in command under Luo, felt it necessary to consult with Chairman Ji, two levels his senior, on whether to release a relatively low-level employee.

2. I was coming to agree with Fernando Moreira, the head of the joint venture life insurance company mentioned in Chapter 7, that the prospects of any JV in China can be summed up by the Chinese saying, "One bed, two dreams." The CCP had a dream in pursuing this JV with us, as did we, and they were much more enamored of their dream than of ours. And in a country where business outcomes are determined more by the government than the market, we could only move forward through the government. And that meant the CCP.

I had an epiphany: if I wanted permission to use Chinese currency without waiting an additional three years, I would need to go to the top—that is, to Xi Jinping himself. I would need to devote all my time to "lobbying" my way up to Xi. I would turn most of my banking responsibilities over to various members of my executive team. I would monitor them, of course, but I would allow them maximum latitude within reasonably broad parameters. In this way I could concentrate my efforts on working with the government to secure permission to use RMB in something less than the mandatory waiting period.

And I needed to be "fit for battle," both mentally and in terms of whatever leverage I could muster, before I embarked on this journey. In my opinion, the Chinese government operates ruthlessly in accordance with *The Art of War*, which I should have read before I arrived because it is woven throughout Chinese life and culture, like the Constitution in the

United States. This slim volume argues that one should seek to win at all costs, primarily through deceit and manipulation rather than direct conflict. I would need favors from friends with whom I had *guanxi* and who stood to benefit from helping me achieve my goal. In addition, they would need to have influence themselves.

Accordingly, I diagrammed the Chinese government, covering the territory between Xi and me. On it, I noted only those people who might be able to influence events at their respective levels and hasten the movement of my message up into the upper echelons of the CCP, all the way to Xi.

There were fundamentally three routes to Xi. The most obvious would be through the government. Almost as obvious would be through the regulators. The third and least obvious was through the press. By "the press," I don't mean the Western press or the public-oriented Chinese press. I mean the internal CCP press.

And here's where it gets complicated. *Xinhua News Agency* is the official government news service for China, which publishes official Chinese news in a number of languages both domestically and in other countries. It also publishes information and analysis for the sole use of the CCP, gleaned both from *Xinhua* reporters and from external sources, collected and translated into Mandarin by *Xinhua* staffers. Its three most important periodicals, from the perspective of the CCP, are *Xinhua News* for the Party and *China Daily* and *Cankao Xiaoxi* (Reference News) for the masses.

For CCP members at the ministerial level or higher, *Xinhua* produces a 3- to 10-page newsletter called *Neibu Cankao* (Internal References) twice a day.[1] Only the most trusted journalists from *Xinhua* and *China Daily* write for this newsletter. Their pieces may be based on articles in *Xinhua* or other sources, or they may be directly written for *Neibu Cankao*, but they are specifically written or edited by this cadre of trusted journalists.

Neibu Cankao is read by a defined set of Party members from the most junior ministers all the way to the most senior. As an issue works its way up to the top, I've been told, various articles are marked by officials at different levels in a way that indicates their importance. The people at the top focus on these markings. If they have a strong opinion, they scribble it in the margin, after which the "internal reference" works its way back down again to the level at which the leaders' wishes can be understood and executed. If I could get some articles in *Neibu Cankao*, the JV's plight might get attention from senior officials, even Xi.

Of course, I did not come to this idea unaided. Lao Ding suggested it, and, upon my bewilderment that I might write, let alone publish, an article for *Neibu Cankao*, he had a solution. Again, of course. Professor Zhao, whom I'd met at a conference a year earlier, could assist. At that conference (need I point out that it was government-sponsored?), I'd found myself—quite by accident, I'm sure—seated at lunch next to the kindly professor. He taught economics at Beijing's Central Party School, a sort of executive education institution for CCP members who might, for instance, want to increase their knowledge of economic policy to position themselves for a particular career path. He had asked that I check in on his daughter who studied engineering at Stanford when we were in California for Christmas, which I did. She eventually became an SVB employee.

I slowly concluded that Zhao was one of the secret team who'd been monitoring us and coordinating our trajectory, and he'd been involved from the outset. At this point, in early 2013, he offered—possibly at Lao Ding's request—to write articles for us that would be published in *Neibu Cankao* and funneled upward. Zhao might even have been part of the *Neibu Cankao* team of writers.

Unsurprisingly, there was no problem in getting those articles into *Neibu Cankao*. Lao Ding was good friends with Ms. Jiang, the head of the Shanghai branch of *Xinhua*, *Neibu Cankao*'s parent, and with her junior associate, Ms. Yao. At his request, they happily met with me several times. Naturally, they knew Zhao well, as he'd written for *Xinhua*'s various publications in the past. His articles would describe our bank and its value proposition, asserting that we could do wonders to help Chinese banks learn how to finance tech companies. Jiang and Yao would publish them and we would see what we could accomplish. All we needed was a small exception (the expedited ability to use RMB), which—if granted—would put the Chinese government back in compliance with the regulations of the WTO, with which China had agreed to comply when it joined the organization in 2001.

Around that time, Zhao also recommended that I ask the government to install a Party Committee in our bank. We would have one inevitably, he said, and we would be the first foreign company in history to have actually asked for one of our own accord. It would please the government so much that they might even find a way to grant us an exception to the "no RMB" rule. I couldn't bring myself to do it. That may have been a mistake.

The secret team that monitored and guided our progress expanded again, this time by the addition of the two charming and talented women who headed the Shanghai branch of *Xinhua*. Once again, I had chased them until they caught me.

Thus, I embarked upon a lobbying effort with four "fronts":

1. Regulators: The CBRC, starting with Mr. Liao in Shanghai, and from there on up to Beijing and all the people I knew in the organization.

2. Government: The Shanghai government, including most of the secret team.

3. The CCP and the press: Lao Ding, Professor Zhao at the Central Party School, Ms. Jiang and Ms. Yao at *Xinhua* and *Neibu Cankao*, Li, and so on.

4. Trade groups: The U.S. Treasury and the U.S. Department of Commerce, through their Strategic and Economic Dialogue with China. The U.S.–China Strategic and Economic Dialogue group had been established in 2009 under President Obama with the idea of ironing out tensions between China and the United States before

they expanded into larger issues on the global stage. To perhaps no one's surprise, the effort was bogged down with tradition and procedure—it took six months to just get on the agenda. Over time, I developed relationships with the U.S. delegation and met with them about three times per year. They were always friendly but offered little hope.

I didn't expect much to come from the *Neibu Cankao* project, but I was willing to give it a try while focusing on the other strategies. What did I have to lose? The effort to get our plight to Xi's attention ended up absorbing most of my time.

9.1 COMPLEXITIES

By 2013, two years into setting up the bank, the picture was, well, complicated. Lao Ding, our "prince," was always there, somewhere in the background. Sometimes he was asking me to help him execute on his most recent assignment from the CCP or to promote his son. At other times, he was offering his assistance in overcoming the challenges posed by the CCP and teaching me more about my new environment.

I'd have liked to turn this mixed bag upside down and empty out the distractions (such as Thomas and the giant tech park) and just keep the *guanxi* that accrued through being connected with Lao Ding. But that's not the way it works in China.

Even after two years in Shanghai, I felt forever on the back foot. I would think I'd agreed on something with SPDB only to find I was wrong. At a board meeting around that time, Luo criticized me for things that we'd discussed and agreed to in private meetings. It was perplexing—board meetings of U.S. companies often give rise to posturing, but in my limited experience, that tendency seems much more pronounced in China. In China, board members in particular and people in general are often (if not *always*) playing to a different audience, frequently one that isn't even in the room. Whether this situation was Luo's last-ditch attempt to convince the Organization Department to keep him on as a hedge against my "transgressions," I don't know, but that seemed the best way to explain it. Needless to say, to my knowledge, no one at the meeting was from or even connected to the Organization Department. I was mystified.

By this time, though, I finally had an inkling about how to succeed in China. If you're an insider (Chinese citizen), express loyalty (*guanxi*, in one of its complicated aspects) to the Party. If you're an outsider (Westerner), seek to build *guanxi* (in the sense of a network of interwoven favors) and use *leverage* because you can never become a Party member. That means you can't express loyalty to it. Only a handful of non-Chinese people have ever become CCP members.

My wording above is a little convoluted because *guanxi* is much more complex than it initially appears. It's not just loyalty or a mutually beneficial relationship. As I described at the start of the book, there's an element of "tit for tat," "I'll scratch your back if you scratch mine," or, more menacingly, "I know where you live." In an economy without contract law, people prefer to do business with family members or at least friends and acquaintances. This isn't just because you can count on the loyalty of family members, but also because pressure can be applied to ensure that they follow through on their commitments. Moreover, by helping others achieve their goals and thus get promoted or look good to the Party, you build a web of interlocking favors that propels you through the convoluted networks of the Chinese business world.

In spring of 2013, SVB headquarters sent over the first of the new team that would eventually replace me and other top execs, such as Tim Hardin. Even though I would stay until the end of 2014, three replacements arrived much earlier to learn the culture: Oscar, our new head of sales, came in the spring; Harvey, our new head of credit, a few months later; and Rudolf, our new president, in September. To our surprise, Oscar's arrival set off a minor firestorm, upsetting our employees, our partners at SPDB, and even the secret team.

In Western companies, senior-level staff changes usually unsettle the workforce to a certain extent, but after a little while, life goes on. When the management team changes in a Western company in China, the upset is more profound unless the Chinese partner has mandated the changes. But if the Western company is making the change, it upsets the Chinese element profoundly. There is an entire matrix of Chinese officials involved in the Western operation and such independent decision-making throws them all off balance.

In our situation, this discomfort manifested itself as objections to many of our requests. Part of this stemmed, I believe, from the fact that you never really know who you're dealing with in China. As I learned over time, people play to the true decision-maker, who is never in the room. In this specific situation, the SVB team had made these changes on our own, and the secret team and SPDB didn't like that *at all*. They wanted to understand everything about our business and how it worked. Oscar upset them simply because he was a new element in the puzzle. Furthermore, the Chinese team was keenly concerned about parity—we shouldn't change the balance. But because Oscar would overlap with his predecessor for a few months to ensure a smooth transition, this shift in parity, even if it were temporary, rattled the Chinese team. While nothing changed—Oscar still arrived—the JV board was not happy and made its objections known by foot-dragging on any decision that had to be made for a time.

I also saw the CCP's attitudes in this response. The CCP was obsessed with control,[2] and this staff change was outside its control. In general, the Chinese don't like change unless they initiate it themselves—and that's particularly true with the CCP.

9.2 MOVING FORWARD, MAYBE

In this timeframe, I had dinner with the past U.S. Consul General (CG) in Shanghai, who had become the president of the American Chamber of Commerce in that city. In his view, SPDB wanted to turn our JV bank into a captive loan-guarantee company, entities that underwrote loans to small and medium-sized enterprises (SMEs) and then got the banks, which were the only organizations that could legally take deposits and therefore had cash to lend, to fund the loans. At one time, there were 20,000 loan-guarantee companies in China. Today, I suspect that there are fewer, as more Chinese banks have begun lending directly to SMEs. But the loan-guarantee companies still exist, and they don't have a happy life.

Loan guarantee companies emerged from Liu Mingkang's resurrection of the Chinese banking industry in 2002. (Liu, you may recall, was the Western-educated economist who set up the CBRC.) Before then, banks focused exclusively on lending to government entities, SOEs, and CCP-connected businesses. SMEs were out of luck. The loan-guarantee companies filled the need for SME financing, acting as loan originators and credit evaluators who then sold the loans on to the banks, which provided the real money. SVB bought part of one such company in 2008 just to learn about how they work. It seemed a miserable existence, barely profitable, and nothing like the innovation-funding role I'd envisioned for our bank. But after the former CG's observation over dinner, I started thinking: *Is this the fate that awaits us?*

My belief in the strategy I'd embarked upon received reinforcement from an unexpected quarter just the week after the Spring Festival, when Vice Mayor Tu and a few members of his team came to visit. Offering advice and encouragement, he urged me to "be creative." He used that phrase repeatedly, and at the time, it baffled me. Eventually, I came to believe, based on discussions with other members of the government, that Tu meant this:

Look for loopholes in the regulatory system and seek to exploit them. Avoid asking permission in advance. If you ask permission in advance, your request will likely be denied, because nobody has enough authority to make an exception for a foreigner. Anybody whom you might ask for an exception will "kick it upstairs" because they don't want to take the risk of being criticized and maybe even punished. Of course, you could always offer an official a "red envelope"—a bribe, which generally does not arrive in a red envelope—to make an exception for you, but it would be expensive, and if you got caught, you'd be subject to fines and/or punishment by the American government under the American Foreign Corrupt Practices Act. So, it's best to find the loophole, and without asking permission, forge on ahead. If you get caught by the Chinese authorities, as long as you have good guanxi *and haven't brazenly broken the law, you'll be forgiven and asked not to do it again.*

Or, to put it differently, seek to build good relationships with government officials. If they don't like you and are out to thwart you, they can do so whether you're in compliance or not. They can even invent a new regulation after the fact simply to prosecute you. However, if you have good guanxi *and you simply exploit a loophole without permission, you'll be forgiven.*

Admittedly, not all my colleagues in the United States agreed with my theory. But, to a person, those who disagreed have never lived in China.

I'd invited Luo to attend the meeting with Tu. Of course, as a member of the secret team, all of whom were in regular communication with each other regarding channeling our JV in a direction beneficial to China, he'd known about the meeting beforehand and was planning to attend. By inviting him, however, I showed him face.

That said, I had explicitly asked him not to dominate the meeting. I wanted to listen rather than talk and develop more of an individual relationship with Tu. Predictably, Luo sought to dominate. When I called him on it afterward, he apologized (a rarity in China), and (even more of a rarity) he told me he'd felt insecure, which was why he'd tried to dominate. It seemed as if my relationship with Luo had really progressed, although, given that we were in China, I will likely never know for sure. In any case, I would never claim to be a "China whisperer."

A few weeks later, Changchang had a talk with me. You may recall that she had been seconded to us by the CBRC at the start of the project, and Luo had insisted that she should be head of "strategy." I'd thought that odd, since she knew nothing (at that time) about our strategy. But, in China, Party membership is often more important than subject-matter expertise. In fact, it's so important that Changchang had been "forced" to join the Party as a prerequisite to becoming our head of strategy—and ended up being our head of compliance.

Changchang disclosed to me that we would, in the not-too-distant future, have a Party Committee of our own, which she would chair. She echoed what Mr. Sun had said early in my tenure. The Party Committee could override management, and we wouldn't even know it. There wouldn't be a confrontation; it's just that whatever I had said should be done wouldn't occur.

The whole process was very secretive. Even I, the president and representative of the 50% JV, would not know who was on the committee. I learned that it would work this way: the Party Committee makes the big decisions and tells the board what they are. If the company is Chinese, the board does what the Party Committee tells it to do. If it's a JV, the Chinese portion of the board acts as if the Party Committee's decisions are their own recommendations.

And that's why Xi wants a Party Committee in all non-state-owned companies, Chinese or foreign.

This would happen whether I wanted it to or not, Changchang said. She also told me that I should not be too upset about the fact that SPDB appeared to be competing with us, even though the shareholder agreement included their commitment not to do so. Changchang assured me: "They are not competing; they are letting the customer decide."

I had heard this before. I did not believe it.

Soon thereafter I learned I was going to receive yet another award. I was starting to feel like a real idiot. Clearly, I was giving away the store, or at least the CCP believed I was. I would be one of about 50 Westerners receiving the so-called Magnolia Award at the annual Shanghai Magnolia Awards Festival that spring. The awardees are selected by the government of Shanghai for outstanding contributions to the development of the Chinese economy. It's interesting to see how proud Americans can be to receive an award for having been cajoled to do things for which you'd be fired in a market-oriented economy—specifically, educating your competitor.

It's interesting to note the extent to which the Chinese government, in the guise of rewarding foreigners who help China develop, engages in behavior that on the surface looks a lot like "buying us off." Recall the Innovation Advisor Award I'd received a couple of years earlier.

As part of this award, I would receive a financial award from the Shanghai government, which sets aside millions of dollars every year to be given to CEOs of Western companies that have gone the extra mile to help China develop. This was not chicken feed—I'd be receiving a few hundred thousand dollars. The money would be mine, I was told, not for SVB. Of course, I contributed it to our JV bank. Conceptually, I was giving half of it back to the Chinese government and earmarking the other half for the shareholders of SVB. I wonder what other American CEOs of JVs in China do with rewards of this sort. I truly have no idea.

9.2.1 How "Letting the Customer Decide" Really Works

And at this time, I finally had an insight into what "letting the customer decide" really meant. Our contract with SPDB pledged that neither "parent" would compete against the "child"—the JV. But I kept encountering situations where SPDB was *clearly* lending to tech start-ups without involving the JV, and the start-ups they lent to were much more promising than those they offered to us as a way to learn our model. Whenever I protested, the SPDB bankers would smile and say they weren't competing, they were "letting the customer decide." As with many things in China, it took me several years and a fair amount of circumstantial evidence to understand exactly what that meant.

I started assembling this body of context as I learned more about the size and operation of Shanghai's innovation technology market. The head of a relevant department of the Zhangjiang Technology Park in Shanghai's Pudong District told me that there are only two *real* tech parks in Shanghai, a city of about 25 million. All the others—and there are several—are just industrial parks, but the Shanghai government is determined to give the impression that all are focused on technology.

Simultaneously, I made friends with Clayton, a senior banker from SPDB who for some reason (thank goodness!) took a liking to me and was willing to cut through the opaque veil of official "spin." According to him, SPDB claimed (at the time) that Shanghai had 20,000 tech companies. Only about 4,000 of them, he said, were truly tech companies, and of those, the city's Financial Services Department tracked only 800 that appeared to hold promise.

In his view, very little real innovation took place in Shanghai, but there *was* a lot of reverse engineering. The Financial Services Department fed these 800 real tech companies to the various banks in Shanghai for financing, and SPDB got the lion's share. The Shanghai government, the banker said, supports SPDB and other Chinese (as opposed to foreign) banks with favorable interpretations of regulations, guarantees the loans these banks make to tech companies (regardless of their true technology status), and recapitalizes the banks when the loans or the companies fail. This could explain what Mr. Liu and others, including Changchang, had meant when they said that SPDB was not competing against the JV but "letting the customer decide." As an entrepreneur, would you rather get a loan you have to pay back or one that is practically a subsidy from the government?

I wondered why anyone bothered with the dissembling. Upon further thought, it's part of the whole Potemkin village facade that the CCP puts out on a regular basis. It wants to appear not just on par with the United States but superior, so a lot of official data are made up or massaged to show China in a good light. You have to triangulate almost any data you receive, so I went through the following exercise: Shanghai in 2013 had a population of about 25 million, larger than all four Scandinavian countries and about five times the size of Denmark. Denmark, which is open about its technology industry, had about 800 tech companies. Thus, Clayton's suggestion that Shanghai had 4,000 true tech companies seemed plausible; 20,000 did not. By now, in 2023, technology in China has made considerable advances, but when we were there, these numbers held.

The truth about China's technology progress, as usual, is somewhere between two extremes. Some experts will say China has no domestic innovation and just copies; others say China is far ahead of us. There are elements of truth in what both say but to get to the facts requires sleuth work.

In 2019, almost five years after I'd left China, an SPDB representative on the JV's board told me that Shanghai had 40,000 tech companies. She claimed to be in charge of banking them, so I figured she might know. The conversation startled me—such openness is frowned upon, but in addition, the number was completely implausible. It's apparent, though, that China is catching up with the United States in terms of technology. While official numbers from the CCP can't be relied upon—consider the COVID counts—they *are* directionally indicative. In a number of technological sectors, the astute reader will find articles suggesting that China is ahead of the United States, but official numbers have nothing to do with it. One of the things I learned during my time in China was the importance of understanding the context and finding evidence for the existence of any metrics I was given.

9.2.2 Making Progress?

One of the things I kept working on was trying to create goodwill and *guanxi* with members of the secret team. Shanghai's vice mayor Chen had asked me to help him achieve one of his KPIs, which involved creating an innovation ecosystem in the region. His portfolio consisted of health care, education, and technology. I wanted to help—because I quite liked him and because I believe in the importance of innovation. Chen asked me to help set up meetings with Plug and Play, one of Silicon Valley's most respected incubators, and with one of the top people at the University of California, San Francisco (UCSF). With considerable effort, I arranged both meetings, hoping as a side effect to enhance my *guanxi* with Chen.

Chen, of course, wanted to learn how Plug and Play was organized so he could replicate it. Ideally, he wanted that operation to establish a division in Shanghai so his team could copy its approach. Arranging the Plug and Play meeting was quite difficult because a member of its leadership team had to travel to Shanghai. Chen couldn't travel to Silicon Valley—like every member of the CCP above a certain level, the CCP held his passport and he couldn't leave the country without official permission. And after everyone moved heaven and earth to make the meeting happen, the entire project just faded away.

I never quite knew why Chen wanted to meet with the UCSF folks. I suppose he wanted UCSF to set up shop in Shanghai so Shanghai could steal all its trade secrets, then allow the operation to fail. This meeting required me to pull additional strings. Because the UCSF representative was unwilling to make an extra trip to Shanghai, the meeting was to take place in Hong Kong, where she would be anyway. Chen didn't need his passport to go to Hong Kong, given that it was technically part of China.

(Note: U.S. visitors to China without multi-entry visas may not zip down to Hong Kong from the mainland so blithely. A friend realized, upon passing through Shanghai security for a quick side trip to Hong Kong, that the gate had literally closed behind her since she only had a single-entry visa for her research trip to China. She would not be able to return to Shanghai after her Hong Kong day trip—even though Hong Kong was ostensibly part of China! Happily, downtown Hong Kong has a bustling business producing last-minute visas for Westerners who have misunderstood this relationship and, $400 and an hour later, she had her instant photos, her passport stamp, and her trip back to Shanghai sorted out. She obtained multi-entry visas for her later trips to China.)

In the end, this project fizzled also. Vice Mayor Chen had to cancel his trip to Hong Kong.

This was not unusual. Members of the CCP seemed to have very little latitude to make decisions. They always needed permission from some undisclosed person higher up. I could have spent most of my time arranging things for members of the CCP that never happened.

Also in May, a woman named Kelly Zhang, who was on the staff of the *People's Daily* in San Francisco, reached out to me. She wanted to interview me for an article in the U.S. edition of the publication. And, for the privilege, she wanted me to pay her $5,000. I declined.

I find it interesting that the *New York Times* is banned in China, but our government seemed, at the time, to have no objection to the publication of either the *China Daily* or the *People's Daily* in the United States. (In 2020, however, *Xinhua* and four other Chinese media outlets, including the China

THE CHINA BUSINESS CONUNDRUM

Daily Distribution Corp., were labeled foreign agents by the U.S. government but are still allowed to publish here.[3]) And even more interesting is that the *People's Daily* thought I'd be willing to pay $5,000 to be interviewed.

9.3 THE DANGER OF HOPE

In May 2013, a few months after I'd started the *Neibu Cankao* campaign, Chairman Ji told me that Vice Premier Ma Kai had read one of our articles and allegedly told the CBRC to let us test our model using RMB. The pilot never came to pass, but for a while I felt as if I'd succeeded. Until I realized I hadn't. It's these sorts of vague intimations of success, always enticing, mostly elusive, that keep a Western CEO going.

In the same time frame, my anonymous advisory board in Beijing advised me to bluff: I should tell the Shanghai government that they needed to give me permission to use RMB *now*, or we would close up shop and go home. I couldn't bring myself to recommend this strategy to our board in Santa Clara for several reasons: 1) I didn't think it would work; 2) we would likely lose the roughly $100 million we'd already invested; and 3) I still entertained the hope that we would prevail over time. I still clung to the belief that if you treated people well, they would reciprocate. After all, the members of my secret team seemed to want us to succeed.

I believe this is the way most CEOs of Western companies think, after they've expanded to China and find themselves caught in a bear trap. In the end, many of them end up having to saw off their own legs to get free.

Takeaways from the Trenches

- The Party can accelerate your progress by granting you licenses. It can impede your progress through denying you licenses. If it wishes to impede your progress through denying you licenses, it can simultaneously seek to keep your interest by granting you subsidies.
- The Party will attempt to give you hope while simultaneously creating obstacles. The intent is to keep you in China long enough that the CCP can learn everything possible about your business while at the same time limiting your success.
- Significant decisions are generally made at the highest level and then trickle down. The Party may, from time to time, grant you access to the higher levels to spark hope and hold your interest. However, you will never get access to the level at which the relevant decision will ultimately be made. That is always at least one level higher than the highest level to which you will be granted access.
- Don't believe anything you are told, unless you hear it directly from the level at which the relevant decision is being made—and that will never happen.
- Agreements mean nothing. Leverage means everything. If you have no leverage, bluff. Never admit that you have no leverage.
- American companies rotate management too frequently within China. It takes years on the ground in China to build *guanxi* and understand leverage. *Guanxi* and leverage are more important than compliance. If you have *guanxi* and leverage, noncompliance will be forgiven. Without *guanxi* and leverage, compliance will buy you nothing.
- Chinese people are as capable of innovation as anyone else, if not more so. On the other hand, why innovate if you can "borrow" for free?

NOTES

1. Michael Schoenhals, "Elite Information in China," *Problems in Communism*, 34 (September–October 1985): 65–71.
2. *The Economist*, "An Obsession with Control Is Making China Weaker but More Dangerous," October 13, 2022. https://www.economist.com/leaders/2022/10/13/an-obsession-with-control-is-making-china-weaker-but-more-dangerous. Also Bertrand Russell, *The Problem of China* (London: George Allen & Unwin, 1922).
3. Conor Finnegan, "U.S. Forces 5 Chinese Media Outlets to Register as Foreign Missions," *ABC News*, February 18, 2020, https://abcnews.go.com/Politics/us-forces-chinese-media-outlets-register-foreign-missions/story?id=69054342.

CHAPTER TEN

THE NEW SHERIFF

XI COMES TO POWER

I n the spring of 2013, the entire business community in China—Chinese government officials, Chinese businesspeople, foreign businesspeople—were on the edge of their seats, waiting to see what kind of a leader Xi was going to be. On the one hand, he'd promised to "reform" the economy in general and the financial services sector in particular. What "form" would "reform" take? And what did he actually mean by "reform"? Whom was "reform" intended to benefit?

At the start of the prior year, Xi had inaugurated his anticorruption campaign with eight (always the magic number eight) guidelines for government officials throughout China, including rules to be followed for business entertaining. In part, these rules were intended to cut back on extravagance—ultimately, to ensnare both high-ranking tigers and low-ranking flies. In early 2013, the Shanghai government, in an attempt to demonstrate its enthusiasm for the new rules, expanded the eight guidelines to 23. But in May, I attended an extravagant dinner for about 14 people at a private club. The host told me afterward that the local officials had already figured out an end run around the restrictions. They paid each other in kind, which meant there would be no recorded expenses and thus no audit trail for their entertaining practices.

Initially, the anticorruption campaign was well-received by ordinary citizens who had been disgusted by the excess. Over time, though, it went too far. Some sources cite 2.3 million people who were rounded up and jailed as of 2023.[1] At that point, support turned to resistance.

But as Xi took the reins, things seemed to be closing down rather than opening up. Theories emerged from all sides, Chinese and foreign alike. The most popular one was that Xi was tightening things up to be able to loosen them later. In other words, to be able to open things up in the (hopefully near) future, he would have to make sure that everything was buttoned down first to prevent this eventual liberalization from engendering chaos. Avoiding chaos was Job Number One. Once again, we were clinging to hope.

For many, if not most, Chinese, the top priority was and is preventing chaos. China has experienced so much turmoil over the past 180 years (roughly since the beginning of the Opium Wars) that it has developed a phobia about the underlying potential for pandemonium. This phobia gave rise to some unintended consequences: in April 2013, supporters of Xi's anticorruption campaign were arrested for "unlawful assembly." Ironically, they'd "assembled" to voice their support for Xi's program. Apparently, in Xi's China, you may not assemble, even in support of his policies.

In May, our newly recruited chief information officer, Robert, suggested to me that the people whom SPDB had seconded to us, most of whom had already returned to the mothership, were likely "moles." Robert had come from a Western bank's Shanghai office and was thoroughly

Chinese although he didn't belong to the CCP. Thus, he had a deep knowledge of and great appreciation for Chinese culture. Because he'd spent so much time working in a quasi-Western environment, he understood both sides. I started to understand more about the motivations of the SPDB secondees.

Shortly thereafter, I spoke at the Tech Fair in Shanghai. My thesis was this: Xi has called on China to develop its innovation space to realize his "China Dream." But there were impediments, and I listed them:

1. The capital allocation process—namely, that the government tries to pick the winners and losers. I argued that this task is best left to venture capitalists because they have more expertise, more time, and fewer conflicts of interest.
2. The lack of intellectual property (IP) protection.
3. The lack of transparency, especially regarding financial results.
4. The lack of a legal system.
5. The lack of a firm understanding of the difference between debt and equity, and therefore the lack of financial instruments like warrants.

I wouldn't feel comfortable delivering a speech with this type of content in China today. It would be taken as excessively critical.

At this same time, Sharon, our wonderful head of HR, and a member of the Party, once again told me that with Xi in charge, our bank would soon have a Party Committee. She was adamant that it was nothing for me to worry about. It would be perfunctory, she explained: Xi was insisting that all foreign companies have one. Besides, I could do nothing to prevent it. Since Xi came to power, I've been told, the proportion of foreign companies with a Party Committee has risen from roughly 10% to 90%.

Also, by this time, we started to see the impact of the so-called Document Number 9, which was promulgated in 2012. It wasn't openly published, but was clearly Xi's work, according to research by the *New York Times*.[2]

THE CHINA BUSINESS CONUNDRUM

According to the *Times*, every Party cell was required to study it and internalize its dictates, which warned against the "seven subversive currents" that might loosen the CCP's grip on power. It explicitly stated that the Party should, "with great resolve," work to ban Western concepts such as democracy, freedom of speech, the rule of law, and so on, from China.[3] In summary, Document Number 9, which is supposed to be a "state secret," criticized Western ideals and prohibited people from discussing them in a public setting. Since its release, several journalists and professors have been jailed for such offenses.

Once that year, I naively asked Dean Lu, our supervisor, about Document Number 9. Lu told me directly that I should forget I'd ever heard of it and not mention it again in China.

At this point—and more troublingly—I learned that the Chinese government was arresting people who worked in Western due diligence companies. Many Western firms hire such firms to help them learn more about the people they're dealing with in China. That's fine, as long as the people they're investigating aren't members of the CCP. To investigate the background of a CCP member can result in arrest, prison, and torture.

A particularly horrifying example is that of Peter Humphrey, a British former journalist and his wife, a Chinese-born U.S. citizen.[4] They had founded one of these due diligence companies, but then made the mistake of inadvertently investigating a CCP member on behalf of GlaxoSmithKline, a British pharmaceutical firm. Humphrey and his wife were arrested in August 2013, held separately in secret prisons without knowing the charges they faced, tortured, and tried a year later in a public trial.[5]

The kicker is that the law prohibiting due diligence firms from investigating members of the CCP was created several months *after* the arrest of Humphrey and his wife. It was aimed explicitly at them . . . and was ultimately used to convict them. They spent more than two years in jail, separated from each other and their son, before being expelled in 2015 to the

United Kingdom. Humphrey was denied medical care for prostate cancer, likely, he said, in an effort to extort a confession.[6]

The possibility that I might be arrested for any sort of infraction, or none at all, always loomed in the back of my mind. People were locked up for lesser transgressions than my inadvertent mistakes. I'm not sure why I was not arrested and, tragically, why some others were imprisoned or, as occurred in *Red Roulette*, disappeared.[7]

And ever since, Xi has tightened his grip. Anti-American propaganda has become more intense. The current American consul general has warned me that China does not treat foreign companies well, especially American ones. And at the end of 2013, it was rumored that a number of professors had been fired for violating Document Number 9's prohibition on discussing Western values.

10.1 THE PARTY COMMITTEE

In June 2013, the idea of us having a Party Committee came up again, this time by Mr. Luo. We would benefit, he insisted. First, the Shanghai government, in its effort to please Xi Jinping, would be delighted with us for cooperating. Second, the 25% or so of our employees who were members of the Party would be thrilled, as it would provide them with a sort of club of their own, right in our own building. Third, it would elevate them above our non-Party employees, from which position they could more easily serve as role models. As expected, Luo argued that Party members were smarter and more productive than non-Party members, but nobody noticed, because we had not yet elevated them by having a Party Committee.

I wasn't persuaded. I didn't like the idea of a two-tiered society right in our own little bank. Perhaps I should have been more amenable. As Sharon and Changchang had told me more than once, we were getting a Party Committee whether we agreed or not, so why not acquiesce gracefully and enjoy the gratitude that the Shanghai government *might* bestow upon us?

I discussed it with Mr. Liu. He took it one step further: the Party members had a *right* to a Party Committee, and who was I to deny them their right? I was still not convinced.

Mr. Zhang, Hannah's father, met with me soon afterward and encouraged me to resist the government's efforts to establish a Party Committee in our bank. Since that reinforced my own preferences, I chose to follow his advice. Again, he told me to hide my true intentions, and never allow myself to become vulnerable.

One of the JV bankers told me that in his Party cell, which was housed at SPDB, they were all reading Document Number 9 and writing self-critiques targeting the extent to which they entertained and practiced Western values such as freedom of speech. In an unexpected moment of confidentiality, he told me he'd been raised by his grandparents because his railroad-worker parents had been constantly on the move, building out the rail system for the New China. His grandfather had owned a small business that made matches (for starting fires, not connecting people). As a business owner, he was severely punished during the Cultural Revolution. And now the grandson was engaging in activity ominously similar to the philosophy that had so abused his beloved relative.

10.2   BUILDING THE BANK'S CULTURE

We had worked very hard on creating a culture for the JV that was neither SPDB's nor SVB's but a blend of both. I am a firm believer in the importance of culture as a way to move companies from "good to great," as the business author Jim Collins said.[8] SVB had "The Sayings of Bill," which reflected the philosophy of our founder Bill Biggerstaff, and I wanted a similar touchstone for the JV. We came up with "Cheng Gong," which translates as "success" and also served as a mnemonic for the Chinese words meaning **C**ollaborative, **H**appy and fun, **E**mployee focused, **N**ew concept, **G**o for it, **G**iving, **O**pen communication, **N**eeds-based client focus, and **G**olden rule.

On May 29, 2013, we held our first "Culture Day," an event created by Arman and Chrystal, on their own initiative. They'd suggested we reinforce the cultural norms we'd been developing by using them for something fun. They had the troops form teams to create a skit illustrating one of our cultural norms, which the two of them chose.

The result was breathtaking. I don't know if we were just lucky or if we'd hired people who were extremely creative. On the one hand, many of our employees seemed disinclined to take initiative without explicit direction. On the other (and maybe the two are related), all we had to do was give them a topic, and their pent-up desires to be scriptwriters, actors, and directors all seemed to emerge from nowhere. Time after time, we would thoroughly enjoy this aspect of life at our bank.

This first Culture Day was all about client focus, because it is conspicuously absent in most Chinese banks. Since Mao "liberated" China in 1949, the retail banking system (to the extent that it even existed during the Mao era) was run like a utility. Everybody is, or at least was, equal in the eyes of the water department or the bank. Everybody paid the same fee, and everybody received in exchange the same identically poor service. Even today, if you're granted private client status by a Chinese bank, you'd be amazed by how terrible that service will be, although it's better than what you'd receive as an ordinary depositor.

As president of SPDB's most prized JV (that's what they kept telling me), I was a VIP client. And yet whenever I went to SPDB to withdraw, deposit, or exchange money, I left feeling depressed. I was greeted by a woman in uniform who apparently had never smiled in her life. Whenever she even looked at me, I felt guilty because her stare seemed so accusatory. I was given a number and told to wait. When my number came up, I was called to a double-paned window, facing a teller who acted more like a prison guard than a service provider. We communicated through microphones and speakers on either side of the double panes, much like what you'd experience if you were conversing with an imprisoned friend. Even a simple transaction could take 20 minutes. I was always amazed by the number of pieces of paper to be signed and stamped just to make a deposit. I always exited the bank feeling like I must have committed a crime.

Each skit depicted good and bad behavior and they were hilarious. After viewing all the skits, we discussed them as a group and voted to choose the best. This was followed by a meal together, and everybody went home in high spirits. Most important, they all went home knowing "what it meant to work at our bank" and proud of being members of our team. Until I left in late 2014, we held these Culture Days every couple of months. And every time, our troops staged a talent show that would have made Hollywood proud.

We inserted these talent shows into every event we could. Every year we had one to celebrate the Spring Festival (Chinese New Year). One year, it involved a dance presentation in which I had to take part. Given that I have no sense of rhythm and was an inattentive student, I was required to undergo private tutoring. The things we had endure to start a bank in China!

But at the end, I had to wonder how well our efforts at culture building actually worked. One day I arrived to find that William Koo, the head of our general office after Luke left, had purchased uniforms for all our customer-service personnel. I was flabbergasted and asked him why. His response: all proper bank customer service personnel wear uniforms.

"But that's why we don't!" I told him. I made him get rid of the uniforms immediately, but he was furious. The fact that he was as incensed with me as I was with him made me realize that our efforts at building a new culture might not be as effective as I'd hoped.

William figured in another cultural spat as well. He had fired Max, one of our drivers, whom everybody loved largely because of his spirit of adventure. For example, one day Max borrowed his mother's ancient, women's-frame[9] fat-tire bicycle and rode it 112 kilometers (68 miles) to Suzhou and then back again to visit a woman he'd met on a train. His enthusiasm was infectious. Despite very little formal education, Max's English was far better than my Chinese, notwithstanding my years of private lessons. He had picked it up watching TV and chatting with his passengers. But Max was dismissed for "borrowing" the company car he drove for us every day and using it for a small personal errand.

I found this interesting. Mao was responsible for the deaths of hundreds of millions of people and yet many regarded him as a "god" for having united China; Max got fired for "borrowing" his company car for an errand. Culturally, views of justice could vary greatly.

In the aftermath of the Max-car issue, Arman's assistant, Karen, wanted him to pretend that he never used the car and driver assigned to him for personal or social purposes. Arman refused. He definitely used the car and driver for personal and social reasons, and he didn't intend to stop. Nor was there any reason for him to do so—the car and driver perk was to make the lives of our senior personnel easier, regardless of the reason for the trip. It was the very policy I'd articulated.

William was flummoxed. He didn't realize that his policy (no personal use of company vehicles) conflicted with mine. Or maybe he did. Or perhaps William was concerned about Xi's anticorruption campaign. I assured him that Xi's policy didn't pertain to us. Our company policy had *nothing* to do with Xi's Party policy. I explained to William that our policy is our policy, and that based on it, Arman could use his car (and driver) for whatever he wanted. William wasn't so sure.

When my successor took over in February 2014, he wasted no time in firing William.

10.3   BUILDING *GUANXI*

In early summer, there was an official "ribbon-cutting" for a marketing project, called the SSVB 3+1 program. Thomas had developed it with help from his father, Lao Ding, and it was designed to get the Financial Services Department of Minhang, a district in Shanghai, to funnel more tech companies to us. It failed miserably—it never produced a single prospect, much less an actual client. My suspicion that the government determined which companies used which banks grew as a result.

Of course, I had to give a speech at this event, alongside various government officials who also gave speeches. I gave mine in Mandarin, and once again, I received the by-now predictable response from members of the audience: "Your Chinese is sooo good; last time I only understood some of what you said, but this time . . ." Even after four years, when we left China to return to the United States, I received that same compliment every time I gave a speech in Mandarin—literally word for word. It must be in the playbook that appears to govern many interactions between Chinese and foreigners.

In mid-June, I attended a conference sponsored by Fosun Enterprises (meaning the government, as Fosun is an SOE of sorts), at which I spoke, this time in English. Fosun is a typical Chinese conglomerate, allegedly private, but in many regards state-owned. The government had appointed its founder to our board in 2011, but after about a year, he was taken into custody for some misdeed, and we never saw him again. (Such events are not uncommon in China.) Vice Mayor Tu and Mayor Han also spoke, encouraging the Chinese members of the audience to recruit as many U.S.-educated Chinese entrepreneurs and scientists back to China as they could, to help build its innovation space. President Obama's secretary of the

Treasury, Tim Geithner, spoke as well. He was overflowing with praise for China and its future. In my estimation, the whole event was so predictable that I could have produced the video without ever attending.

The next day, Changchang advised me that I should quit my lobbying efforts to use RMB. By now, she claimed, everybody of any importance—all the way up to Xi Jinping himself—knew of our plight and my lobbying, which had left scores of lower-level officials sick of writing white papers for their bosses on why or why not the government should grant us an exception. "Would you please just stop?" she pleaded.

Of course I didn't.

Also around then, Mr. Luo told me that I was his "role model." Both his wife and his daughter wanted him to strive to be more like me, he claimed. In my experience, such over-the-top flattery is ubiquitous in China. It is usually a means to an end. I'd like to believe it was genuine in this case, but in China, you should always assume you're being played.

At the end of June, government officials from Guangdong Province came to Shanghai to visit us—a trip of almost 1,500 kilometers (950 miles). Of course, they wanted us to teach them our business model. I told them that we wouldn't teach anybody our model unless the central government granted us permission to use RMB. They seemed to accept this. They knew I'd be speaking at the Lujiazui Forum in a couple of days, and strongly suggested I use that opportunity to plead for permission to use Chinese currency.

Two days later, I served on a forum panel where we discussed how to increase lending to SMEs. It didn't seem appropriate to follow up on the suggestion to ask for RMB. What I found most interesting was that most of my fellow panel members had been here several times in the past. They told me it was hopeless. The government would encourage them to lend more to SMEs, but it was all just talk. Nobody was really interested in changing regulations to make it possible.

At that time, we were also enmeshed in a dustup with the government of the Yangpu District for whom we'd been managing an investment fund since 2011. The relationship had been strained from the start. The government team insisted we should invest in the best funds, global or domestic, but then require them to fund companies only in Yangpu. We chose to interpret that last bit as "suggest" that they consider Yangpu companies. The government had also wanted our investment professionals to agree in advance to accept the government's investment decisions, which were often based more on *guanxi* than on the track records of the funds in question. We had ignored this stipulation as well.

The particular issue now was their insistence that we invest in a fund with no track record whatsoever, due of course to *guanxi*. The founder was the son of a former governor of the Yangpu District. This youth had studied at Harvard and started a venture fund upon his return to China. He wanted the Yangpu government to invest in his new fund using the capital they had placed with us. The founder had never worked for a VC fund and knew nothing about VC investing but, in his view, expertise was unnecessary as long as he had good *guanxi*—and he did, through his parents. We refused. The Yangpu government officials were furious.

To even the score, they vetoed our next investment decision: to invest in the most successful American VC fund in history. I think that's called cutting off your nose to spite your face.

Around this time, Thomas, Lao Ding's son, gave me some advice. For the bank to succeed, he said, we should do two things: First, we should get rid of all of the white faces (Westerners) and replace them with Chinese—ideally, Party members or their progeny. Second, we should do a better job of helping the CCP achieve its objectives. By this, he meant we should organize seminars for government officials taught by Harvard and Stanford professors, on any subject that would help the Chinese government make faster progress in building an economy that would surpass ours. Oddly enough, I followed up on neither of these suggestions, nor did I relay them to my successor when he arrived.

10.4   THE CARROT OVERHEAD

In mid-2013, we still had no sense of whether we'd be able to use RMB anytime earlier than the late-2015 date our license stipulated. I kept meeting with people, including members of the secret team, who held out hope.

Professor Zhao assured me that his articles in the *Neibu Cankao* were making their way up the chain of command. Soon they would be read by Xi and China's then-premier Li Keqiang, and we would over time see change—that is, we'd be able to use RMB.

He also told me that Americans and Chinese have similar values, but tensions arise around power and money. Otherwise, we get along with each other very well. According to Zhao, the drivers of the Chinese economy are SMEs (the Chinese are an enterprising group); urbanization (the fact that the CCP has moved hundreds of millions of people from rural peasantry to the urban middle class); the Chinese work ethic (historically, the Chinese people have been masters of deferred gratification); and technology (whether through theft or invention, China has acquired an astounding amount of technology in an amazingly short period of time).

Zhao promised to get me another invitation to speak at the Central Party School in Beijing, where he taught. And, of course, he hoped that his daughter, Zhao Ye, would do well in her career at SVB in California. As a closing shot, just to keep me completely unbalanced, he declared that within two years, China would be in a hot war with either Vietnam or Japan, and the United States should not interfere.

Shortly thereafter, Lao Ding reiterated his vow to assist us in getting our plea in front of Xi. In Shanghai, he'd once worked with a man who was now on Xi's staff. This gentleman would undoubtedly assist us in getting a message to Xi. I'm not sure if that was yet another head-fake or a sincere effort that just didn't work out.

In mid-August, I attended yet another foreign bankers' meeting at the CBRC in Shanghai, led by the Shanghai office's top two executives, Mr. Ma and Mr. Liao. In front of roughly 100 bankers, Liao singled us out, expressing his disappointment that the government hadn't granted us permission to use Chinese currency. He said he believed it was unfair. I kept hoping.

Around then, the head of research at the Central Party School in Beijing came by to write a case about us. He claimed he, too, wanted to help us get permission to use RMB. He admitted that by refusing to let us use Chinese currency, China was violating the terms they'd agreed to when they joined the WTO in 2001. The government *should* play fair, he told me. It was nice to know that someone else was in my corner, but I didn't see how this was going to help. It didn't.

My VC advisory board met with me in Beijing that month and gave me straightforward advice. Our bank needed to be less cautious and less worried about the regulators. Instead, we should spend more time with government officials, tell them politely what we needed to succeed, emphasize how much our success would help China, find out what their goals and concerns are, offer to help (as appropriate), and, above all, praise them for their hard work and wise decision-making. Also, we had to spend more on marketing—we needed to be better known, especially among the financial services bureaucrats. We had underestimated the extent to which the bureaucrats were instrumental in determining who banked with whom.

As part of the marketing effort that followed this advice, we created a book about SVB and its history. It was a standard coffee-table piece, full of beautiful glossy photographs that illustrated the organization's history and the many start-ups it had banked. We were very pleased with the result and gave copies away whenever we met with anyone. This practice positioned us as culturally sensitive and was perfectly legitimate—and everyone seemed to like the book.

While I was in Beijing, I met with Wang Hong, the head of financial services for the city (and province) of Beijing. She was embarrassed by the fact that we'd located our headquarters in Shanghai and promised to do everything she could to help us get permission to use Chinese currency, if only we'd put our first branch in Beijing—sooner rather than later. Although we weren't planning to have a large branch network, it was a no-brainer to put our first branch in the capital city. Using my newfound skills in diplomacy, I assured her that we'd be happy to oblige.

Shortly thereafter, Mr. Luo and I traveled to Beijing to visit the CBRC's national headquarters. Luo argued eloquently for permission to use Chinese currency, and I was proud of him. Sadly, it was to no avail. After the meeting, we went to the Shangri La for tea. I was stunned—tea for two cost us $71. Not only had we failed in our aim, but we were out almost a hundred bucks for two cups of tea.

Doggedly, I kept on with my campaign to accelerate our ability to lend RMB. In an early September lunch with Professor Zhao from the secret team, he told me that the articles he wrote about us for *Neibu Cankao* made it all the way to Xi and Li. Again, he invited me to speak at the Central Party School, where he taught, and he advised me to *ask* for a Party Committee in our bank. He repeated that we would be the first foreign company in the history of the PRC to request one. By doing so, he thought, we would likely receive permission to use RMB much sooner. I still couldn't do it.

Shortly thereafter, Mr. Liu relayed a request from Chairman Ji. Ji, it turned out, was good friends with the head of SPDB's branch in Wuxi and wanted us to go to Wuxi to teach that branch about our business model. For free. So it could better compete against us once we could use RMB and do business, I thought cynically. But on the other hand, there was always the suggestion that such helpfulness might, just might, build a little more *guanxi* at high levels . . .

By now, I had learned enough to decline this chance to create yet another competitor, but that it was in Wuxi made it even worse. I had history with Wuxi. In 2011, shortly after my arrival, I accompanied our employee Ming to talk to the Wuxi mayor about our fund management services, which she led. Wuxi had several hundred million RMB and wanted to invest it in VC funds. Such services were an area of expertise for SVB, and my attendance at this meeting gave face to both me and the Wuxi mayor.

We arrived in Wuxi early that morning and met with the mayor and several people from his financial services department. The mayor had his own interpreter, a woman in her early twenties who looked like she could have played the role of Marian the Librarian in the musical *The Music Man*. She was the epitome of both demure and nerdy.

The meeting wrapped up at midday and we all adjourned for lunch in the mayor's dining room, complete with the usual big, round table. The Party Secretary of Wuxi joined us. Almost immediately, the baijiu appeared. I tried to beg off, honestly explaining that I never drink before evening. If I do, it puts me to sleep. But the mayor wasn't interested in my well-being. He signaled to his henchmen to start pushing the drink on me. Within a few minutes, the interpreter joined the assault. She plunked herself down next to me, poured me another glass of Baijiu, and began screaming in my ear, "He jiu, he jiu!" ("Drink! drink!")

The remainder of the lunch was sheer hell, as was the trip back to Shanghai. Ming had grown up in Taiwan and for whatever reason, appeared to believe that all Chinese customs must be followed, regardless.

As a result, I had no interest in going to Wuxi a second time, for any reason. I told Liu we were too busy.

In the meantime, though, Mr. Wang, the head of SME banking at SPDB, had approached Elwood Dong with the same request, and—without conferring with me—Elwood said yes. As CEO of the bank, I countermanded that approval. Nothing came of any of these Wuxi interactions.

Not long thereafter, the SPDB branch in Tianjin relayed the same request through Chairman Ji. In true Chinese fashion, they'd already built a 36,000-square-foot "tech center" with nothing to put in it, and they wanted us to teach them how to build and train a team of bankers focused on technology companies that they could incubate in this facility.

I talked with Mr. Luo about this. Luo, whom I respected even if I didn't always agree with him, told me that we *should* help the SPDB branch in Tianjin. Banks in China help each other, he said. I pointed out that *of course* they help each other—all 3,000 or so of them are owned by the Chinese government; and by American standards, they're all the same bank. As often happened when I pointed out facts that the Chinese wish I hadn't noticed, Luo scowled and had more tea.

Later, I learned that the Tianjin government officials thought I was "arrogant" because I refused to teach the local SPDB branch how to compete against us using our own business model.

I intuited that, at a subconscious level, many Chinese believed that because of the Century of Humiliation, we Westerners owed them—owed them the use of our precious technology, of our business models, of things that could boost their development. I could understand that. And yet, at some point, it had to end. We couldn't have a true peer-to-peer relationship until they viewed themselves, and us, as equals, and until we did the same. Currently, it seems that the West is so eager to do business with China that we'll sell them anything they want, including our very means of competitive differentiation. Remember that Lenin is said to have written, "When it comes time to hang the capitalists, they will sell us the rope."[10]

Takeaways from the Trenches

- In general, Chinese people prefer order to freedom as we define it. They fear chaos.
- To understand China today, you have to understand Xi's thoughts. Fortunately, he's codified them, so it is possible.
- Xi's thoughts are an amalgamation of Confucius, *The Art of War*, Marx, Lenin, and Mao. Our Bill of Rights is anathema to him.
- In China, you can be detained for breaking a law that does not exist. A law can be created specifically for you, months after you've been arrested and served time.

NOTES

1. Keyu Jin, *The New China Playbook: Beyond Socialism and Capitalism* (New York: Viking, 2023).
2. Chris Buckley, "China Takes Aim at Western Ideas," *New York Times*, August 19, 2013, https://www.nytimes.com/2013/08/20/world/asia/chinas-new-leadership-takes-hard-line-in-secret-memo.html.
3. Buckley, "China Takes Aim at Western Ideas."
4. BBC News, "China Frees Wife of UK GSK Investigator Peter Humphrey," June 11, 2015, https://www.bbc.com/news/world-asia-china-33090372.
5. Peter Humphrey, "'I Was Locked in a Steel Cage': Peter Humphrey on His Life Inside a Chinese Prison," *Financial Times*, February 15, 2018, https://www.ft.com/content/db8b9e36-1119-11e8-940e-08320fc2a277.
6. Carrie Gracie, "Investigator Peter Humphrey Warns Over GSK China Ordeal," *BBC News*, July 10, 2015, https://www.bbc.com/news/world-asia-china-33490446.
7. Lest my fears seem extreme, the Humphreys' experience was not unique. Desmond Shum recounted the experiences of his wife and him in *Red Roulette: An Insider's Story of Wealth, Power, Corruption, and Vengeance in Today's China* (New York: Scribner, 2021), and how their life of elite business privilege came crashing down. He and his son have been exiled to the United States, while his wife is held in custody in China without charges.
8. For more, see Jim Collins, *Good to Great* (New York: Harper Business, 2011).
9. Also known as a "mixte" or "step-through" frame.
10. Vivid though this image is, the exact phraseology cannot be found in any of Lenin's authenticated writings or statements. The earliest close match dates from 1955 when Major George Racey Jordan stated, "Lenin wrote, 'When it comes time to hang the capitalists, they will vie with each other for the rope contract.'" But Lenin died in 1924. *The Commonwealth*, 31, no. 33 (October 31, 1955), 268, with additional information from Quote Investigator, https://quoteinvestigator.com/2018/02/22/rope.

CHAPTER ELEVEN

IRRECONCILABLE DIFFERENCES

THE MORE WE KNEW, THE WORSE THINGS LOOKED

Toward the end of September 2013, Arman and I shared a car ride to a company event a couple of hours outside of Shanghai. The whole bank (about 200 people including spouses) dined outdoors on hairy crab and pig tails. Both are, in my view, acquired tastes.

During the ride, Arman shared his feelings of discouragement. He believed we would never succeed in China. His reasoning was predictable and, to me, justified. His points were:

- We can't use warrants. This eliminates our opportunity to cover losses with small equity gains. Lending to start-ups is risky and invariably results in losses.
- Loans have no collateral. China has nothing like the Uniform Commercial Code in the United States, which officially records the fact that an asset is being used as collateral to secure a loan. As a result, taking a security interest in an asset is very difficult, if not impossible.
- We're not allowed to use Chinese currency, and no one in China needs anything else. Therefore, we're unnecessary.
- Compliance is difficult. In the West, banks require borrowers to disclose their "use of proceeds"—how they will use the loan—but they need not actually document the use of every single dollar. In some situations, such documentation is impossible. For instance, proving the use of a working capital loan would involve mountains of paperwork. In China, regulations say the loan must be used exactly as described and closely documented. This is very difficult even with the best of intentions. The bankers would have to spend all their time tracking down the borrowers' actions, and the borrowers themselves would have to devote vast amounts of time to the necessary paperwork if they wished to comply. (It's always seemed to me that the stricter regulation becomes, the better people get in executing end runs.)
- The playing field is uneven. The multitudinous regulations are applied to favor Chinese banks and hurt foreign banks.
- As Westerners, we have no *guanxi*. And we will *never* have *guanxi* (Arman is proficient in Mandarin, but he is *not* Chinese and never will be).

This litany foreshadowed Arman's eventual decision to give up and return to SVB's headquarters in Santa Clara—and, honestly, my own decision to return to California too. We were slowly concluding that this project was not going to work. But at this exact moment, we could hardly abandon the effort.

Actually, we *could* have given up. And maybe we should have, because there were some fundamental roadblocks.

- First, the West has a series of institutions that safeguard the banking system—not just the Fed, but the IRS, accounting standards, financial transparency, the requirement for regular audits, accounting firms that perform these audits, the rule of law, contract law, and the like. They're so fundamental to our way of looking at the world and doing business that we don't even think about them. China doesn't have any of this. Most of the business practices that we simply took for granted in the United States did not exist in China. Trying to implement a U.S.-based banking system in China would simply not work.
- Second, none of the Chinese leaders nor the CCP has anything to gain by creating a self-sustaining business-and-banking system. It's much more effective for them to keep the economy reliant upon guidance and occasional bailouts from the central government. Moreover, the state banking system serves as a helpful patronage tool.
- And finally, the Chinese don't want JVs to be successful. They want to learn from the JVs and then let them fail.

It had taken us years to figure this out—but now it was finally coming together. And the outlook was bleak.

Shortly after this depressing conversation, I visited Mr. Jin, formerly governor of the Yangpu District, and later the deputy head of the Shanghai Financial Services Bureau. Jin is, I believe, a genuinely nice person. He told me that I was more successful than most foreign CEOs working in China. He said that the key was to be persistent, direct, respectful, a good listener, and responsible. I agree that those were some of the important qualities. However, I believe he left out the most crucial one: to understand leverage, how to acquire it, and how to apply it.

Furthermore, I've learned to beware of compliments from Chinese officials. Invariably, they follow a pattern: "You are much smarter than your countrymen, and you alone have the insight to appreciate China." In many cases, I believe, this line softens up listeners, rendering them receptive to requests for favors and less resistant to unreasonable demands and ridiculous rationalizations.

In retrospect, Jin's compliment may have been genuine. But it may also have been yet another head-fake. Head-fakes are the order of the day in China, and that's what wears you down.

11.1   THE SUCCESSOR IS NAMED

Our original plan had Ruth and me in China for two years. But as the saying goes, "Humans plan; gods laugh." I had failed in my efforts to find a successor to lead the JV, and Greg, the CEO of SVB Global, worried lest I might leave before a new CEO was firmly settled.

Greg wasn't alone in his desire to bring me back home. Ruth missed our grandchildren, and, in truth, I was growing ambivalent as well. The tightening under Xi Jinping, coupled with all the talk about a possible war, made me feel anxious.

Still, the ongoing thrill of discovery kept me engaged. I really didn't want to go home now, just as I felt I was finally beginning to understand China. Furthermore, I began to see that continuity was critical for our success. It takes at least three years to get acclimated and develop even semi-productive relationships. The huge emphasis that China places on *guanxi* means that without it, nothing gets done. To develop even a modicum of *guanxi* takes at least three years. Many Western companies send their executives to China with the expectation that they'll be there only for three years—the minimal amount of time to be effective. Then they rotate the execs back home and send over new ones. Because successor CEOs seldom choose to learn from their predecessors, many corporations spend most of their time in China reinventing the wheel.

In mid-2013, Greg chose as my replacement Rudolf, who had been a senior executive with SVB for 15 years. Beginning in August, I started telling people, starting with Mr. Luo, that Rudolf would be arriving in September and overlap with me until February, whereupon he would become CEO. I would stay on until the end of 2014 as his advisor, helping him as best I could to acclimate and introducing him to the people with whom I'd developed some level of *guanxi*.

To be frank, I had concerns about Rudolf's suitability. Succeeding in China requires a combination of flexibility, determination, and steeliness. Part of Rudolf's success as a credit expert was his adherence to rules. He had spent his entire career in a control position; he interpreted and made the rules, and when he said no, it stuck. But China, I'd learned, was far less about rules—it was impossible to follow them all—than building *guanxi* and having the determination not to be pushed around. You had to walk a delicate line: being friendly without being a pushover; tough without being aggressive. Rudolf had some of these qualities, but I feared he lacked the full suite. While I didn't doubt his toughness, I had concerns about his friendliness. And Rudolf was anything but flexible. This is a double-edged sword: you can survive more easily in China by being **in**flexible because you're less likely to be pushed around, but you won't succeed because everything is about flexibility.

But Rudolf had distinct strengths—otherwise he wouldn't have done so well at SVB. He was an absolutely indefatigable worker. I don't know how he did it, but he could work nonstop. In addition, he had an astounding memory. Whenever he was in a meeting, it seemed as if he'd just read the credit report of every company that came up for consideration. He had all the details absolutely top of mind. Finally, with one $50 million exception, his credit decisions were top notch. Like many bankers who join SVB, it took him a few months to get the feel of the SVB approval process, but once he'd figured it out, he was absolutely on the mark.

Perhaps, I told myself optimistically, he'd become more flexible in the two years that I'd been gone.

The drums of war kept beating, albeit in the background. My art-appreciating friend Huang insisted that war was imminent. China must fight Japan to save face over, first, the atrocities committed by Japan during World War II and, second, the disputed islands (most of which are uninhabited outcroppings of rock) in the East China Sea. The United States would have to support Japan, so the result would be a war between China and the United States. Nor was this just a single conspiracy theorist's daydream: Back in 2011, a new computer game called Glorious Mission had appeared on the Chinese market. It featured a war with Japan. Of course, in that version, China annihilates Japan.

Rudolf, my successor, arrived in the office on September 3, as planned, to get a head start on climbing the learning curve before he officially took over in February 2014. Unfortunately, we did not get off on a good foot.

His first act in the new environment was to grow a beard, which is highly unusual in China's business world. Modern Chinese society prefers a clean-cut look, and beards are perceived as messy and unhygienic—or indicating an artistic temperament. In addition, beards are associated with the persecuted Muslim Uyghur minority in western China, so it's just better not to bring up the topic of beards at all, or to wear one. No matter, Rudolf did.

His second act was to begin contradicting my directives in front of the executive team—or behind my back. I put a stop to it, but it was only temporary. Only a few months after I left China at the end of 2014, he resumed the direction he'd tried to pursue initially.

A good example of our inability to work together was Rudolf's view of a branch in Beijing. By the summer of 2013, I'd concluded we needed one. Beijing had far more tech start-ups than Shanghai. Furthermore, we were gaining support for the project from Beijing's city/provincial government and the CBRC. And I'd promised the head of financial services for Beijing that our first branch would be there. It just made sense!

Accordingly, I gave my direct reports the go-ahead to start hiring. Within two or three weeks of Rudolf's arrival, I learned that he was telling my people, behind my back, to stop recruiting for Beijing. I went directly to Rudolf's office and confronted him. Unaccustomed to being challenged, Rudolf was furious. He turned red and told me that I was wrong to hire for Beijing. I told him *I* was in charge, he wouldn't be running things until February, and to deal with it. He finally accepted that fact, but once I'd left China, he did his best to erase as many of my policies as possible.

Shortly thereafter, I visited another member of the secret team, Mr. Liao, the head of the Shanghai CBRC. I gave him a copy of Lee Kuan Yew's most recent and ultimately last book, *One Man's View of the World*. Liao had just returned from a seminar on governance at Yale University, and we discussed the one-party system. Liao wondered why I liked the two-party system. In his view, there were pros and cons, but the one-party system was better. I told him that I'd prefer a multiparty system to either.

This exchange reminded me of a similar interchange I'd had just after arriving in China. At a dinner to welcome me, eight of us sat around a large table holding the typical massive turntable of dishes. The guests—except for me—practically chain-smoked cigarettes, creating a pall of smoke that rivaled London's famous fogs. At the end of the meal, one of the attendees challenged me: "You say Americans live in a free country. But you can't smoke in a restaurant! Here, we can smoke wherever we want! How can you say we're not free?" That stuck in my mind—but the strange codicil was that a few years later, this same individual asked me to invite him to the United States. He wanted to visit his much younger wife and their child, who were living in California, but he needed permission from the Chinese government as well as a U.S. visa, which entailed a formal corporate invitation. I didn't zing him then about who was freer.

I found it strange indeed that the more senior a member of the CCP was, the more their movements were conscribed. For instance, it was with great pride that my assistant Victor told me his wife had reached a level in the Party where she could no longer hold her own passport. It was locked in a vault, and she couldn't access it without permission.

11.2   FILLING IN THE BLANKS

In October 2013, Clayton, the friendly senior banker at SPDB, spent several hours with me explaining the intricacies of the relationship between SVB and SPDB. Once again, it could be described with the Chinese proverb "One bed, two dreams." SPDB wanted knowledge from us, he said, and the marketing benefits of the SVB brand. This explains why they referred to the JV as "SPD SVB" (as opposed to SSVB, as most people in Shanghai, including myself, called it), and why they had wanted the JV to use their SPDB logo rather than having its own—as if the JV were just a division of SPDB. I had suspected this as we went through those epic battles back in 2011, but the confirmation was nice.

He also articulated my suspicions about the license issue. In China, because everything is forbidden unless it's explicitly permitted, banks need a specific license for every discrete activity. SSVB, the JV, wanted the maximum number of licenses so that it could leverage its entire business model and not just parts of it. Because it's possible for one bank to borrow or rent licenses from another, SPDB only wanted us to have a few ourselves and then to borrow the rest—from it, of course. This would limit what we could do without their permission and thus reduce our ability to compete against them.

In addition, he said, SPDB employees gained nothing by being seconded to us, which explained why no one from there wanted to join us and, when they did, why they wanted to return to SPDB as fast as they could. Their bosses wanted to appear cooperative with their own supervisors, but nothing encouraged the staff. Part of the tension was the difference between cultures, both corporate and "national." But furthermore, SPDB had no stake in creating a new, third blend of the two cultures. SSVB did and tried, but SPDB's lack of support and the enormous cultural differences between the two made it almost impossible.

Clayton also confirmed a nascent suspicion of mine: that SPDB didn't care if the JV survived long term, as long as it lived long enough for the SPDB team to gain every last bit of relevant knowledge. To that end, he continued, the United States rotated its people too fast. Instead of staying for three to five years, we should have stayed for eight to 10. It took that long to learn the system and to develop *guanxi* and leverage.

Most important, he explained, the United States didn't appear to understand two key things:

1. The Party determines economic outcomes. Clever strategies and expert execution help, but the Party ultimately determines the results.
2. There is very little risk in Chinese banking. No bank had ever been allowed to fail. SPDB would not and could not fail, and with sufficient *guanxi*, the JV, SSVB, would not fail either. What would keep SSVB afloat, he said, was good relations with the government (the Party) and any knowledge it possessed that SPDB wanted and did not yet have.

Illuminating as it was, this discussion on top of Arman's bleak assessment of our project plunged me into gloom, which was intensified by one of the most disappointing experiences of my life. As described earlier, Oscar had arrived in Shanghai during the spring of 2013 as part of Rudolf's new crew. He replaced Elwood Dong as head of banking (that is, head of the sales team). I'd known Oscar for almost 30 years, since we worked together in Boston. A Brit, he was famous for closing a sale by literally throwing himself at the customer's feet, as a knight might kneel before a king, and swearing eternal fealty. Everybody loved Oscar and found him immensely amusing. Ruth and I had always found him charming and had gone out of our way to help him acclimate to China.

By the time Rudolf arrived in September, Oscar was well-acquainted with, and involved in, our plans to establish a branch in Beijing. I knew that in February, when Rudolf became CEO, he would obstruct those efforts.

In late October, Oscar and I were returning from the celebratory meetings of Dean Lu's International Advisory Board and Mayor Yang's International Advisory Council. I took the opportunity to appeal to Oscar, saying something to the effect of: "You've been with us now for more than six months as head of banking. You know how important it is for us to forge ahead in Beijing. And you know that Rudolf is against it. Rudolf likes you—and you know that he's wrong about Beijing. Would you be willing, for the sake of the bank, to try to change his mind?"

It turned out he either wouldn't or couldn't.

11.3   WRAPPING UP 2013

Throughout 2013, I continued to meet interesting people—no surprise in a country of 1.4 billion. In one instance, Chairman Ji sent me a message through another member of the secret team requesting that I meet XuFei, whom he had just promoted to president of Shanghai Guaranty Company, another subsidiary of the Shanghai International Group, SPDB's parent. Ji thought there might be opportunities for us to collaborate.

Over lunch, XuFei told me her life story. In her youth she'd fallen in love with the law. She believed that the Western legal system was superior and wanted to see it adopted in China. Over time, however, she came to realize that the Chinese system, based on *guanxi*, would work better in China, and now she believed that all legal systems worldwide should be replaced by the Chinese system. Her advice to me: never speak at conferences; turn to her for guidance; and let her screen all my contacts to make sure that I wouldn't get into situations where others could take advantage of me. I was startled but said nothing.

At our next meeting, she was wearing a very tight-fitting, leg-revealing *qipao* dress. I complimented her on it, and she told me she was wearing it just for me. At that point, I decided to cut off all contact. I did not need that sort of collaboration.

But before I left the meeting, XuFei told me that I would never understand China, not because I was stupid, but because no Westerner could *ever* understand China. According to her, I should never approach a prospect by myself, but always rely on a referral from a member of the CCP. Nothing could be accomplished in China without the help and guidance of the Party. She may have been right on that point.

I also decided to find out more about Chinese venture capitalist/political scientist Eric Li. He came to widespread notice with his TED talks and has written a number of opinion pieces for the *New York Times,* the *Wall Street Journal,* and other Western publications. He is so one-sided in his anti-American rhetoric and so arrogant in his delivery that I felt compelled to meet him. It was easy to justify an introduction. After all, our bank dealt only with VC firms and venture-backed companies.

Eric was the founder of Chengwei Capital, and some of his portfolio companies were clients of the bank. He was born and raised in Shanghai, and then went to the United States for his BA (Berkeley) and MA (Stanford), following which he returned to Shanghai to earn his PhD from Fudan University. Based on his writings and his speeches, the United States is the worst country ever, and China is the best. It's tempting to theorize that he was dead set on pleasing the CCP. We just don't know why.

Our visit lasted 90 minutes, and Eric gave me about 90 seconds of air-time. During the other 88 minutes and 30 seconds, he blasted me with how horrible the United States was and how amazingly great China was. It made me wonder: Exactly what happened to him at Berkeley and Stanford? How was it possible to be so one-sided? How thickly was his bread being buttered? And by whom?

Mr. Guo, the head of Z Park, an industrial park in Beijing, was once again lobbying us to set up a branch there. He'd approached us many times in the past, and I remained skeptical of his motives and intentions. Whenever we showed interest, he seemed to lose it. When we lost interest, he regained it. My guess is that he wanted to learn more about our business model. I doubt if he had any real interest in building a bank with us and I believe he had even less interest in sharing the profits.

I believe that here again we were operating with different mental models. The American view of someone who runs an industrial park is fairly simplistic: he would want to attract various rent-paying businesses that will make the operation profitable. But Guo wanted to demonstrate to the government that he could build an important technology park. Having our bank locate there, I suspect, would be a feather in his cap and also attract other businesses eager for a spot close to a bank with our pedigree.

I was skeptical for several reasons. There was just something about him that seemed disingenuous. We had met before I moved to China, and in that four-hour meeting, he'd pushed very hard for me to sign a memo of understanding (MOU). I wanted to take it home and review it before I signed it—this was before I understood that Chinese MOUs weren't worth the paper they were written on—and when I called him back with questions, he never returned the call. Finally, he was just pressing so hard that something seemed amiss—and then he would completely fade out of view.

This happens quite frequently in China. People respond to pressure from their superiors to produce something that shows movement on a certain trajectory, but if nothing happens in a day or two, the matter is dropped completely. There was also a quality in many of those interactions that I've encountered in four-year-olds. The counterparty will ask the same question over and over, apparently hoping for a different answer. Eventually, they get distracted and drop it altogether.

At the end of 2013, Bob Eccles, my organizational behavior professor at Harvard Business School, introduced me to one of his former students, a Chinese woman living in Shanghai named Zhang Ying. She was the progeny of a "Revolutionary family," members of the group who joined Mao on his "Long March" from 1934 to 1935 from Jiangxi Province in the south to Shaanxi Province in the north, retreating from the Nationalist army, which at that point was in its ascendency. These Revolutionary families are held in the highest regard in China today, and their offspring are very high-level officials in the CCP, very rich, or both.

In our meeting, I learned that Zhang was a strong believer in the "Thucydides trap," an idea propagated by the American historian Graham Allison. This philosophy held that there was seldom a smooth transition between a rising power and a descending power. Usually, either or both became insecure and initiated war. I found Zhang charming, amusing, and affable—but not convincing. I think the Chinese latch onto this concept as a pretense for making it appear that we, not they, are the aggressor in any given situation.

In December 2013, my friend from the CBRC in Beijing told me that we might be getting permission to use Chinese currency soon. Hope springs . . .

The same day, I met Hui, a close friend of Zhang Ying, and also a well-educated member of a Revolutionary family. She wanted SVB to fund a study of the effects of so-called shadow banks on the banking system in China, a study that she would lead. Because Chinese banks are all owned by the CCP and have focused almost exclusively on servicing SOEs, a number of financing entities have emerged to serve the needs of those sectors of the economy ignored by regular (state-owned) banks. These organizations—such as the loan guarantee companies mentioned in Chapter 9 and the shadow banks—have no counterpart in most Western countries.

Because these "unofficial" banks are relatively unregulated, they caused dislocations in the financial system that gave regulators ulcers due to their own lack of control. I say "relatively unregulated" as opposed to "unregulated" because everything in China is regulatable if the CCP wants it to be. If you're in China and you're not regulated, it's because the CCP has determined that you're not important enough to be regulated. If you succeed in realizing your growth ambitions, you *will* be regulated.

I found it interesting that Hui would ask a foreign bank that wasn't even allowed to use RMB in China to fund a study of an aspect of the Chinese banking system that was causing a problem for the Chinese government—with a straight face. Even more intriguing, she told me that Westerners couldn't understand the Chinese economy because we were all imbued with a Western understanding of the principles of economics, which didn't apply in China. Maybe she was right.

And immediately after saying this, she told me she couldn't tell a Westerner what the corresponding Chinese economic principles were, those that would enable us to understand the Chinese economy. It reminded me of a feature of the late Qing dynasty, when to teach the Chinese language to a Westerner was a capital offense. However, she assured me that the truth was "hiding in plain view."

On the topic of plain view—the pollution in Shanghai at this time was the worst we'd seen in the prior three years. Ruth compared photos that she'd taken from our balcony with identically positioned shots taken earlier. At the beginning of 2014, the view was crisp and clear. By the end of that year, you couldn't see anything. The light was night-dim even though it was only 3 p.m. Pollution in Shanghai has now subsided because heavy industry has been moved further west.

Also in December, I gave another speech on our JV at the Central Party School in Beijing. I shared the podium with Rudolf. The same thing happened as the earlier time I spoke. We received a warm welcome and an enthusiastic response.

"We love your bank," the audience said. "We want one of our own."

We told them, "You have one. It's the very bank we're describing. Your bank is right here in China, and 99% of the people who work there are PRC citizens. All its customers are Chinese technology companies."

They replied, "We understand, but we want one of our own."

If you're not Chinese, you will never be accepted as Chinese.

Takeaways from the Trenches

- In China, if a bank needs a specific license, it can "rent" that license from another bank that has it.
- In China, banks almost never fail. They are all effectively owned by the government. The government has no interest in letting itself fail. If a bank generates large loan losses, the government arrests those in management whom they deem guilty, throws them in jail after a very short and seemingly perfunctory trial, and quietly recapitalizes the bank with government funds.
- To understand the way the Chinese economy works requires a working knowledge of an entirely different set of principles and concepts than Western economists are used to. That's why the predictions of our economic pundits are so often wrong.

CHAPTER TWELVE

WRAPPING UP MY STAY

STAFF CHANGES, MORE LESSONS, STILL NO RMB

Our fourth year in China started with lots of change. Sheila, our first employee here, who had opened the office on Huaihai Road back in 2005, decided to leave us for greener pastures.

In addition, Mr. Liu, Luo's second-in-command, was "asked" by the Organization Department to move out of SPDB and into a new position in another part of Shanghai's network of SOEs. His new job entailed combing through these SOEs to determine which assets should be held and which should be sold to fund new business lines that were more relevant to the

CCP's ever-evolving goals. Teresa Li, our long-time head of banking for larger companies, was interviewing with East West Bank, one of our competitors. And Ruby, my mentee, decided to move to Taiwan to be with her Taiwanese American husband, whose business was based there.

In time, none of these moves proved to be permanent. To help retain valued employees, Liu and Mike Descheneaux (SVB's CFO in the United States) went halves on a retention fund to boost the salaries of employees who were being poached by other banks, such as East West. And we did some coaxing. As a result, Sheila and Teresa both decided to stay and are still with us in late 2022. They were attractive to many Chinese banks because they knew our business, but their futures were less secure in banks that fundamentally did not understand technology banking. Ruby got divorced and stayed in Shanghai. She eventually left SSVB to join a government-owned private equity firm whose purpose was to purchase semiconductor companies (at any price) to help China achieve its dream of semiconductor independence.

Within just a couple of years, Liu returned to SPDB as president, replacing Mr. Zhu, whom the Organization Department had brought in to replace Mr. Luo. All these higher-level changes were instigated by the Organization Department, the CCP's national HR office that was independent of SPDB.

Soon thereafter, our employee Christina quit to join her father's "family business" in Hong Kong. Such a loss represented a typical pitfall for "foreign" companies like our own. Christina was a very smart young woman who grew up in Beijing. Her father was a "red hat" (a businessman with ties to the Party, which increased the probability of his success) who ran a family business. While his wife didn't really participate, Christina, who'd been educated in London, was being groomed to take it over.

Christina had been referred to me a few years before by a friend who taught at the London School of Economics. When we hired her, she promised to be with us for many years. In total, she lasted three. When the siren song of the family business rings out, all former promises to Western employers are forgotten. Family first. Goodbye, Christina. We spent tons of money every year training young Chinese employees who would take that training, leave us, and put it to good use elsewhere: family businesses, competitors, government-owned entities, and so on.

Also, in January we had our semiannual evaluation process. Interestingly, I saw a parallel between how our U.S. parent, SVB, evaluated its employees and how SPDB in China evaluated *its* staff. In both cases, part of the evaluation was based on "production," and part of it was based on what some refer to as "soft factors."

But there was a difference on the "soft" side. In the case of SVB, the soft part of the evaluation was based on the extent to which employees demonstrated behavior that reflected our corporate values (a willingness to help colleagues, a strong desire to help clients, determination, creativity, and ethics). In the case of SPDB, the soft part was largely a function of the extent to which the employees were seen as loyal to the CCP.

By mid-January, members of our secret team—Ms. Jiang of *Xinhua*, Professor Zhao of the Central Party School, and Madame Wang of the CBRC in Beijing—all told me that they thought we'd be getting permission to use RMB soon. Also, they all thought the Shanghai government would continue to prop us up with subsidies. However, while we were waiting, they encouraged us to help other banks learn how to copy our business model . . . as a sign of good faith vis-à-vis the Party.

The carrots were always large, but the stick from which they dangled was long, and it was always moving even faster than we could run in our eagerness to catch it. Some of us, including me, were getting disillusioned.

As the year started, there was growing tension between our Beijing "branch"—it wasn't a formal branch but just an office—and the new management team in Shanghai involving Hannah, Mr. Zhang's daughter, who managed the effort. Apparently, Hannah didn't like working with the new team (Oscar, Rudolf, and Harvey, our head of credit), who felt she was "entitled." Others believed that Hannah was right, even if she *was* entitled.

At issue was Hannah's approach to prospecting (finding new customers). The new regime wanted Hannah to spend her time cultivating relationships with Chinese VC firms that had American origins, such as Sequoia. Hannah thought the bank would be more successful if she cultivated relationships with government officials and with VC firms founded by children of Revolutionary families who had access to government capital and who had been asked by the government to invest in technology. As for who won, let's put it this way: Hannah is still running the successful Beijing branch. Oscar, Rudolf, and Harvey have all left China.

When I met with Chairman Ji to tell him that Rudolf was replacing me, he chastised me for leaving. As I'd heard from others, he said American companies regularly made the mistake of rotating out their executives too early, about the time they'd started to develop *guanxi* with government officials, but before they had a chance to make use of it. He encouraged me to stay and continue my lobbying efforts. He said I was making progress. Both Xi and Li had reportedly read the articles that Professor Zhao had written (with my help) and published in *Neibu Cankao* (with the help of Lao Ding, Ms. Jiang, and Ms. Gao), and sent them back down with encouraging notes in the margins. Chairman Ji was sure that we'd have access to RMB soon.

Lao Ding's response was similar when I told him of Rudolf's arrival. He praised my lobbying and promised, of his own volition, to support my efforts. Then he asked for a raise for his son so that Thomas's wife (the daughter of a People's Liberation Army general) would be proud of him.

Mr. Liao, one of our regulators at the CBRC, told me in private that he was personally ashamed of the way the Chinese government had treated us. He admitted that Chinese banks didn't follow the rules yet got away with it all the time. His advice to me was: "Innovate first and ask permission later." He followed this up by urging us to "lobby, lobby, lobby" all the way to Beijing, to Xi and to Li. Since I'd been doing this for a full year, I was glad to receive his blessing, even belatedly.

I had finally learned that *"innovate"* in this case was a synonym for *"execute an end run."* Liao also suggested that we ask Mr. Jin (formerly governor of Yangpu, and currently deputy head of financial services under Mr. Zheng) for special permission to set up a "lending fund"—a pool of money to lend out—so that we at least could get started using RMB.

Apparently, I may have taken my lobbying campaign a little too far. A bit later, Mr. Ma, the deputy head of the Shanghai CBRC, told me that everyone at the highest levels of government in Beijing knew of our strong desire to use RMB. He thought that I should stop lobbying. I'd made my point, he said. In the end, the wheel that's *too* squeaky gets punished.

I learned more about the nuances of "innovation" from Zhu Xiao Hong, a very nice woman in the compliance group at SPDB, who advised me that the regulators used a secret language. They encouraged "innovation," which in Chinese-regulator talk meant end runs—but they didn't really mean it. A bank couldn't possibly follow all of the plethora of rules and regulations. Simply to do business, banks were forced to execute end runs ("innovate"). If the regulators caught you, you'd be reprimanded—but the extent of the correction depended on the level of *guanxi* you'd developed. The lesson: government relations are of the utmost importance. *Guanxi* counts!

I was very fond of Zhu. Most of my person-to-person experiences in China, and particularly with members of the CCP, were cordial. The people weren't the problem; the problem was the Party as an organization and the belief system to which it clung. That belief system looked a little like this: The Chinese are a superior race. They had led the world for centuries, until the 1800s, when they were overrun by Western Barbarians. Thus ensued the Century of Humiliation. Only the CCP could reunite China and lead the Chinese back into a position of leadership among nations. Of greatest importance, the CCP should lead China, and China should lead the world. Not *run* the world, just *lead* the world. At least in the near term.

Like most superiority complexes, this one was accompanied by a deep-seated inferiority complex, which motivates the Chinese to work hard, and for them, justifies the one-sided approach they took to competition: "Because the evil West brought us to this low level, we must fight to return to our original position of superiority; and because we have been degraded to this extent, anything we have to do to succeed (such as implementing an extremely slanted playing field) is justified."

Most Westerners go to China to create a "win-win." They're gratified to hear the Chinese profess to be targeting a "win-win" as well. What so many Westerners don't understand is that the CCP's "win-win" means China wins twice. The Party will often flatter you into believing that you are "so Chinese" that you've earned the special status of being an "old friend." Beware of this special status. It is a fiction intended to soften you up for further manipulation.

Soon thereafter, I attended another "foreign bank meeting" at the CBRC. Liao told the entire group that—on the whole—we foreign banks were more responsible and took less risk than the domestic banks. He lauded us for being more conscientious than our Chinese counterparts. *So, what about the RMB?* I wondered privately.

And then in mid-February, Rudolf took over as president of SSVB.

12.1 I COULD HAVE GONE HOME

I could have gone home once Rudolf took the reins, but I decided to stay in China, for two reasons.

1. It was apparent that Rudolf didn't understand the critical need to develop working relationships with government officials and members of the CCP to get things done. To this day, I don't believe that

Rudolf ever learned that the Party, government, and business were pretty much all the same thing in China. During the six years after I left China at the end of 2014, while Rudolf led the JV, various government officials consistently asked me to advise him to spend more time with them. His failure to do so slowed our progress. The more we learned, the less we understood.

2. Both Ruth and I were enjoying ourselves. Simply put, we loved living in China. Every day was an adventure. So, for another year, we had a front row seat to the evolution of the bank and of China.

As a result, even after Rudolf took over, I continued my program of building *guanxi* for the bank and asking the government for permission to use RMB. I kept receiving requests from Lao Ding for favors—and fulfilled them as best I could. A particular example occurred around this time, when he asked Victor if I could help the daughter of a friend of his get into Stanford. I asked Victor to explain to Lao Ding that I had no influence over the Stanford admissions office, but I'd be willing to meet his friend, hear him out, and offer any advice that might be helpful.

Lao Ding's friend turned out to be a real estate developer, apparently with very good ties to the government based on his almost limitless access to capital. He'd moved to Los Angeles a few years earlier, and his daughter was in junior high school in Vancouver, British Columbia. He was dressed entirely in black, with the top two buttons of his shirt undone to display a very large gold necklace. His daughter was wearing the shortest pair of cut-off jeans I'd ever seen. She was about 14, and radiated disinterest.

After showing me pictures of real estate that he'd purchased on the Embarcadero in San Francisco, the father segued into the reason for the meeting. He wanted his daughter to go to Stanford—not now, of course—but in four or five years when she was old enough.

I explained that, while neither I nor any acquaintances had any influence over the Stanford admissions program, I did know a woman who ran a small company specializing in helping Chinese youth earn admission to noteworthy U.S. universities. The daughter was, if nothing else, the perfect age to begin the process of building an attractive résumé for a high-caliber Western institution. I have no idea how this project ended up, but I think Lao Ding believed I'd fulfilled the duty of friendship, by Chinese standards. And that, honestly, was all that mattered (that and doing so within the bounds of U.S. law and my own integrity).

During the remainder of 2014, President Xi stepped up his anticorruption program. He was going after both tigers and flies (big guys and small guys). Hardly a week went by without a rumor about some government official or red hat in Shanghai in trouble, a list that included one of our own board members (the independent director on the Chinese half of the board). People were definitely scared, and at least a handful of them even told me directly how frightened they were.

The atmosphere in China was gradually but unwaveringly becoming more charged and less comfortable. On March 1, 2014, a group identified by the Chinese government as Uyghurs undertook a terrorist attack on the public at the Kunming railroad station in Yunnan Province. Wielding long-bladed knives, they attacked innocent passengers, resulting in 35 deaths (31 passengers and four terrorists).

During this period, Peter Humphrey and his wife were languishing in a Shanghai prison, as described in Chapter 10. I knew nothing about this until my return to San Francisco in 2015, which makes me feel sad and undeservedly blessed. In retrospect, I wonder how many similar stories were percolating, still underground, in that last year in Shanghai. Personally, I was always vaguely afraid, but there was nothing to do apart from building *guanxi*.

But I was starting to feel the impact of Xi's crackdown. In May, Xi and the heads of some other Asian countries gathered in Shanghai for a pan-Asian conference. To deter protests, Shanghai was under a curfew and people were encouraged to stay close to home. One afternoon during this period, while walking down the street to our local grocery store, a five-minute walk from our apartment, I was stopped by two policemen. They wanted to see my passport. In the three years I'd lived in China, no one had *ever* asked me for my passport while on my way to the grocery store. When I couldn't produce it, they scolded me severely and told me to have it with me at all times or I could be in real trouble.

Around this same time, a Chinese journalist, Gao Yu, was accused of sharing state secrets and arrested for emailing a copy of Document Number 9 to another Chinese journalist in New York City. This was unsettling because it was already in worldwide circulation—and searchable on Google.

But life went on, and some things didn't change. Now that I had better *guanxi* with Luo, he asked me for favors. He wanted me to go to Vice Mayor Tu and tell him that the new president of SPDB, Mr. Zhu, was too busy to be the chair of our JV, so Tu should really arrange for Luo to return to his old position as our chair.

This was clearly infeasible, as the Party had already decided that Luo had to retire. Having learned a few lessons in negotiating Chinese bureaucracy, I chose to find it impossible to get on Tu's calendar. I simply couldn't see that any good would come of this effort. And frankly, Zhu was easier for me to deal with than Luo.

On the other hand, Zhu wanted us to teach the intricacies of our SVB business model to every applicable branch in the SPDB system. If he stayed as chair—which seemed entirely likely—I needed to figure out how to pretend that I was complying with his wishes without actually doing so.

12.2 BECOMING VICE CHAIRMAN

A few months later, at the annual shareholders meeting, I was to be named vice chairman of the JV bank. We'd never had a vice chair, but for several reasons, a number of board members thought it appropriate for me to have that title:

1. After serving as president for almost four years, I would soon be retiring and returning to the United States, returning quarterly for the board meetings.
2. I was by far the oldest in the room, and China reveres age.

That said, the Organization Department had been mulling over this question for months and had still not made a decision. As Changchang explained, it was an issue of parity. Because each owner (SPDB and SVB) had 50% of the operation, the Organization Department felt that naming me vice chair (a purely ceremonial title) would upset the balance. If I—a representative of SVB—became a vice chair, the Chinese side must have one too.

The Organization Department felt that their vice chair should be Mr. Jiang. Because there was constant turnover on the Chinese side, thanks to the Organization Department's habit of moving people around every couple of years, Jiang was a relative newcomer to the board. In addition, he distinguished himself from others, in my opinion, by the inverse relationship between how much he knew and how much he said. No other board member knew as little, nor felt compelled to say as much. With reluctance, I accepted the vice chair title during the meeting, and Jiang did as well, with obvious (and loquacious) enthusiasm.

In February 2014, Rudolf assumed the mantle of CEO. To my surprise, he immediately embraced the idea of the Beijing branch and enthusiastically forged ahead. I could only suspect that he wanted to get credit for it. Unfortunately, he pretty much ignored building relationships with the government, much to the detriment of the JV's progress. He did fire William, the head of the general office who had forbidden the personal use of cars. I continued trying to get permission for the JV to use RMB, while building the bank's *guanxi*. And I put up with the unending head-fakes of doing business in China. It was exhausting.

12.3   WARRANTS AT LAST

On a muggy Saturday afternoon in July (government officials in China work seven days a week), our head of credit, Harvey, and I met with a group of government officials from Beijing. The topic was warrants. Harvey, by the way, was an amazing guy. He could have starred in a television series: "Everybody loves Harvey."

To review: Our SVB business model depended on our ability to take warrants. The reason was simple—globally, about 10% of our loans by value went to start-ups.[1] We banked them because it helped ensure that we would be able to bank the larger companies they would become (assuming they survived). Companies that started with us typically stayed with us. For the most part, start-ups usually had only one choice for a bank, and that was us because no one else had a model that could manage banking loss-making enterprises. As the companies grew, they had many more banking options to choose from. (As an analogy, consider Tom Brady, the former New England Patriots' quarterback and seven-time Super Bowl winner. He was the 199th pick in the sixth round of the 2000 NFL draft. Only Bill Belichick, the iconoclastic New England coach, was willing to risk adding him to the roster. By 2005, when he had won three Super Bowls, there was no question about Brady's talent and any team would have gladly taken him. At SVB, we banked the start-ups that turned into Tom Brady–quality companies. No one else did.)

To get access to these would-be superstar companies, we *had to* bank start-ups. In addition, it was part of our culture and we loved it. But the problem with start-ups is that the loss rate is much higher than for larger, more mature companies. We couldn't afford a high loss rate—we're a U.S. bank. The solution was warrants (in effect, extremely cheap stock). When a start-up failed, we might lose money (although our model reduced the odds), but if we had warrants in every start-up we banked, a few of them would pay off big. Those big payoffs would offset the losses. It was as simple as that.

In China, it's illegal for banks to hold warrants, largely because there's no law that says banks *can* do so. For years, we told the Chinese regulators, over and over again, why we needed to be able to take warrants as part of our pricing. They routinely objected that Chinese banks aren't allowed to own companies, or even parts of companies.

I don't know how many times I explained to the regulators that by taking warrants, we didn't own companies, or even parts of companies. When we asked risky borrowers to give us a warrant, we were asking them to give us a written promise that at any point in the future, we might buy a small percentage (usually less than 1%) of their company, at an extremely low fixed price. If the company succeeded and we exercised the warrant, we didn't hold the stock—we sold it immediately. And by selling it immediately, we eliminated the possibility of owning stock in the borrower.

That day, there were at least 10 government officials and regulators in the room with Harvey and me. The topic was warrants. I explained it again, for the umpteenth time. Miraculously, on that day, by pure happenstance, I hit on the right words. Spontaneously, and without premeditation, I blurted out: "Think of the warrant as a success fee! If the start-up is successful, we get a reward for our efforts in seeing it through to success."

A light went off in the brains of several attendees simultaneously. Enough people there had the same insight at exactly the same time that all the rest of them felt compelled to pretend they did as well. Fortunately, among those who "got it" was someone perceived by the others as the most senior person in the room.

Suddenly, they were all laughing and screaming out together: "We get it, we get it! Why didn't you just say that in the first place? Of course you can take warrants. Just don't call them 'warrants'! Call them 'success fees.'" We all laughed, wound up the meeting shortly thereafter, and parted company.

Everybody went their own way to enjoy the remainder of that Saturday. Now *that's* what's meant by the word *innovation* in China.

Although we were now allowed to use warrants—oops, success fees—we still couldn't use RMB. But in mid-August, Mr. Liao told me that Mr. Zheng (the head of financial services in Shanghai now that Dr. Fang had been promoted to a much more senior position in Beijing) would give us yet more subsidy to tide us over. On SVB's books, we'd again show a loss.

12.4 CONVERSATIONS IN CONTEXT

During those final months in China, I continued to have conversations with all sorts of people, both inside and outside our JV bank, on various topics. I gained much more insight from these than my earlier ones, for two reasons. First, my frame of reference was larger, so I could contribute to and benefit from in-depth dialog with these perceptive people. And second, as I knew many of my conversation partners better than I had before, they were more willing to share their views.

I was also attuned enough to the audience to understand some comments that were previously unintelligible. I gave speeches at several organizations, including the advisory board of Fudan University's Graduate School of Management, where I was a charter member. I also gave my final speech at the Central Party School during this period and received the exact same response from the audience that I'd had previously. They *loved* our bank's business model, and they wanted *one of their own that was just like it*. Once again, I pointed out that they already had one—namely, this one—and they replied as they had in the past. They understood but they still wanted *one of their own*.

I had the insight then that our half-ownership of the JV rendered it somehow tainted. Even the facts that they owned 50%, that 99% of the employees were PRC Chinese, and that *all* our clients were Chinese companies, couldn't make it "one of their own."

Conversations with non-Chinese friends were also illuminating. Arman and I shared another long ride to visit a prospect. To put his thoughts into perspective, he was the only American from SVB to attain fluency in Mandarin. Additionally, he was probably the most open-minded of all the SVB expats. During those two hours in the car, Arman told me all the reasons that he continued to think we could never succeed in China:

1. **Turnover:** It had taken us four years to reach our current understanding of how to do business in China. Soon he and I would be returning to the United States, and the new team would be in charge. By the time they reached our level of understanding, they, too, would be replaced by yet another team.

2. **Hierarchy:** The Chinese are extremely hierarchal. Our employees had a ranking system in their minds based on which they knew every single person's place in their (imagined) hierarchy—and no two people were on the same rung of the ladder. This created a problem. SVB couldn't have both the CEO and the chairman positions as long as we were in a partnership with SPDB. SPDB would insist on the chair position because that was the higher of the two. That left us with the CEO position, which consisted of two parts: government relations and running the bank. Rudolf, my successor, who was also very hierarchal, would want to do both rather than share power. But doing both was too much for one person, so he would be forced to ignore one task and focus on the other. Rudolf would gravitate toward running the bank because he discounted the importance of government relations. He would appoint someone to go through the motions of government relations, but that wouldn't work. The government

ministers *expected* the CEO to be their point of interaction and wouldn't settle for anyone else. Government relations would be deemphasized, creating suboptimal results, at best.

3. **Senior staffing:** To truly succeed, we needed to have non-SPDB Chinese in each of the two top positions (CEO and chair). That was impossible.

4. **Localization:** We needed to "localize," that is, to rethink our value proposition. Chinese clients wanted "operational excellence," not "customer intimacy"—and they weren't willing to pay for it. In China, banks were viewed as utilities: everybody gets the same electricity; and it should be dirt cheap.

   Rudolf was unlikely to take the necessary steps to localize. His idea was to superimpose our American value system—which they didn't want—on China.

5. **Relationship:** The Chinese wanted an algorithm, not a relationship, and insofar as they wanted a relationship, they wanted one with another Chinese person, not a Westerner. Yet our bank was perceived as a Western bank, despite our overwhelming majority of Chinese staff.

6. **Government control:** The government controls interest rates, so we couldn't charge to reflect the level of risk. Because outcomes are controlled (by the CCP steering the best companies to its own banks), we could be only as successful as the government wanted us to be. Our partners (and the government) were pushing us toward a high-volume, low-margin business. While that may be reasonable in the dairy business, it would not work in technology lending.

As you might guess, I emerged from the car with my few remaining illusions in tatters.

Friends of ours in Shanghai, an American couple who had spent several years there—he ran a division of an American chemicals company while she was engaged with several charities—had a similarly dire view of

U.S. business prospects in China. His company, in fact, was preparing to pull out of Shanghai, and he said that the Chinese government "sucked" the margins out of Western companies through capriciously imposing fines, taxes, and regulations.

On my last visit to Mr. Zhang, the head of the Shanghai People's Bank of China/State Administration of Foreign Exchange (SAFE), he faulted me for having visited him too infrequently during my years in Shanghai. Ironically, almost every time I'd asked Changchang to call his office about getting on his calendar, his handlers had said he was far too busy.

When I called on Hanscom Smith, the then-current U.S. consul general in Shanghai, I took Victor with me. Afterward, I commented that Smith was openly gay and lived with his Taiwanese partner.[2] Victor was amazed and remarked that he'd love to live in a country where that would be permitted.

12.5 BODY COUNT

Toward the end of our stay, I was becoming profoundly disillusioned. I wasn't alone. Of the thousands of Western companies that have entered China since it first began opening up, the successes are minimal. In fact, to my knowledge, one of the few *truly* successful Western companies is the venture capital firm Sequoia, which succeeded, essentially, by becoming Chinese. In short, the Chinese division of Sequoia, the world's most successful VC firm, was led by Neil Shen, a Chinese national who received his MBA at Yale. He ran it in a truly Chinese fashion, ruthlessly competing for and winning deals like JD.com, ByteDance, and Didi. The firm managed to raise a $9 billion China-focused fund in mid-2022, even in the midst of Xi's tech crackdown and the chaos of the COVID pandemic. But in June 2023, Sequoia announced it would spin off its Indian and Chinese entities from the U.S. operation. Since March 2024, these groups operate completely independently, reflecting concerns about the Chinese environment for private equity, particularly the increasing willingness of the CCP to take stakes in promising technology companies.[3]

Some people may find my assertion surprising, as companies like GM and VW have long histories in China. But even so, they too are failing. During the 1980s, many of the large international carmakers piled into China, licking their lips at the prospect of large profits. Unsurprisingly, they ended up in JVs, through which they transferred their technology, willingly or not. Over time, the CCP created brands of its own, in many cases using the foreign technology. Now, except for Tesla, China no longer wants or needs foreign car makers.[4] Jeep, Suzuki, and Mitsubishi have already pulled out; VW, Ford, Hyundai, and Nissan are said to be departing by 2030. Chinese sales of GM—formerly the star of U.S. companies in China—have fallen by 50% from their peak in 2017.[5]

Here again, it's "one bed, two dreams." Michael Dunne, the expert on the history of U.S. carmakers in China, has argued that the only reason China encouraged the foreign automakers in the first place was to learn from them and eventually develop a world-leading domestic auto industry.[6]

Across history, companies (or invaders) that succeeded in China did so by becoming Chinese. The Mongols successfully invaded China in 1271, ending the Song dynasty, and the Manchu invasion ended the Ming dynasty in 1636—but there are fundamentally no Mongols or Manchus in China today. They've been absorbed by the culture of the conquered and become Chinese.[7]

But apart from Sequoia, entry to China appears to be a fraught experience, even for Asian companies. In 2018, Arm Technology, a British chip maker owned by SoftBank Group, the Japanese conglomerate, had entered China in a joint venture with Hopu Investments, a government-funded private equity firm. The Chinese division became Arm's most profitable operation. In 2020, the board fired the CEO, Allan Wu, for apparent conflict of interest. Not only did Wu refuse to accept that he'd been fired, but he took the company chops (the seal) with him, giving him legal control of the entire operation because no official documents could be attested without the chops. It's important to understand that while Arm licensed most of its chip designs, Arm China was developing its own chips as well, much to the interest of the Chinese government. Wu set up a replica of what had been Arm China and brought all the employees with him, leaving Softbank with an empty shell. The local government did nothing to address the situation. Only two years later did the local government agree with SoftBank and Arm to recognize the new management team and issue a new set of chops for the company, allowing SoftBank to pursue a long-planned public listing for the company.[8]

Nor are large companies the only ones to struggle in China. Icon Aircraft was a start-up founded in 2006 by Kirk Hawkins and Steen Strand to design a super-light amphibious aircraft with foldable wings. Its investors included Eric Schmidt of Google and a former Boeing CEO, but developing the product took longer and cost more than expected. As a result, the founders accepted capital from the Shanghai Pudong Science and Technology Investment Company (PDSTI) in 2015 and by 2017, PDSTI was the company's controlling shareholder. At that point, PDSTI took over the board, removed Hawkins as CEO, and began implementing a "tech transfer" agreement with China. The Pentagon had allegedly been exploring the application of this technology to unmanned aerial vehicles, but now it will, by Chinese law, be transferred to the Chinese army. In 2021, the founders and the PDSTI group filed lawsuits against each other alleging the tech transfer was illegal and drawing the attention of the Committee on Foreign Investment in the United States (CFIUS).[9]

The willingness of Chinese government-backed investment groups to step in when U.S. venture capitalists have lost enthusiasm for start-ups developing various groundbreaking technologies makes one despair of the short-termism of the U.S. V.C. industry—and the lack of a U.S. industrial policy. Two cases come to mind, both of them in the green energy space.

MiaSolé was a start-up that designed a new and less expensive way of making flexible solar panels, while A123 Systems was a Boston-area battery company, both founded in the mid-2000s. Both received backing from top tier VC firms and raised considerable amounts of money—over $1 billion for A123 and about half that for MiaSolé. Despite shipping product, both went bankrupt or close to it and both were acquired by Chinese companies for pennies on the dollar (A123 for $256.6 million; MiaSolé for $30 million). A123's batteries are now propelling the Chinese electric vehicle market, while MiaSolé's technology is being applied by Hanergy, its acquirer, to the solar panels that Americans are now enthusiastically buying.[10]

Certainly, the West can't ignore China. But neither can we allow them to scoop up our innovations because we're too short-sighted or profit-focused to fund them while the industry catches up, as occurred with A123 and MiaSolé.

In addition to the societal and economic costs of doing business with China, there's also a human cost. More than once in our four years in China, Ruth would come home from an American Women's Club event with a story about an impending divorce. In time, we discerned a pattern: an American multinational sends an executive to China for what is anticipated to be a four-year stint. The executive is male, the "trailing spouse" is female. He's away all day every day, she's unhappy and alone at home. Every night he comes home, and she is grouchy. In time, he despairs.

But there is a light in his life—his assistant. He's in his fifties, she's in her thirties. And she is nice! She dresses fashionably, she is always supportive, and she caters to his every whim. In time, the range of his "whims" expands. Or does she expand it for him? In any case, he starts succumbing to his inner demons. His wife finds out, throws a fit, packs up and goes home, hires a lawyer, and serves him with papers. He seeks solace in his new relationship. While I don't have any hard data on this phenomenon, it is widespread, and all American executives should be aware that this is a bigger danger in China postings than in many other parts of the world.

12.6 REVOLUTION ON THE DOORSTEP

Between September 26 and December 16, 2014, during the Umbrella Revolution, Ruth and I traveled to Hong Kong. As a refresher: when the CCP ruled that Hong Kong residents could only elect their chief executive from a pre-approved list of candidates, protests erupted, led by students and eventually involving up to 100,000 people who occupied areas of the downtown for 77 days. They used umbrellas to defend themselves from tear gas fired by the police.[11] The protests fizzled out without any change;[12] 266 people were prosecuted and 118 convicted.[13] We found a dizzying variety of reactions and explanations.

The younger people in SVB's Hong Kong office said that the struggle was between young and old, rich and poor, capitalists and communists. The youth felt hopeless. The rich owned more than 90% of the assets, and the younger generation didn't think they had a chance.

Many of our Chinese friends said that the people in Hong Kong looked down on mainland Chinese. In return, the mainland citizens looked down on the Hong Kong youth, seeing them as condescending, entitled, self-centered, and bratty.

Some of our older friends in Hong Kong said that the CCP's unwillingness to negotiate stemmed from its need to maintain credibility with the mainland citizenry. Others (mostly Hong Kong Chinese) told me that the protests were instigated by CCP operatives hoping to create a pretense for a crackdown in response to a pattern of "foreign" interference.

Many of my Chinese acquaintances believed the protests were instigated by the CIA. One member of the CCP told me that there were 1,000 CIA operatives in Hong Kong. That idea struck me as ludicrous.

Hannah and her father told me that the protests were driven by American stock market manipulators who hoped to drive down the Hong

Kong exchange, buy low, and then wait for it to rise again so they could later sell high and make a profit.

Lao Ding said it had nothing to do with the Americans but was driven by right-wing professors. Xi, he said, would deal with it effectively, at a time of his choosing.

To me, the CCP's decision to pre-approve Hong Kong's candidate slate was seen by Hong Kongers as a final disavowal of the much vaunted "one country, two systems" promise made when Hong Kong was transferred from British rule. To the CCP, I assumed, it was simply business as usual.

12.7 LEAVING

Even in our last few months, there were additional adventures. After six years of Mandarin lessons, I finally passed the HSK 3 test in the government's language proficiency program. I'd reached the proficiency level of a 12-year-old. I could read and speak somewhat, but I could comprehend only my teacher and a few highly educated individuals who spoke a dialect-free version of the language. As you may guess, those are few.

Ruth and I spent some time doing the tourist circuit. One such event was riding the "Maglev," which connects the Shanghai Pudong International Airport with the District of Pudong. It uses a German technology, which employs magnets to both levitate the train and move it forward—at 270 miles per hour! And oh, so smooth!

And there was the inevitable sadness of leaving the haunts that, once so foreign, had become familiar. One was GL Japan, the grocery store across the street from our apartment complex. I had always taken my SVB tote bag on my shopping trips, and the cashier had always admired it. She did it again on my final trip, so I gave it to her. She seemed pleased.

On November 19, 2014, our apartment had that echoing air of sad emptiness indicating imminent departure. Our belongings were packed. It was time to leave. Xiao Meng, our driver, drove us to the airport, and Victor accompanied us. We were all sad, I believe, to such an extent that just thinking about that day still makes me feel bad. We loved China—the people, the culture, the fascinating history. It's true, we weren't enamored of the Chinese Communist Party and the gratuitous aggravation they'd put us through, but the overall experience had been wonderful. When people ask us, we still refer to our time in China as the most interesting four years of our lives.

Sixteen hours later, we were home again in Silicon Valley. Not long thereafter, our belongings arrived at our door: 70 boxes in total, including an entire closetful of gifts. We have enough tea sets to last several lifetimes!

Takeaways from the Trenches

- When Chinese people use the word "innovate," they are often referring to successful efforts to get around the rules.
- The Chinese government encourages the Chinese people to believe that they are a superior race and that China's problems are due to things that foreigners have done to them. That's why we foreigners "owe" them.
- In China, "win-win" usually means that China wins twice.

NOTES

1. In terms of numbers of client companies, this was much higher—about 75%—but the loans were smaller.
2. In fact, two years later, Smith and his partner, Eric Lu, got married in San Francisco. Since gay marriage is illegal in China, this caused "a bit of a stir." Edward Wong, "U.S. Diplomat's Same-Sex Marriage Causes Stir in China," *New York Times*, May 3, 2016, https://www.nytimes.com/2016/05/04/world/asia/us-diplomats-same-sex-marriage-causes-stir-in-china.html.
3. The Economist, "Why Sequoia Capital Is Sawing Off Its Chinese Branch," June 8, 2023, https://www.economist.com/business/2023/06/08/why-sequoia-capital-is-sawing-off-its-chinese-branch.

4. Michael Dunne, "Why Everyone Except Tesla Should be Terrified of BYD," The Dunne Insights Newsletter, January 2, 2024, https://newsletter.dunnein sights.com/p/why-everyone-except-tesla-should.

5. Dunne, "Why Everyone Except Tesla Should be Terrified of BYD."

6. Michael Dunne, "The Sudden Death of Detroit in China," The Dunne Insights Newsletter, March 12, 2024, https://newsletter.dunneinsights.com/p/the-sudden-death-of-detroit-in-china?utm_campaign=email-half-post&r=ck&utm_source=substack&utm_medium=email.

7. For a readable history of China, see Jonathan Spence, *The Search for Modern China*, 3rd Edition (New York: W.W. Norton, 2012).

8. For more detail, and you can believe there's much more detail, see Zhang Erchi, Qu Yunxu, and Guo Yingzhe, "In Depth: How SoftBank Wrested Back Control of Arm China," *Nikkei Asia*, July 5, 2022, https://asia.nikkei.com/Spotlight/Caixin/In-Depth-How-SoftBank-wrested-back-control-of-Arm-China.

9. Kate O'Keeffe, "U.S., Chinese Investors Feud over Startup Icon Aircraft During National Security Review of Deal," *Wall Street Journal*, February 8, 2022, https://www.wsj.com/articles/u-s-chinese-investors-feud-over-startup-icon-aircraft-during-national-security-review-of-deal-11644340248.

10. For MiaSolé, see the discussion in Josh Lerner and Ann Leamon, *Venture Capital, Private Equity, and the Financing of Entrepreneurship*, 2nd ed., (Hoboken, NJ: John Wiley & Sons, 2023), Chapter 3. For A123, see Annaliese Frank, "Battery Maker 123 Systems to Lay off 42 as It Steps Back from Manufacturing Work in Michigan," *Plastics News*, August 8, 2019, https://www.plasticsnews.com/news/battery-maker-a123-systems-lay-42-it-steps-back-manufacturing-work-michigan.

11. BBC Newsround, "Hong Kong Protests: What Is the 'Umbrella Movement'?," September 28, 2019, https://www.bbc.co.uk/newsround/49862757.

12. Tyler Y. Headley and Cole Tanigawa-Lau, "Why Did Hong Kong's Umbrella Movement Fail?" *The Diplomat*, April 6, 2016, https://thediplomat.com/2016/04/why-did-hong-kongs-umbrella-movement-fail.

13. Austin Ramzy, "9 Hong Kong Democracy Advocates Convicted for Role in 2014 Protests," *New York Times*, April 8, 2019, https://www.nytimes.com/2019/04/08/world/asia/hong-kong-umbrella-revolution-occupy-central.html.

CHAPTER THIRTEEN

SUCCESS IN A FASHION

CHINA'S NEW TECH BANK (WHICH WASN'T US), AND BEING VICE CHAIRMAN

S ix months after Ruth and I left China, on May 19, 2015, the Shanghai government announced that the JV could use RMB. The bank had technically opened in August 2012, so May 19, 2015, was three months ahead of the prescribed three-year waiting period. I was in China for the occasion—primarily to attend our regular board meetings.

When the officials told me in person, their announcement was filled with praise. We were receiving permission three months early largely because I'd done "such a brilliant job of lobbying the government; seldom has anyone done so well," they said. In fact, I'd done so well that the State Council had decided to change the law altogether. Henceforth, any new bank with any element of foreign ownership would only be subject to a one-year prohibition on the use of Chinese currency, rather than the three-year prohibition we'd been subject to. And not only that, but they purported to be thrilled to give me this really excellent news.

As a footnote to this "really excellent news," these same officials also told me that the Chinese government held our business model in such high regard that they'd made the executive decision to copy it. Four days later, the Shanghai government would hold the opening ceremony for the brand-new Huarui Bank, 100% owned by the Shanghai government, to deploy our business model. Finally, they would have "one of their own"! Oh, and one other thing: even though they'd studied our business model for a number of years, there were still a few things they didn't quite understand. Would I mind meeting with the new bank's management team just to help them understand some of these finer points about which they were still unclear?

I was invited to attend the opening ceremony. Out of 250 people in attendance, I think I was the only Caucasian.

Almost two years after I left, I received bits of information that suggested the *Neibu Cankao* campaign was indeed my most fruitful undertaking. People at lower levels told me that Professor Zhao's "internal references" praising our model and describing how it could help finance Chinese technology companies had successfully worked their way up the chain of command, all the way to the top, then back down, annotated by Xi, Premier Li Keqiang, and Vice Premier Ma Kai, arriving at the level where they could be executed.

I believe the effectiveness of this approach stems from the widespread Chinese unwillingness to make a decision. Making a decision exposes the decision-maker to criticism. No one wants to be criticized. In the extreme, all decisions must be made by Xi—and the *Neibu Cankao* route was the only one of the four I'd devised that led to Xi. This insight didn't occur to me at the time; I just had four potential routes to get approval and worked all of them.

From the end of 2014 through the end of 2019, I continued to travel to China every quarter for board meetings. Initially, I stayed for two weeks each time, trying to maintain my relationships with relevant government officials and old friends. In time, it became clear that Rudolf, who'd never seen the value in building relationships with government officials, didn't feel comfortable with that aspect of my itinerary. And many of the expats among my friends moved on. Under Xi Jinping, the atmosphere became increasingly less expat-friendly. Before long, it seemed as if there were no expats left.

And then, even before the pandemic ended all travel, I stopped going altogether for a cultural gaffe that still galls me. Mike Descheneaux, our former CFO and then the president of Silicon Valley Bank, also attended the board meetings of SSVB in China. He is a black-and-white, "show me the numbers, that's all I need to know" guy, with a brittle personality. He has a tendency to lose his temper and (I think, I hope) regret it afterwards, but he lacks the capacity to acknowledge it.

At one of the last board meetings I attended in China, just before the onset of the pandemic, his frustration reached the breaking point and he exploded. The situation was this: the CCP had withheld numerous licenses from us over the years for no clear reason, which had a profound impact on our bank's profitability. The most crucial of these is the so-called custodial license. This would functionally allow us to bank VC firms, the key component of our business model. We discussed renting a custodial license from another bank, as we had done in the past with other licenses that we'd been denied. That strategy would be completely inconceivable if we were dealing with the U.S. Fed, but not necessarily for the CBRC. For Mike, though, it was a complete nonstarter. In the board meeting, I voiced the opinion, shared by the Chinese members, that we should consider renting licenses. No sooner had I stopped speaking but Mike screamed, "That's stupid." I tried to calm him down, suggesting that we discuss this further in private, but he persisted in berating me anyway.

Of course, I was insulted, but in the eyes of our Chinese board members, this was an important turning point. Either I was being "purged" by my American colleagues, which is the only circumstance that could justify this show of disrespect to the former CEO, or Mike would be removed after the board meeting. Because he wasn't removed, they thought I was being purged. In effect, he ended my usefulness in China.

A lot has changed since I left, in China and for the bank. Hostilities between the United States and China have intensified immeasurably. As of this writing, the trend line is still downhill. The election of Donald Trump certainly didn't improve things; nor did the COVID pandemic. In all honesty, I'd attribute much of the relationship's degradation to Xi himself.

The bank, sadly, has lost much of its allure. When we first started hiring in 2011, we attracted many young people who were enthusiastic about the idea of working for an American company. In the meantime, due to the rise of Xi with his incessant anti-American propaganda and the influence of Trump who succeeded in making America look like a nation of buffoons, we are nowhere near as attractive as we once were.

And what happened to the secret team? As of this writing in mid-2022, here's what I know—but some details may have changed.

Yu Zhengsheng, the man who convinced us that we should build a bank in China, was promoted from Party Secretary of Shanghai to a seat on the Standing Committee (making him arguably one of the seven most powerful people in China). He has since retired.

The extremely affable Chairman Ji also retired. I'm told that his health deteriorated. I'm sorry about that, because he was a very likable man.

President Luo also retired, despite his pleas to the Organization Department. I understand that he spends most of his time with Mrs. Luo, taking care of Ke's children while she and her husband work. She is still at the state-owned "private equity" firm; her husband is at a Western investment bank in Hong Kong. I miss discussing history with Mr. Luo over dinner, and both Ruth and I miss Mrs. Luo and Ke.

Mr. Liu, another of our favorites, was promoted from his role as president of SPDB up into the holding company that owns it. He is now the president of the Shanghai International Group.

Mr. Tu was promoted to be the head of the largest sovereign wealth fund in the world, China Investment Corporation, and has since retired. He would easily win a popularity contest, if there was one, in our JV bank.

Party Secretary Ding (Lao Ding) has since retired, I believe altogether. He was held in such high regard and loved by so many people that the Party found many jobs to keep him busy after his initial retirement.

The extremely competent Dr. Fang is now the deputy chairman of the China Banking and Insurance Regulatory Commission, the top regulator for banks and insurance companies in all of China.

Liao Min, my personal favorite, was promoted from head of the Shanghai CBRC to deputy director of the general office of the Central Financial and Economic Affairs Commission and vice minister of finance. In that capacity he is Vice Premier Liu He's deputy. As Liu became the chief trade negotiator during the Trump administration, I often saw pictures of Liao from a distance at these meetings.

Zheng Yang, another good friend, was promoted from deputy head of the Shanghai SAFE to head of financial services in Shanghai. More recently, his career has skyrocketed. He is now chairman of both SPDB itself *and* our joint venture, SSVB. I understand that he's happy, he likes our bank, and our bank likes him.

Dean Lu, at one point in time the youngest academic dean in China, continues as the dean of the Graduate School of Management at Fudan University. He is very well liked and extremely competent. Without his help, the secret team could not have been as effective as it was in helping us succeed, to the extent that the CCP wanted us to.

THE CHINA BUSINESS CONUNDRUM

Our CEO as of 2022 is Jade Lu. She's a member of the CCP, and she completely understands the value of government relations. I understand that our employees appreciate her warm and caring leadership style. Until the onset of the pandemic, Rudolf remained in China, significantly setting back the JV's progress through strategies that ranged from ignoring the Beijing branch to neglecting our marketing efforts. Shortly after my departure, he loaded all the coffee table books we'd produced as marketing collateral and gifts to government officials and took them to the dump.

Chrystal, my other assistant, left us to start a fashion boutique. I don't know what COVID did to her business, but pre-COVID, she was extremely successful. The cashmere garments she designs, has others manufacture, and sells online and in her shop are gorgeous.

Finally, Victor, my wonderful assistant, is still with our bank, now as the head of the general office. Without him, we never would have done as well as we did in China. Victor is amazing.

One final point: periodically, people ask me how well our bank in Shanghai is doing. I always give them the same answer: as well as the CCP wants us to. What do I mean by that? Well, the Party, operating through, and for that matter, as, the government, has a multiplicity of methods for determining outcomes, including selective application of regulation, issuances of licenses, and general "encouragement" versus "discouragement." As mentioned earlier, every discrete banking activity requires a separate license, and the CBRC won't grant us the critical custodial license. As a result, we're "fighting with one hand tied behind our back."

Whenever I say, "as well as the CCP wants it to," whether I'm speaking with Party members, government officials, or simply well-educated Chinese businesspeople, they always answer the same way. They give me a knowing grin and say, "I understand."

PART III

THE CHINESE COMMUNIST PARTY

CHAPTER FOURTEEN

THE CCP'S ROLE AND INFLUENCE

Over the course of our stay in China, I learned a vast amount about the CCP and the Chinese people overall. Because anyone trying to do business in the country will interface with both, I wanted to share these lessons, in the spirit of reducing the oh-so-American tendency to reinvent the wheel.

14.1 "PARTY, GOVERNMENT, MILITARY, CIVILIAN, AND ACADEMIC, EAST, WEST, SOUTH, NORTH, AND CENTER, THE PARTY LEADS EVERYTHING."[1]

Oddly enough, I had a completely irrational sense of personal connection to the CCP. It was founded 1921 in Shanghai—in a building that was barely a five-minute walk from our apartment. We walked past that building every day. There was a plaque on it and on weekends, when it was open, there were long lines of people seeking entrance.

The CCP operates with a self-reinforcing dynamic. Initially, it was composed of the Revolutionary families who were part of Mao's Long March and then made up his government. Now, though, the machinery of the CCP identifies and recruits the best and the brightest, regardless of their parentage, although offspring of CCP members get advantages simply based on their pedigree. CCP members or their children receive spots at the best schools, the best internships, the best study abroad opportunities and, eventually, jobs with the best companies where their progression is nurtured. I'm not sure when the Organization Department gets involved in their careers, but at some point, that occurs, and they continue to move through the ranks.

As I've mentioned, there is no clear distinction between the government, the CCP, and business in China. Extensive research by journalist David Barboza shows conclusively that many, if not most, so-called private companies in China are owned at least in part by the state or government entities or officials. Furthermore, even those that are not, are controlled—to a much greater extent than their American counterparts—by the state, through Party Committees, regulations, and arbitrary government intervention. In an interesting contrast, many of the Chinese government officials I met believed that the Chinese economy would perform even better with less government involvement.

Not only is the CCP in charge, but that control is obvious in every gathering. For instance, in 2013, when I attended the first meeting of the International Advisory Board of the Fudan Graduate School of Management, the Party Secretary sat on a higher tier to indicate his superior position. Dean Lu, our JV's supervisor, was the dean of the school and although he presided over the meeting, he deferred to the Party Secretary. Lu was apparently the subject matter expert, while the Party Secretary was the "top dog."

This control gets into minute details. Not long after the Fudan meeting, the Yangpu District insisted that we fire our internationally recognized accounting firm, KPMG, and replace it with a Chinese accounting operation. I inferred that this was a matter of national pride. To my knowledge no one in Yangpu had ever questioned KPMG's competence. Furthermore, virtually everyone who worked at KPMG's Shanghai office was Chinese. But KPMG was not Chinese. And it never would be.

The Chinese banking system and economy have unique characteristics as well. Approaching them as if they're the same as the Western systems—even though China's accession to the WTO should imply some degree of similarity—sets one up for failure. My long battle with "letting the customer decide" is an example. Because banking and the economy were fundamental parts of our business, I studied them in depth, and share my findings next.

14.2   THE CHINESE BANKING SYSTEM AND ECONOMY

Back in 2010 when we decided to accept Yu Zhengsheng's invitation to build a bank in China, we at SVB (myself included) were unfathomably naive. We envisioned taking our business model and superimposing it on the Chinese innovation sector. We envisioned helping China learn how to finance technology, with the active assistance of the Chinese government in achieving our own success. We thought of SPDB and ourselves as partners as we worked toward this shared goal—"one bed, one dream." It never occurred to us that such arrangements don't exist in China. We never imagined that our partner might have another, very different dream, and hog the blankets.

Now, with the advantage of hindsight, I can see the problem was much bigger than I'd ever thought. Not only did the CCP have a different dream, but the landscape onto which we were attempting to superimpose our business model was not at all what we'd expected. The Chinese banking system, in particular, and the Chinese economy in general are so incredibly different from what we'd experienced in other countries that we never could have foreseen the extent to which this landscape would not and could not mesh with our business model.

Let me attempt to describe the differences:

When I began my banking career in 1982, there were more than 20,000 banks in the United States. Today, there are at most 5,000 and the number is steadily declining. Since 1980, the industry has lost at least 15,000 banks, many to acquisition and others to failure. Within that same time frame, China went from having fundamentally *one* bank (the People's Bank of China) to about 5,000. Almost all those banks are new bank formations. They are *all* owned by the Chinese government, and as such, by the CCP, whereas none of the banks in the United States are owned by the government. And in that 40-year period, virtually no bank in China has failed, and virtually no bank has been acquired.

How did all of this happen? Well, in 1949, when Mao "liberated" China, he set about dismantling the quasi-capitalist system that had existed under the Nationalists. Among the first to go were the banks. All of these were dismantled, leaving only the People's Bank of China (PBoC). Until the end of the Mao regime, this bank served first and foremost as a repository of money for the CCP. The Party would call the bank and tell it to send money to XYZ state-owned enterprise (SOE) and the PBoC did so. Individuals didn't use or need money.

After Mao died, the Party began to reestablish a number of institutions that had disappeared in the wake of the "Liberation." Among them were the banks. Even today, though, one can make a reasonable argument that there's only one bank in China. That's because 75% of the banking activity of the 10 largest banks is performed by the top five institutions,[2] and those five freely share strategic plans and executives with each other, as if they were one team.

Even as recently as the early part of this millennium, all the banks in China operated in the same way that the PBoC had under Mao. Conceptually, the Party called a bank and told it to send money to XYZ SOE, and the bank did so. There was no such thing as underwriting—that is, the assessment of a borrower's underlying risk. There was often no specific repayment schedule. And, in general, there was no conceptual difference between debt (which must be repaid) and equity (where the provider of money receives an ownership share in the company). There was only the concept of "money."

Not all of these "loans" were repaid. No matter—when a bank ran out of money, the Chinese government simply and quietly recapitalized it. No banks failed. But nobody would have known anyway, because almost all information about the banking sector was considered a "state secret." It still is today.

In the first part of this century, the Party decided it wanted to join the World Trade Organization (WTO). One of its goals in doing so was to attract Western capital to—among other things—aid in recapitalizing the banks. To make this possible, the Chinese banks had to look a little bit more like their Western counterparts. Therefore, the CCP created a banking regulator, the Chinese Banking Regulatory Commission (CBRC), and appointed the brilliant economist, UK-educated Liu Mingkang, to lead it. He introduced the concept of underwriting, as well as the distinction between debt and equity and other details, all of which made Western investors more comfortable. And yet, to the extent that those Western investors paid attention, they had little reason for comfort. Chinese banks *still* swap management teams at the whim of the Organization Department; they share strategies whenever they wish; and their activities and accounts are anything but transparent. Finally, major decisions are often made by the Party Committee rather than the board, and the makeup of the Party Committee is, well, a "state secret."

The way that Chinese banks operate is fundamentally different from the Western approach. Some of the major differences include the following:

1. **Operations.** There is still far less emphasis on underwriting than a Western bank analyst would imagine. There's almost no correlation between risk and pricing in Chinese banks. *Guanxi* plays a greater role than risk in pricing. The Chinese view banks like Americans view utilities. Everybody pays the same price for the same dreadful service.
2. **Staffing.** In China, the Organization Department decides a bank's CEO, putting more emphasis on Party loyalty than on banking experience.
3. **Lending targets.** Most of the lending is directed at SOEs— including government entities—and very little at small and medium-sized enterprises (SMEs).
4. **Securities.** It's not evident that the distinction between debt and equity is important to Chinese banks.
5. **Growth.** Chinese banks are expected to grow much faster than Western banks. If a Western bank grows much faster than 10% in a year, banking analysts fear potential danger. Yet, Chinese banks commonly report growth at 25% or higher.
6. **Recapitalizations.** Chinese banks never fail. Instead, they're quietly re-capitalized by the government.

7. **Compensation.** In the United States, banking regulators prefer that individual bankers receive 80% of their pay as a base salary, and only 20% as a reflection of new business development. In China, those proportions are often reversed.

8. **Regulations.** Chinese regulators have many more regulations in place for their banks than do American regulators. Accordingly, Chinese banks labor under more controls and impose more rules on their borrowers than do U.S. banks—but both the regulations on the banks and the rules banks impose on borrowers are applied somewhat arbitrarily. In the case of the United States, there are fewer rules on both banks and borrowers, but those tend to be inarguable.

9. **Approvals.** In general, all commercial banking activities in China are forbidden unless expressly allowed. Theoretically, China agreed decades ago to switch to the Western standard of "negative lists"— that is, everything not expressly forbidden is allowed. Although the *concept* is understood, it doesn't suit the CCP's purpose, which is to keep ultimate control while retaining plausible deniability. Therefore, the positive lists remain.

10. **Loan qualification.** *Guanxi* determines loans, terms, and restrictions to a much greater extent than regulation, whether we're talking about rules imposed on banks by regulators or on borrowers by banks.

11. **Licenses.** In China, every activity in which a bank can become involved requires a separate license. For example, setting up a website to show your customers their account balances requires a separate and discrete license. In fact, almost any discrete activity requires a separate license. And yet, if bank A has a license that bank B covets, it's not uncommon for bank A to "rent" its license to bank B. They can both use it, but A gets a new income stream of rental payments from B.

12. **Goals.** The main goal of a Chinese bank is to support state industrial policy (still). The main goal of a Western bank is to achieve

a high return on equity (ROE) and a high stock price—and to avoid getting into trouble with regulators.

13. **Foreign ownership.** Foreign banks in China are in a different category altogether. The regulations are more strictly applied to them than to their Chinese competitors. Also, the public perception is different. Everyone in China knows which banks are foreign and which are Chinese. That is not true in the United States. Almost no Americans know that the Bank of the West (in California) is French, or that Citizen's Bank (in Massachusetts) is Scottish.

14. **Customer service.** Customer-service standards are different in China. I was a VIP client at SPDB, yet whenever I went to the bank to do personal banking, the interaction, as described in Chapter 10, left me feeling more guilty than appreciated.

15. **Efficiency.** Chinese banks are remarkably inefficient, especially with regard to consumer banking. That's one of the reasons that the Chinese government has begun to put the brakes on so-called private entities, like Ant Group (formerly known as Ant Financial).[3] That company has so much better customer service than the retail banks that the government is afraid that China's 1.4 billion people will abandon the banks for Ant. This would remove their deposits from the pool of low-cost capital available for government projects.

14.2.1   Chinese Economics

Banking plays a major role in an economy. For as long as I've been studying China, which is about 25 years, economists on both sides of the Pacific have dramatically disagreed about how its economy works and what it will lead to. Usually when economists disagree, it's about whether economic conditions will improve or deteriorate. But in the case of China, it often seems to be about whether its economy will skyrocket or implode. Should other countries adopt the China model or a Western model? And these days, at the beginning of 2022, as Xi is now praising the Chinese system as a model for other countries to emulate, the debate is even more engrossing.

Toward the end of my stay in China, I encountered an extremely intelligent and well-educated daughter of a Revolutionary family, who was willing to answer my questions. (I met a number of intelligent, well-educated daughters of Revolutionary families.) Over tea in the lobby of the St. Regis in Beijing, I asked: "What is the secret to understanding the way the Chinese economy works? Western economists regularly predict a collapse, but the collapse never comes. Why? How does it really work?"

"The answer to that question," she said, "is a 'state secret.' I can't tell you." But, she assured me, "it is hiding in plain sight."

For months I pondered her mysterious response. Western friends told me her claim was "pretentious BS." Chinese friends said she was being painfully obvious.

Choosing the latter explanation, I began exploring "the obvious." There are plenty of theories, mostly in articles written by economists.

Here are some (more-or-less) facts:

There are no reliable statistics about the Chinese economy. Perhaps, on the other hand, there are, but there are so many of them and they're so different from each other that there's no way for a banker like me (as opposed to an economist) to reliably tell which are correct. Therefore, I looked at the context.

For thousands of years, China has been home to millions of very poor people and a relatively small number of wealthy people. Of course, this is true of many other countries as well. We can reasonably infer that this small group of wealthy people has had thousands of years of experience with, and practice in, extracting wealth from everybody else for their own benefit.

That said, China has, relative to other countries, perfected the art of wealth extraction. In 1949, after the Liberation, Mao spent years killing off all the landlords. Some historians believe that he did away with about 4 million of them, but—and here's the kicker—*he didn't redistribute the land*. Instead, it is all owned by the government, and the government is controlled by the CCP. *Ergo*, the CCP owns all the land that was formerly owned by the landlords, whom Mao killed. They lease it out to Chinese citizens for 70 or 90 years at a time.

The CCP comprises about 7% of the population. In a sense, Mao succeeded in taking all the land from the landlords and giving it to the CCP. That's a learned skill. And many of the other 93% (who are not in the Party) lease buildings from the government and then re-lease them to other members of the 93% who are *less well off* than they are—functioning, in essence, as landlords themselves.

The Chinese government (and the CCP) is highly secretive. It's very difficult to find out who owns what, or even how much specific people, or even classes of people, either own or earn. There must be a reason for this secrecy.

China has the largest number of government employees as a percentage of the population of any major country in the world today. In a sense, China has the most expensive government in the world. It pays for itself by owning a higher percentage of the country's total assets than any other major country.

We in California often resent the fact that so much of our income goes to the government in the form of taxes—most of them transparent but some relatively hidden. But the Chinese government makes California's look like novices. For example, almost a quarter of this book described our frustrations with the inability to use RMB for three years. We could only use "onshore" dollars, which no company or individual needed or wanted, even to pay foreign vendors. And, in the context of the economy, this warrants more discussion.

The distinction of onshore versus offshore dollars is one we don't have in the United States. In China, though, it very much exists. If a Chinese company has a shell in the Cayman Islands, for instance, the dollars it uses there are called "offshore dollars." If the parent company wants to bring those dollars into China, they must go through the State Administration for Foreign Exchange (SAFE). Once the dollars go through SAFE, they become "onshore dollars." But generally speaking, Chinese companies don't have onshore dollars because SAFE (and the CCP) wants to control the currency.[4]

If a Chinese company wants to buy something from a foreign supplier, it can't directly pay for it from foreign exchange it owns—because companies can't own foreign currency. The government does. For a company to pay a foreign vendor (for simplicity, let's say it's in the United States), it usually has to go through an agent or a trading company (typically government-owned) that provides the dollars to them. They might go to a bank, which, being government-owned, is also the government. The importer gives the trading company RMB. The trading company converts the RMB to dollars to pay the foreign vendor by using dollars from SAFE, held in the Treasury. All those dollars in the Treasury come from exports—because export transactions work exactly like import transactions, only in reverse. The exporter doesn't hold the dollars it receives in its own accounts. Instead, the company that has the dollars gives them to the trading companies (or banks or agents), which present them to SAFE. Then the Chinese exporters receive RMB (see Figure 14.1). This is only one of the many ways the Chinese government gets rich. And this, by the way, lies hidden in plain sight.

One of my questions about the Chinese economy had been whether, indeed, that approach should be adopted around the world. Was it better? Clearly, as described above, it's better for the CCP. But is it better for the people?

One way to compare economic systems is by how much benefit accrues to the government relative to the people. China's system is very low on one

Figure 14.1   Exchange of foreign currency for RMB and vice versa.

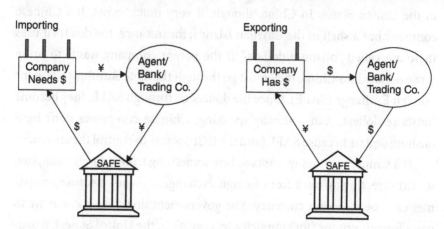

end of the spectrum—it provides a relatively few benefits to its people—and very high on the other end, providing a very high level of benefit to the government. This means meager "social benefits"—fewer intensive care beds per capita (4.52/100,000 people[5] vs. 29.4/100,000 in the United States[6]), nothing resembling Medicare, and almost nothing resembling Social Security; additionally, there is a relatively low standard of living for the vast majority of the population and a relatively high standard of living for the roughly 98 million members of the CCP.

One other important thing: the Chinese government has far more controls in place and leaves far less to chance than most Western governments. Along with its control of capital flows in and out of China through the SAFE, it goes much further than the Federal Reserve (for example) in controlling interest rates on both deposits and loans, as well as the amount of money banks are allowed to borrow or lend. The Chinese government has so many levers to pull, and at least at its highest levels, so much collective experience and unchecked unilateral control, that it can, and for the most part does, control many more economic variables than its counterparts in most Western countries.

In fact, the Chinese government can control pretty much anything it wishes to, including, according to recent news, the weather.[7] Many Westerners go to China thinking that the economy consists of two parts: state-owned companies and private companies. Accordingly, they believe that the government controls the state-owned companies, and the private sector can make decisions for itself as long as it follows regulations. That's what Americans are used to. And it's a misunderstanding. The government can control any company it wishes to control, regardless of regulation or law.

Jack Ma, the cofounder of Alibaba, learned this lesson in 2020 when he attempted to take Ant Group public. The Chinese government stepped in and stopped the process. I wouldn't say that doing so was a violation of any specific regulation, law, or right. It was, simply, what the government wanted to do.

For my part, I wouldn't predict an implosion of the Chinese economy. The Party contains a lot of smart people, and it can do pretty much whatever it thinks is right—with no objection from an opposing party and no viable objection from its own people.

14.3 OPINIONS OF OTHERS ABOUT THE CCP

The general opinion of the Chinese I encountered was that the CCP was extremely corrupt. One of the most senior employees of our bank, a member of the Party as well, told me flat out that the Party is corrupt, through and through, and nobody respected or liked it. As if to confirm the assertion, Mr. Ma, the deputy head of the Shanghai CBRC, told me in 2013 that significant reform was on its way right after the next plenary session (meeting of the Central Committee of the Communist Party). He was referring to President Xi's anticorruption campaign.

SPDB's Mr. Liao told me that only the senior people of the CCP are trustworthy. Those in the "middle" are corrupt and always stick to policy to collect graft and avoid exposure.

In contrast, Mr. and Mrs. Luo argued in front of Ruth and me about the CCP, displaying different perspectives. As a banker, Mr. Luo was a lifelong Party member, but Mrs. Luo had never joined. She felt that the Party was disingenuous, and they were forcing her husband to retire against his will because his *guanxi* wasn't good.

Young people provided additional insights. My mentee Ruby was a member of the CCP, and she fervently believed in its wisdom and benevolence. To my astonishment, she'd never heard of Pol Pot, his "murder" of about 25% of the Cambodian population in the 1970s, nor the extent to which the CCP had supported him. Our employee, Changchang, told me the Party mistrusts all foreign companies, believing that they're all "wolves" who want to "eat" China. The Party's job, she said, is to get as much knowledge out of the foreign companies as possible, then drive them back out of China.

But the approval of the CCP among the youth was not universal. Mr. Luo's daughter, Ke, told me that her contemporaries were growing impatient with the *guanxi* system as practiced by her father's generation. She and her colleagues in the state-owned "private equity" firm would have preferred to select their investment targets based on their merit as opposed to their founders' *guanxi*.

Intriguingly, in my last meeting with Professor Zhao of the Party School, he said something similar, based on what he'd learned about the VC investment process as he wrote articles on the bank for the *Neibu Cankao*. China, he thought, could do a much better job of funding innovation if the government were less involved in selecting the companies that were funded.

We saw the CCP's corruption in practice with an illusory Free Trade Zone (FTZ). This was a few acres of Shanghai where companies could get 70-year leases and operate as if they were off-shore (to a certain extent). Starting in 2012, any number of government officials tried to cajole me into leasing real estate in that area. In fact, the FTZ's acting head claimed that the rules for the area had been written specifically to benefit our bank. To this day, I've never understood what was supposed to be done in the FTZ, how it would have benefited us, or why it failed. In short, my BS alarm went off early on. That's something you develop as a banker, and it has stood me in good stead many times.

Every month the cost of space in the FTZ went up. Finally, in 2013, Dr. Fang (on our board and the secret team) advised me it would never happen. By the time we left to return to San Francisco, it was widely rumored to be a scheme perpetrated by the family of Jiang Zemin, former General Secretary of the CCP. It was rumored that his family "owned" the land in question—that is, the government had given it to Jiang for an indefinite amount of time for his own use—and they were hoping for a killing.

This is an odd tendency of senior members of the CCP. They will simply appropriate to themselves land or other state holdings and act as if they can sell, rent, or otherwise profit from it.

Oddly enough, attitudes of Westerners toward the CCP ran the spectrum. Many, like me, had come to believe as I did: that it wanted to entice your company to come to China where the CCP could extract its information and cast the carcass aside once it was of no further use. Others, though, were almost embarrassingly subservient, as I learned when the head of McKinsey (the consulting firm) sat next to me at one of Vincent Lo's dinners at his "clubhouse." He was French and purported to love the one-party system. The level to which people would stoop to ingratiate themselves with the Party was nothing short of heartbreaking. The Party knew this and did everything it could to perpetuate it.

14.4 ATTITUDES OF THE CCP

In August 2013, I invited a Mr. Yang, the head of the Propaganda Museum, to join me and a few of my colleagues for dinner at the Key Club. The

Propaganda Museum in Shanghai is a collection of CCP-commissioned art from the period between the "Liberation" in 1949 through the end of the Mao era, roughly 1978. It consists of posters in the style of socialist realism. The primary themes are the glories of life in the New China under Mao, and the evils of the American Imperialists.

Of less interest to most visitors, but fascinating to me, was a large collection of "big letter" (character) posters. During the Cultural Revolution, those whom the Red Guards had decided to target as enemies of the people—in most cases because of the social class of their ancestors—were publicly denounced, often through these posters. Not uncommonly, someone would wake up in the morning to find big posters all over their neighborhood defaming them as enemies of the people. At that point, they knew they were in trouble, often because someone had disclosed that their grandparents were intellectuals, landlords, or businesspeople. The only group that was really safe were those who traced their lineage back to uneducated peasants and could prove it.

The Cultural Revolution's whole campaign of naming and shaming neighbors by each other reinforced a culture of secrecy that appears even now in the Chinese business world. You'll note that my advisory team was called the secret team (my term, not theirs)—I never once met all of them together in a formal setting. I simply surmised, based on what they knew about me and our progress, that they acted as a united advisory group. I met with Dean Lu secretly at the tea house; the letter trying to renegotiate our agreement was "secret." This secrecy has created huge problems for people seeking to do research even on topics that would seem to be unexceptional. In 2007, an English-speaking, U.S.-resident, Chinese-native geologist was thrown in jail on the grounds that he had shared "state secrets" two years before, when he uploaded information about 30,000 Chinese oil wells to a database widely used by global firms, including Chinese oil companies.[8] It also makes due diligence extremely difficult for foreign banks and investment firms.

But to give it credit, the CCP gets things done. In early September 2013, I met with Zhu Ge, the governor of the Yangpu District. He'd been instrumental in the construction of the Yangshan deep water port in Hangzhou Bay in 2005. Having worked on a freighter for a few months when I was 20, I displayed genuine interest and he arranged a tour for Ruth and me. A few weeks later, we spent a day at the port, which was at the end of the Donghai Bridge. Built explicitly to serve the deep-water port, this bridge extends 20 miles from land into the ocean and accommodates ships that draw as much as 50 feet of water. It can accommodate any freighter in the world and processes more freight than any port anywhere in the United States. It took 6,000 workers just under three years to complete. It was *very* impressive. And it was built *very* fast.

Attitudes within the CCP constantly surprised me. Many CCP members had told me they felt the government—that is, the Party—was being unfair in its prohibition on our use of RMB. Yet somehow the policy remained in place.

But this was not the only situation where individual opinion conflicted with CCP actions. Also of interest was a situation that Professor Zhao of the Central Party School described to me. His daughter worked with SVB in Palo Alto, and while her professional life was fulfilling, she had been lonely until she found a Chinese boyfriend in the area. Upon learning of the relationship, however, Professor Zhao's wife, also a CCP member and a professor at the Central Party School, insisted the girl break up because of the young man's inferior social standing! I had thought Communism was all about creating a classless society. But that may not be the case when it's your potential son-in-law.

14.5 CHANGES WITH XI

It's worth a moment to explore Xi Jinping's background. Xi was cut from a different cloth than his immediate predecessors. First of all, he *is* from a Revolutionary family (his father, Xi Zhongxun, joined Mao at the end of the Long March). The elder Xi was purged from the Party in the early 1960s for being too moderate. At the start of the Cultural Revolution in 1966, he was persecuted, and his daughter (Xi Jinping's sister) either committed suicide or was killed by the Red Guards as they ransacked the family abode (the record is unclear). In 1968, the elder Xi was jailed, and his wife (Xi Jinping's mother) was forced to denounce him in public. In 1969, Xi Jinping himself was sent "down to the countryside" to learn from the peasants and engage in hard labor. According to the theory of cognitive dissonance, someone with this history would be likely to either completely reject the CCP or to embrace it fully. Xi Jinping chose the latter path—the Stockholm syndrome[9] at work.

In November 2012, Xi was named General Secretary of the CCP, and in October 2022, he was named to an unprecedented third term as the Party's leader. As described earlier, he has introduced much harder-line policies across the board. In a small example from May 2013, an art historian friend in Shanghai, a U.S. citizen who had lived and worked in Shanghai for several years, was unceremoniously kicked out of the China Art Museum by armed guards for taking notes on the artwork on display. What earthly threat could she have posed?

The CCP held its Third Plenary in November 2013, a year after Xi was named General Secretary. (China has a system of Five-Year Plans. Each year, the CCP Congress holds a plenum or plenary meeting, where it discusses and announces policies for the coming year. At the first plenum of a given CCP Congress session [in 2012, it was the 18th], the Central Committee names the slate of leaders. The second plenum of the 18th CCP Congress was held in February 2013, and the third in November of the same year.[10]) In the third plenary of the 18th Central Committee, the CCP vowed to create a "level playing field" on which foreign companies could compete on terms equal to those governing the indigenous companies.

It is now almost a decade later and so far, nothing has changed for the better. Since Xi came to power, things have only gotten worse, from a Western point of view. Some Western companies will tell you the opposite. In my assessment, they believe what they're saying. The Party is treating them well because they possess knowledge that the Party has not yet accrued. When the CCP has learned everything it wants to know, these companies, too, will feel as I do. Pay attention to the words of the scorpion. In the end, he will sting you.

As Xi continued to make his mark, the threats of war amplified. In mid-2014, we held a dinner in Shanghai for an American winery, the Staglin Family Vineyard, to which we invited 40 or so Chinese natives, mostly entrepreneurs. An entrepreneur in his late thirties sitting near me insisted, quite loudly, that China and the United States would be at war soon. The United States, he claimed, was a bully and didn't want China to rise. China had recently declared ownership of the airspace over the disputed islands in the South China Sea.

Yet the United States was not the only country to have tensions with China. Shortly after that dinner, the Vietnamese protested their own government's failure to force China to remove the giant oil rig that Sinopec, China's state oil and gas company, had dragged down the coastline into waters claimed by Vietnam for centuries. One deeply held belief among the Chinese is that China has never attacked another country. Yet Vietnam was annexed by China about 2,000 years ago and held for more than 1,000 years. The Vietnamese people, almost to a person, hate the Chinese government.[11]

In addition, Xi has been demonizing Japan in an effort to whip up nationalism, and this has international implications. Mr. Luo correctly predicted that China would support Putin in his invasion of the Crimean Peninsula in early 2014. The CCP had to support Putin, Luo said, to punish the United States for siding with Japan on so many other issues.

In fact, one can argue that Japan is responsible for the fact that China is ruled by the CCP. By 1933, when Japan attacked China, the Kuomintang had almost vanquished the CCP. The Kuomintang used all its resources to repel the Japanese, allowing the CCP years to regroup and gain strength.

NOTES

1. Mao Zedong, 1973; repeated in a statement from the 19th Party Congress, published in *Xinhua,* October 24, 2017, cited in Charlotte Gao, "The CCP Vows to 'Lead Everything' Once Again," *The Diplomat,* October 28, 2017, https://thediplomat.com/2017/10/the-ccp-vows-to-lead-everything-once-again.
2. Data from the China Banking Association in Meemi O., "Comparing China's Largest Banks," *Investor Insights Asia,* December 7, 2023, https://www.investor insights.asia/post/comparing-china-s-largest-banks.
3. Another reason was increased criticism of the CCP by Jack Ma, Ant's founder. See Li Yuan, "Why China Turned Against Jack Ma," *New York Times,* January 20, 2021, https://www.nytimes.com/2020/12/24/technology/china-jack-ma-ali baba.html.) News reports have speculated on the likelihood that Ant would be nationalized. See Lingling Wei, "Jack Ma Makes Ant Offer to Placate Chinese Regulators," *Wall Street Journal,* December 20, 2020, https://www.wsj.com/articles/jack-ma-makes-ant-offer-to-placate-chinese-regulators-11608479629.
4. One might think that such control of foreign exchange would eliminate a currency black market in China. But that would be incorrect. Not only does a black market in foreign exchange very much exist in China, but the CCP is involved. See John F. Tobon, "Chinese Communist Party Members Move Money in Plain Sight, Threatening Security," *Defense Forum,* March 24, 2022, https://ipdefense forum.com/2022/03/black-market-foreign-exchange.
5. Jason Phua et al., "Critical Care Bed Capacity in Asian Countries and Regions," *Critical Care Medicine* 48, no. 5 (2020): 654–62.
6. Neil A. Halpern and Kay See Tan, "United States Resource Availability for COVID-19," Society of Critical Care Medicine blog, March 13, 2020, https://www.sccm.org/Blog/March-2020/United-States-Resource-Availability-for-COVID-19. Number of ICU beds: 96,596 (divided by population of 328.2 million).
7. For details, see Eyck Freymann, "Climate Changers," *The Wire China,* December 18, 2022, https://www.thewirechina.com/2022/12/18/u-s-china-geoengineering.
8. James T. Areddy, "China's Culture of Secrecy Brands Research as Spying," *Wall Street Journal,* December 1, 2010, https://www.wsj.com/articles/SB10001424052748704584804575644470575141314.

9. Stockholm syndrome refers to a coping mechanism for people in a captive or abusive situation, in which they develop positive feelings toward their captors/abusers over time. (Cleveland Clinic Health Library, "Stockholm Syndrome," February 14, 2022, https://my.clevelandclinic.org/health/diseases/22387-stock holm-syndrome.)

10. Ryan Ong, "The Third Plenum of the 18th Chinese Communist Party Congress: A Primer," *China Business Review*, September 16, 2013, https://www.chinabusi nessreview.com/the-third-plenum-of-the-18th-chinese-communist-party-congress-a-primer.

11. China's six-week invasion of North Vietnam in 1979 did nothing to change this attitude.

CHAPTER FIFTEEN

PRACTICAL GUIDELINES FOR WORKING WITH THE CCP

U nlike in America, in China there is no substantive difference between the government, the Party, and business. Likewise, there is no fundamental difference between SOEs and private business. We want to superimpose our Western mental models on China and they simply don't fit. I learned, eventually, that if a business or industry is not under the purview of the CCP, it's because the CCP doesn't think it's important. If it were important, the CCP would be managing it. In my experience, the absolute overarching power of the CCP is difficult to grasp for people who grew up in the United States, not only because this is foreign to us but because we don't want it to be this way. And the CCP encourages us to believe in our version of reality.

For example, when I would meet with Mr. Luo or Mr. Liu, I initially believed I was meeting with bankers who were my partners in the joint venture—that is, who shared my goal in making it succeed. And, in fact, I was. But were they thinking of themselves as bankers during those conversations? They were. Or were they thinking of themselves as members of the CCP, who had other goals for the joint venture? Which they were. Or were they thinking of themselves as relatively important figures in the Shanghai government? Which they were as well. I can't read minds, but my best guess would be that they did not make these distinctions. For them, all three are the same thing.

I'm guessing that this is parallel to the famous example from Linguistics 101 textbooks of yesteryear involving the Inuit people of the Arctic. They were said to differentiate between different types of snow, both linguistically and practically, because those distinctions are meaningful to them, whereas they aren't to White people in the Lower 48. For most of us, snow is snow, either just regular snow or perhaps powder (if we are skiers) or slush (if we're worried about ruining our shoes).

The CCP listens carefully to the things we Westerners say, and then they curate what they say to make it sound like what we clearly want to hear. For example, knowing that we like to think of the private sector as being clearly separate and distinct from the state-owned sector, they make a point of describing things in a way that will appease us.

That said, if an entity is in China, the CCP can control it. A "private" company in China that the CCP wants to control has no defense. That company cannot sue the CCP or the government (they are the same). It cannot appeal to the law. The CCP has an uncountable number of laws at its disposal. Some of them contradict each other. If the CCP deigned to refer to the law, it would simply select the one that provided the most leverage and apply it. If an appropriate law doesn't exist, the CCP just makes it up.

Also, any business owner who believes that they can take comfort in their ownership position is sadly mistaken. Whether the "owner" has 20% or 50% or even 90% is totally irrelevant. It's China. The CCP is in control.

As I was writing this section, I spoke with a longtime SVB employee who is native Chinese but not a member of the CCP. He pointed out that from the Chinese perspective, the process of establishing Western companies in China has two parts. One of them is the implicit deal that a company agrees to at the start: it receives market access in exchange for providing China with access to its intellectual property and/or business models. This deal is widely viewed by Chinese in general as completely fair and reasonable. That the Western companies in question did not share this perspective was not a concern—after all, no one has held a gun to their heads.

But the deal has a second part, and that, even by native Chinese, is viewed as dirty pool. Once a company has engaged with China, the CCP uses various tactics to prevent it from making progress, thus ensuring the Party's continued leverage. We saw this with the joint venture in the various impediments we confronted, including the impossible deadlines, the refusal to give us all the licenses we needed, and the prohibition on using RMB for three years, among others. According to my colleague, the CCP was well aware of the degree to which this strategy contravened business mores and the WTO rules China had ostensibly agreed to abide by. As we heard from both members and nonmembers of the CCP during our long effort to use RMB, this behavior was viewed as unfair.

What does this dichotomy mean for Western companies? Probably very little, but it's something to be aware of if you're considering entering China.

What I learned far too late was that the single most influential tome in China's intellectual history is *The Art of War*, written in roughly 500 BCE by Sun Tzu. This amazingly short book epitomizes the idea that "all is fair in love and war." It recommends deceit as the most effective method for success. As a result, there is absolutely no correlation between what the Party says and what the Party means.

This applies not just to war but to everything, including negotiation. In negotiation, the CCP will employ two tactics: deceit and leverage. Members of the Party will never say what they mean and *never* mean what they say. You must do what you can to make yourself impervious to whatever leverage they seek to apply, and you must find leverage of your own that you can apply. Without extreme skepticism and without leverage, you will be lost.

I personally encountered a clear example of this "art of war" approach to negotiation. At a conference in late 2013, I met an affable Chinese businessman who eagerly shared his life story. He'd graduated from high school immediately after Deng Xiaoping began ushering in the era of "Reform and Opening." With permission to go to the United States for college, he studied computer science at the University of Maryland.

After graduation, he found a job at a tech company and earned enough money to bring his girlfriend over to marry her. Now, years later, he had his own company producing cybersecurity tools. He'd just been in Washington, DC, peddling them to the Pentagon. After the conference, he was going to Beijing to try to sell them to the PLA (People's Liberation Army).

If both sides were interested, I asked him, to whom would he sell? He grinned from ear to ear and laughed. "The highest bidder, of course. Or maybe both."

15.1 CONTRACTS AND THE CCP

The CCP's approach to contracts is not at all similar to how Western businesses view them. To a CCP businessperson, a contract is a momentary codification of the parties' perception of the relative leverage of their respective positions. As relative leverage changes, in the eyes of the CCP, the contract is no longer valid. It can be rewritten in a way that reflects these changes.

The CCP only adheres to a contract because it believes the counterparty has leverage, never because a contract is seen as binding. Leverage almost always derives from the counterparty's possession of something that the CCP wants. Also, to qualify as leverage, the Party must believe that the counterparty recognizes its leverage and is willing to deny China access to whatever it is that China wants if it doesn't get what it wants in return. To a counterparty, this means you need to insist that you get what you want *first*, before you give China what it wants. It will also serve you well if you don't give China what it wants all at once, but rather in small increments, demanding concessions in exchange for every increment, before moving on to the next concession. If you give first, you've lost your leverage, just by the act of giving. Giving first to prove your good intent is foolish and useless.

The CCP's desire to renegotiate contracts repeatedly will make your impatience grow by leaps and bounds, which may motivate you to give more, more quickly, hoping to get more, more quickly. Don't give in to your impatience. You will only lose your leverage, and ultimately your whole reason for having gone to China in the first place.

In SVB's case, we should have held off on educating SPDB about our model until we had the bank set up and ready to operate in RMB. Whether that would have been feasible, I'm not sure.

15.2   CCP NEGOTIATION

The Chinese negotiate in a way to make most people infer that they view negotiation as a zero-sum engagement. I believe this mental model derives from *The Art of War*, as I described earlier. To elucidate that approach, consider reading Lucian Pye's famous book *Chinese Commercial Negotiating*

Style.[1] I read it in 2010, before my four-year sojourn in China, and was astounded. Pye must have been extremely jaded, I thought. Within a year, I'd become familiar with every one of the techniques he described.

The core tenet is this: it is not only okay, but necessary and appropriate, to deceive your "opponent" in the course of a negotiation. By now, we all know what win-win means in China.

The CCP negotiates in the manner of a child who has all the time in the world whereas you, as a parent, are typically in a rush. You have to go to work, you have deadlines, and you have responsibilities. When my sons were children, I often took shortcuts in our negotiations because I was under time pressure. They, on the other hand, had all the time in world, a distinct advantage in a negotiation. They, like the CCP, can hold out for everything they want, they can be insistent, they can be stubborn. They can simply wait you out.

The pace of events in SVB's case was excruciatingly slow. I would try to get on the calendar of a government official from whom I needed some sort of permission. Government officials can ignore you for as long as they wish, because they have no competition. You can't approach an alternate official, because there is no alternative. Often, I would wait for months (prodding seemed to do no good; in fact, it often seemed to impede my progress). And then, suddenly, a call came out of nowhere. I needed to clear my schedule. The official could see me tomorrow at 9:30 a.m. That was the time, and there was no other. I had to be there.

But when I showed up at 9:30 the next morning, the "news" would not be definitive. The official might dangle a vague promise in front of me, just enough to give me hope. But nothing was certain. Decisions had to be made by vaguely identified decision-makers, and at vaguely described points in time. There was always a carrot to chase, but no matter how fast I chased it, it always moved faster than I did. It was always somewhere out there in front of me, but never within reach. Dealing with government officials in China is very much like one of those bad dreams where it is imperative that you move from point A to point B, but you are wading through porridge, and progress, regardless of how imperative, is impossible.

Over time, you learn the wisdom of differentiating between the system and the individual. Yes, you will say, the system is stacked against you. It has been designed to inhibit your progress; on the one hand, keeping alive a small flicker of hope, while at the same time preventing you from accomplishing the necessary items to legitimately claim success. But the individuals who operate within the system, guiding your case, aren't really that bad. In fact, some of them seem really nice. You are, as they describe you, an "old friend." In fact, you are one of the smartest foreigners they have ever met. You really care about China, and you really understand China. For these reasons, you will receive preferential treatment. You alone will crack the code.

Don't be fooled.

First, these same individuals, however nice they may be, have very little latitude. They operate within a very narrow band. Their behavior is circumscribed by a playbook that you will never see but that you will, in the course of time, be able to infer. Interesting in this regard is Peter Martin's book *China's Civilian Army*.[2] According to this book, when Zhou Enlai created China's diplomatic service in 1949, he imposed a set of rules that are fundamentally unchanged today:

- No one is allowed to say anything that is not in the playbook.
- Diplomats may never meet with foreigners alone. They must always meet in pairs so that either of the two can report on the other if one deviates from the playbook.
- Diplomats may appear to establish friendships with foreigners, but it is forbidden to establish a real friendship. They must always maintain a veneer.
- And they must never let a foreigner penetrate their private space. You may hear, over and over again, that you are an "old friend," but

you may never actually become a friend, much less an old friend. If you think you are, you are kidding yourself.

More recently, this has all taken an interesting turn for the worse. Under Xi, the Chinese government has developed a new concept, termed "wolf warrior diplomacy." To protect themselves from their own natural human tendency to make themselves vulnerable to actual friendship, diplomats (and, in a sense, every government official is a diplomat) must assume a veneer of confrontation.

For example, after returning from Shanghai, I became the chair of the Asia Society in Northern California. Every year, I was invited by the Chinese consul general (CG) in San Francisco to bring a handful of my board members to the CG's house for dinner with him and an equal number (having an equal number was always of the utmost importance) of his colleagues. At the last of these dinners that I attended, in 2019, the CG began the dinner discussion with the following words: "We all know that tensions between our respective governments have increased in recent times, and we all know that the behavior of the U.S. government has been the sole cause of this increase in tension. So, with these things in mind, let's have a great discussion tonight." Although the members of my own contingent were perfectly comfortable disagreeing with anything I said at the dinner, no member of the CG's contingent would have even considered saying anything that did not reinforce his opening statement. As you might expect, conversation was somewhat stilted.

One of the guides to success in China for Westerners, published just before our move there in 2011, advised among other things, helping the relevant decision-makers achieve their KPIs. This, the author declared, would motivate them to help you achieve yours. I found this to be completely off the mark, as I spent vast amounts of time, energy, and personal capital helping Chinese officials achieve their KPIs by arranging meetings for them with key figures at prestigious universities or successful tech incubators, only to have them flake out at the last minute. They might cancel due to a change in plans or priorities, or they'd actually attend the meeting you spent weeks arranging without any reciprocation. In retrospect, I would never agree to help anyone unless it was the counterpart to a *quid pro quo*, and they fulfilled their half of the deal first.

The CCP's drive to control all aspects of business is part of a "whole of society" effort to control all aspects of China. For this reason, *when you are dealing with a Chinese company, as either a competitor or a collaborator, you are dealing with "China, Inc."* By law, all companies located in China and Chinese companies located anywhere in the world are required to help the Chinese government, which includes the military. (So, the U.S. government is not being unreasonable in its concerns about Huawei.) As a result, you are never collaborating with just one entity, you are—at least in theory—dealing with all Chinese entities, and you are never competing against one Chinese company, you are—in theory—competing with all Chinese companies, or at least everyone in your industry. I have come to believe that state capitalism, as practiced in China, is like a dominant gene. Western companies cannot win, because they are always "going it alone." They are not backed by our government, certainly not by our political parties, and definitely not by other companies in their industry. Chinese companies are.

From the point of view of the Party, rules are not absolutes. They exist to help the Party achieve its goals. If a rule required at any given moment is not available (because it doesn't exist), the Party assumes its existence and proceeds on the basis that, in fact, it *does* exist. It is okay to make end runs around rules if you have good *guanxi* with the Party and if you apologize should you get caught. Even without having broken rules, you may be indicted. Or you may break a rule and not be indicted. *Of greatest importance: have* guanxi *with the Party and always give the Party face.*

These lessons apply to the U.S. government's approach to negotiating with China as well. A personal friend who heads a bitcoin business in Asia recommends that the United States adopt the following approach:

- We must show respect, admiration, praise, and "give face" in public. Any criticism must be reserved for private meetings.
- Our negotiators must be realists and operators, not scolders, chest-pounders, romantics, or apologists.
- We need to draw clear lines but leave China enough space behind them.
- We must be fair—we cannot insist that we can protect our airspace, but they cannot protect theirs. But we cannot expect fairness in return.
- China responds best to leverage. The best leverage is understated strength and purity of heart. You don't learn that in business school.

15.2.1   Random Observations

I learned other useful points that don't fit neatly into categories. For instance, another area of difference between China and the West is the concept of sales. Dean Lu lectured me on the idea that sales in China are largely about *guanxi*. People buy from people with whom they have good *guanxi*. While I think he was right, I would word it a little differently. "Sales" as a profession means something quite different in China as compared with the West. Sales in the United States is often combined with the adjective *consultative*; that is, the salesperson is trying to help the customer solve a problem. In China, the practice of sales invariably involves *guanxi*, and sometimes kickbacks.

Contrary to the old Western idea that China merely copies Western innovation, the Party supports innovation and the Chinese are very good at innovating. In some regards, Chinese people are even better at innovating than Americans, because they have perfected the art of rapid iteration. Americans should not rest on their laurels. First, the Chinese have proven their ability to innovate. Second, if they fail at innovation, they may still succeed at stealing.

I also came to the following conclusions:

- Nepotism and conflict of interest are not a problem in China because they are foundational. You do business with people you know and with whom you have an ongoing network of favors. Therefore, it only stands to reason that you'll help them because they will help you. The benefit of this connection outweighs the drawback of hiring someone who may not have the best skill set, simply because they can ensure success not through performance but through influence.
- China controls—Chinese citizens, Western businesses trying to do business in China, and other countries—through propaganda and fear. Within China, the social credit system's rewards encourage compliance, while the penalties for transgressions are harsh indeed.
- China does not want to be like us. And we cannot change China. China thinks it is owed the world dominance it craves, after the Century of Humiliation and its supposed history of peaceful coexistence. (This is debatable as discussed in Section 4.)
- China's game plan: find great technology; entice it to come to China; support it to the extent that it hopes to succeed; block it to ensure that it cannot successfully compete; steal its intellectual property; and—in the end—send it home empty-handed.
- The goals of the CCP: 1) continue to be the ruling party in China, 2) economic success, and 3) world domination, to eliminate any external threats to its continuing existence. In essence, it wants to make the world safe for autocracy.

15.3 THE CCP AND CONTROL

But the CCP is also directly engaged in the lives of foreigners, like me. In May 2012, our friends the Xues invited Ruth and me to travel with them to Qufu, the birthplace of Confucius, in Shandong Province. It seemed like a gesture of friendship. Because neither couple could speak the other's language well enough to hold an intelligent conversation, Chrystal accompanied us.

What we received was a clear demonstration of the CCP's power. As a minor example, upon our arrival in Jinan, the capital of Shandong, the flight attendants ushered us off the plane first, before anybody else, and down a jetway that funneled us into a luxurious VIP room for CCP members and important guests only. A number of higher-level officials representing Shandong Province waited for us there.

For the next four days, we were never alone with the Xues. We were often without them altogether, but we were never alone. The officials who accompanied us were always polite and generous—even trying to force us to stay *gratis* in government-owned, gratuitously ornate hotels that seemed almost empty except for us. In deference to our audit committee in the United States and the Foreign Corrupt Practices Act, we refused, which unfortunately denied them face (but kept us in good graces with a number of important regulatory groups at home).

Over dinner one night, an official presented me with a book in English on the teachings of Confucius. I would be more successful, he said, if I read it, particularly the chapters on authority. Confucius, he announced in pedagogical tones, had devised the perfect system of governance, which was still practiced in China today. The emperor made all the decisions, and his ministers did exactly as he dictated, with unquestioning fealty extending down the chain to the provinces and the municipalities.

To demonstrate, the man stretched out his arm as far as he could, pointing first at his head and then edging his fingers slowly down his arm and ending at his fingertips. In the end, if the emperor made a decision, it trickled all the way down to him (meaning me), so that all of China could easily be on the same page—in theory, in a matter of minutes. He ended this dissertation by saying he hoped I'd learn from this.

The oddest event, however, occurred on the last day of our visit. The Xues and a few of their CCP friends checked our luggage for us ahead of time and took us all to a teahouse next to the airport to say goodbye. As the departure time came and went and our hosts showed no inclination to leave, Ruth became increasingly agitated. She prefers to arrive early at airports and hates to be separated from her luggage.

"She doesn't understand, does she?" I heard one of them say. Actually, she did, and the overt display of control by the CCP was exactly what was annoying her. Finally, five minutes after departure time, we all piled into a van that drove us right up to the airstair. The officials accompanied us into the first-class section (tucked us in, as it were), said goodbye, and disembarked. As soon as they hit the ground, the plane took off. The CCP members had demonstrated that they had total control, including over commercial airline schedules.

This capricious demonstration of control is not unique to members of the CCP. A friend returning to the United States from a research trip in Russia recalled waiting on the tarmac at Moscow's Sheremetyevo Airport as the oligarchs' private jets took off for weekends at Black Sea resorts, aware that time was ticking by and he—and many others on the flight— were missing their commercial connections. Regardless, their flight left only after all the oligarchs were on their way.

And in our last few months in China, *guanxi* came to our rescue. Ruth and I flew to Beijing in June 2014 for a couple of meetings with government officials and a little sightseeing on the side, but we were waylaid by thunderstorms and the plane was forced to land in Shijiazhuang, the capital of Hebei, the province just south of Beijing. As the delay extended, I called a Chinese friend to see if his wife, who had a middle management position in the Chinese Air Traffic Control agency, had any insights. He told us to sit tight, and he would do what he could. Thirty minutes later, he called to say that our plane would be in the air on its final leg to Beijing in just a few minutes. Mum's the word, he advised.

Meanwhile, a famous marketing expert, allegedly a 20-year-plus veteran of China who'd been on the plane with us and was in the same situation we were, sat next to us in the waiting room screaming obscenities at the China Eastern personnel in pretty good Chinese. He was really angry, and he wanted China Eastern's management to know it. A few minutes later we were back in the plane again *en route* to Beijing. I'm certain that this guy was convinced that his tirade had saved the day for everyone. Later, my Chinese friend assured me that such a tirade had nothing to do with our departure. In my experience, anger never wins in China. The only reliable tools are *guanxi* or leverage. Whether my friend's wife was able to speed us on our way, or merely provided the information of our imminent departure, I never knew.

15.4   THE CCP AND HISTORY

As a student of history, I'm keenly aware that it's written by the winners. Only recently have Americans learned that the Native settlements regarded by their colonizing forebears as "encampments of disgusting savages" housed elegant and nuanced societies that enabled a self-sustaining existence in environments that were hostile to the Europeans. Such concepts are viewed as so threatening by some groups that their teaching has been banned from some schools, which is a huge loss in my eyes.

Even since I've read the novel by Stella Dong called *Shanghai: The Rise and Fall of a Decadent City*, I've been fascinated by her account of the evening of May 23 and the morning of the 24th, 1949, when the Communist troops "liberated" Shanghai. Dong paints a picture of anxious farm boys clad in rustic PLA uniforms marching into the city, while equally frightened families hid in their houses peeking out from behind their curtains. Both sides were terrified of the other.

The "invasion" took place almost without incident.

I would have loved to find a time machine and experience that era myself. So, during my entire stay in Shanghai, I was regularly looking for people who were old enough to remember what it was like for them on those two days. It wasn't easy, but Lao Ding was willing to help. One day in the spring of 2013, he rounded up a man in his late eighties who'd been there, could remember it all, and was willing to talk with me about it over dinner.

While I was grateful, it wasn't terribly satisfying. First of all, we had multiple Party officials with us, which I think intimidated the old guy and ensured that he would stick to the Party line. Second, it all felt very rehearsed. And third, my informant was clearly putting on a show. He was dressed in a black leather coat, even though the restaurant was well-heated, and he wore sunglasses all evening, even though the lights in the restaurant were not very bright. And finally, if he'd experienced any of the anxiety that Dong described in her book, he did his best to hide it. His description was all about how dumb and cowardly the Kuomintang were, and how brave and clever the Communists were.

The extent to which history has been rewritten in China is remarkable. In 2013, Ruth and I toured what remained of the Lunghua Internment Camp, where the Japanese interned about 2,000 Westerners living in Shanghai during World War II. It inspired the writer J.G. Ballard to write his semi-autobiographical novel *Empire of the Sun*, which Steven Spielberg made into a movie. Due to the ongoing hatred of the Japanese, perpetrated by the CCP, the camp receives virtually no publicity. Where it once stood, there is currently a school, as I believe was the case prior to the Japanese invasion. You have to seek out information about it aggressively if you want to take a look.

A much more ballyhooed landmark, which also has a rewritten history, is the Sihang Warehouse, located north of the former French Concession on Suzhou Creek in Shanghai. I'd learned about it from Teddy, a local Shanghainese businessman and fellow history buff whom I'd met at the wedding of Lao Ding's son, Thomas. From October 26 to November 1, 1937, 423 Chinese soldiers held off a much larger number of better-equipped Japanese troops before escaping into the British Concession. This battle was particularly meaningful to the Shanghainese—so much so that the building has never been fully repaired. The outside walls teem with pockmarks inflicted by Japanese artillery. Ruth and I drove over to take a look.

In 2011, this event was hardly mentioned. Since Xi has come to power and CCP propaganda has fanned nationalism, though, it's become a much bigger deal. An issue that no one wants to talk about, however, is that the Chinese soldiers who acquitted themselves so honorably were the Kuomintang, not the Red Army.[3]

At the time, hatred of Japan was running high, fanned by the Party's propaganda machine to stimulate a higher level of nationalism and—by implication—support for the CCP. The enemy without strengthens the hold of the Party within.

Another aspect of Chinese history that encouraged some debate is the Cultural Revolution. My Mandarin teacher (and not a Party member) told me that most people hated the Cultural Revolution, but not everybody. His grandmother, for example, loved it, seeing it as her opportunity to punish her enemies by spreading lies about them and getting them in trouble. Also, as an extremely poor peasant, she'd always hated landlords. The Cultural Revolution afforded her the opportunity to get even.

NOTES

1. Lucian Pye, "Chinese Commercial Negotiating Style," Rand Corporation, January 1982, R-2837-AF, https://www.rand.org/content/dam/rand/pubs/reports/2007/R2837.pdf.
2. Peter Martin, *China's Civilian Army: The Making of Wolf Warrior Diplomacy* (Oxford: University of Oxford Press, 2021).
3. The event was the basis for a blockbuster Chinese movie that took a decade to make and was released in 2020, called *The Eight Hundred*—always that magic number eight. Steve Rose, "The Eight Hundred: How China's Blockbusters Became a New Political Battleground," *The Guardian*, September 18, 2020, https://www.theguardian.com/film/2020/sep/18/the-eight-hundred-how-chinas-blockbusters-became-a-new-political-battleground.

PART IV

THE OTHER
93 PERCENT

While much is made of the CCP, it's important to understand that only 7 percent of the population (98-100 million people) belong to it. The balance, about 1.3 billion people, don't. And they have their own set of attitudes about many things, including the Party.

CHAPTER SIXTEEN

CHINESE BELIEFS

One of the most useful insights I gained about the Chinese population came from Mr. Liu, Luo's second in command. China had changed so much since the Liberation in 1949, he said, and the Chinese people had endured so many mass movements and deprivations that the year in which one was born could say a lot about a person's experiences and world view:

- **Pre-1949:** These are the true Communists, ideologically pure.
- **1950s:** Those born in this decade came of college age during the Cultural Revolution. They lost their chance for an education and are resentful.
- **1960s:** This group had the chance to go to college; they are well adjusted.
- **1970s:** They became adults during the Reform and Opening. They enjoyed huge opportunities and are often quite happy.
- **1980s:** They became adults in the twenty-first century and enjoyed great opportunities, but their lives are Darwinian and stressful.
- **1990s:** These people also enjoy lots of opportunities, but many are entitled and lazy.

There's another angle that needs to be considered, which is the mismatch of men and women. Mao's one-child policy and the cultural preference for males resulted in high rates of female abortion or infanticide. According to U.N. data for 2020, China ranked behind only India in terms of gender imbalance: it has 37.17 million more males than females, or a population of 48.71% women to 51.29% men.[1]

Moreover, even with the relaxation of the one-child policy, women find themselves getting the short end of the stick. At least once a month, a Chinese person would tell me about the "quality mismatch" through which the smartest and best educated women ("A" women) were left out of the marriage structure. Typically, "A" men have the choice of partners and choose "B" women—ones who are smart and educated but not at a level to push them. "B" men choose "C" women; "C" men "D" women; and "D" men are left single. As are the "A" women.[2]

Ironically, the head of the Propaganda Museum, Mr. Yang, was adamant that education was the only answer to the population explosion that Mao had created in his quest for more workers. In all of history, Yang pointed out, educated women had fewer children. It was that simple, he insisted: education. No need for a one-child policy—just education.

Our first Mandarin teacher (in China) was YanYan, who'd grown up in Henan Province as the daughter of two lower-level government officials. Her parents had sent her away to a boarding school in Shanghai when she was too young, we thought—not to be rid of her, but to help her get the best education they could afford. But both Ruth and I felt that YanYan's early separation from her parents had left her chronically lonely and a little depressed.

Ruth, a natural mentor who missed our sons and grandchildren, took YanYan under her wing and tried to provide some emotional support and maternal guidance. She also coached her as she looked for a better job than teaching Mandarin to foreigners.

When YanYan finally found one, her parents were so grateful that they drove all the way from Henan to Shanghai—a full day's journey—to take us to dinner and shower us with gifts—14 of them! We could have opened our own gift shop with the inventory they provided. Their gratitude was humbling.

16.1   CHINESE BELIEFS

People everywhere harbor beliefs about themselves and about the world they live in, and the Chinese are no exception. What makes them unique is the extent and effectiveness of the CCP's propaganda machine in reinforcing these beliefs. There's not a lot of competition for the minds of the people in China; the Propaganda Department is dominant. For that reason, a section on common beliefs is more appropriate in a book on China than would be appropriate in one about almost any other country.

Not everybody in China believes the following, but most of the Chinese people I know do. Also, I'm not claiming that these beliefs are wrong; I'm only saying that I personally think they may be somewhat out of step with reality.

- **The Century of Humiliation**

   Virtually everyone I have ever met in China believes in the "Century of Humiliation."[3] To understand China today, you *must* understand and acknowledge this belief.

   Up until the First Opium War, starting in 1842, the Chinese believe theirs was the largest, most important, and most advanced country on Earth. But it was unforgivably humiliated by foreign powers for 100 years as the result of assorted invasions, which are perceived foremost as an insult to Chinese sovereignty: first the British (1839–1842 and again 1857–1859), then the Japanese

(1894–1895), then various other Western powers during the Boxer Rebellion (1899–1901), and Japan again (1937–1945).

We in the United States tend to think of ourselves as the "good guys" because we contributed money to the founding of Tsinghua University after the Boxer Rebellion, funded the Peking Union Medical College Hospital in 1906, and contributed to the Chinese government in the 1930s for rural development and to help support the war against Japan. But China does not focus on these things. Instead, the Propaganda Department, and therefore the Chinese people, tend to emphasize the following:

- The Chinese Exclusion Act of 1882, prohibiting Chinese citizens from coming to the United States for several decades.
- The Treaty of Versailles, which took Germany's colony in China away from the Germans and gave it to Japan at the end of World War I.
- America's support of the Nationalists during the Liberation War, which ended in the victory of the Communists in 1949.
- The Korean War, which, according to the Propaganda Department, *we* started.
- Our alleged intention to invade China in the 1950s.
- The Vietnam War.
- Our allegedly intentional bombing of the Chinese Embassy in Belgrade in 1996.

- **Beliefs about the United States**

According to the CCP, America has been its enemy from the start in 1949. We've always wanted to undermine the Chinese and slow their progress. We are believed to have started the Korean War with the ultimate purpose of invading China and taking it over. Thus, Mao had to enter the war himself—both to help the North Koreans and to preclude an American invasion. It's also why Mao had to move as much industry as possible from the coastal regions into the interior: to protect it from the first wave of the impending invasion.

The United States supports Taiwan, Xinjiang, Tibet, Japan, and others to thwart China. Most Chinese believe that Taiwan, Xinjiang, and Tibet have all been part of China since the beginning of time. As a reality check: according to Western historians, China invaded Xinjiang in the eighteenth century during the Qing dynasty.[4] The same is true of Tibet[5] and Taiwan (seventeenth century by the Qing dynasty and twentieth century by the Chinese Nationalists).[6]

Japan is a somewhat different case. One of my first Mandarin teachers insisted that the Japanese (as well as the Koreans) were just Chinese who'd wandered "off the reservation" long ago. But Japan invaded China from 1894 to 1895 and then again in 1937. According to the Chinese belief system, the Red Army defeated the Japanese in 1945 and drove them out of China. According to most Western historians, the Red Army did its best to avoid fighting the Japanese in World War II, leaving the job to the Nationalists and the Americans. This strategy allowed it to be prepared for the battle for supremacy that occurred after the war (1945–1949) between the CCP, refreshed and rebuilt, and the Nationalist Party of China, the Kuomintang (KMT), weakened by fighting the Japanese.

The so-called nine-dash line is the most recent addition to this collection of beliefs. According to most Western experts, the U.N., and an international tribunal in The Hague, there's no basis in fact for the claim that everything in the South China Sea west of the nine-dash line has always belonged to China.[7] Nonetheless, even the best-educated Chinese I know purport to believe that the nine-dash line has always been there.

Chinese people believe that the United States is constantly interfering in the affairs of other countries, especially in the affairs of the PRC. Human rights in China are within the purview of the CCP, and the United States is wrong to interfere in any way.

Yet many Party members want their kids to go to school in the West! At Mr. Luo's request, I made some introductions on behalf of Eric Zhou, the son of a colleague of his when he had worked at the Bank of Shanghai. Making such introductions for Eric wasn't difficult because he spoke perfect English, was extremely smart, and made a very good first impression. I passed his résumé to the California branch of SVB; Eric got an interview and soon became an employee. Eventually, he left us to join a U.S. VC firm, taking all the training he'd gotten at SVB with him.

Eric told me that most of the members of the 18th Party Congress (which took place in November 2012) had children who were studying at American universities. He thought that most educated Chinese admired the United States and wanted their children to be educated there. I suspect that "most" is an exaggeration.

- **Beliefs on China's Foreign Policy**

The Chinese people believe that China was the dominant power in the world for thousands of years until the Opium Wars in the 1840s. Prior to these wars, all of China's neighbors stood in awe of the superiority of Chinese culture, Chinese science and technology, and the Chinese method and style of governance. They all voluntarily submitted themselves to the will of China, as "client states," and were grateful for China's generosity in sharing its superior cultural and governance institutions with them in exchange for nominal tribute.

The Opium Wars brought this scenario to a screeching halt. For 100 years, China was overrun by "barbarians" (a synonym for "foreigners") from various European countries, as well as Japan. The CCP takes credit for having purged China of barbarians during the course of World War II, and for protecting it from further incursions after the Liberation in 1949.

An important part of this belief system is the idea that China has never invaded nor interfered in the internal affairs of another country. This is completely false. Most Chinese are not aware of China's many invasions of its neighbors, ranging from the occupation of Vietnam in 257 BCE (which it then ruled for more than 1,000 years until 938 CE), through Deng Xiaoping's second invasion of Vietnam in 1979 to "teach [the Vietnamese] a lesson"[8] about getting too friendly with the Soviet Union.

But Vietnam was not the only target of Chinese aggression. Tibet has been invaded and occupied by China multiple times. In 1720, the Qing dynasty expelled the forces of the Dzungar Khanate from Tibet and gradually took over the administration of the nation.[9] Tibet remained a Chinese protectorate until 1912.[10] In 1950, China invaded Tibet again, forcing the Dalai Lama to sign a "Seventeen-point Agreement" that affirmed China's sovereignty. In the aftermath of the 1959 Tibetan uprising, the Dalai Lama fled to India and established a government-in-exile, which rescinded the agreement. Some of Tibet was absorbed into China as the Tibet Autonomous Region in 1965; the rest became part of neighboring provinces.[11] There is nothing autonomous about the Tibet Autonomous Region.

According to this belief in China's glorious and benevolent history, though, the United States is not content to see China rise. Our whole goal is to keep them from becoming number one again. Given their glorious history and inherent superiority, the Chinese have a historic mandate from heaven to return China to its original status as the number one power in the world. Everyone else connects to heaven through the intermediary of the Middle Kingdom—that is, China is in the middle between heaven above and all the other countries and cultures on the Earth below.

- **Families**

The family is the most important unit in society. The top eche-
lon of the CCP consists of the descendants of the Revolutionary
families (those who marched with Mao from the south of China to
Yan'an in the north). The CCP is entitled to rule for the same reasons that various dynasties were allowed to rule. First, they consisted of families who had received the heavenly mandate to rule.
And second, the fact that they'd received the heavenly mandate was
evidenced by their might and success. If this reasoning appears cir-
cular, that's because it is.

In the end, the family is the basic building block. One must not
only worship one's ancestors, but also spare no effort to ensure the
success of one's children. This support extends into helping the children of friends as well, through *guanxi*. I was constantly being asked
to help the children of my acquaintances and "friends." I made many
introductions for children or even godchildren of friends. I never
interfered thereafter, and these individuals would get hired or, if
hired, eventually promoted on their own merits.

Usually, in the spirit of give and take, there was a *quid pro quo*.
If I helped a child, their parents would offer to help my bank, usually through introductions to their connections. In the spirit of
obeying the Foreign Corrupt Practices Act, I would demur.

Because of the importance of the family, primary allegiance is not
to the government, but the family. I think that it's often difficult for
the Chinese to feel allegiance to the government. The family is above
all else, with the sense of being Chinese—belonging to the family in
the larger sense—second to that. The government comes third.

This allegiance to the family explains a lot. In Chapter 15, I
described the entrepreneur who was willing to sell his cybersecurity
software to the PLA or the Pentagon or both, depending on the
price. He wanted the money. What for? The family.

- **Laws and regulations**

Rules and regulations are guidelines; they're not set in stone. Creativity is expressed through workarounds. For a couple of years, I was confused when government officials would say to me, "We encourage you to be creative." In fact, it felt almost mocking. They knew I was caught—and powerless. Why would they admonish me to be more creative? Then, members of the secret team, frustrated by my ignorance, took me aside and explained.

The goals are set by the people at the top, people whom I might know about from the news media but would never meet. The regulations and laws have been established by the government to help the local officials achieve the goals set for them by their superiors. The laws and regulations should be used, as appropriate, to achieve these goals.

Here's the catch: consistency in applying the rules isn't particularly important. It's all about achieving the goals. Helping the leaders achieve their goals is "good government relations." Following the rules is important only to the extent that it aids you in helping the leaders achieve their goals. If you follow the rules but don't help the leaders achieve their goals, you will fail; however, if you break the rules while helping the leaders achieve their goals, you will succeed.

- **Mao**

Mao is a god. I've heard that from so many Chinese, particularly those who are less educated. Educated Chinese don't say that, but they do say that everyone else thinks Mao is a god. Why? Because he unified China, saving it from the ravages of the Western powers.

According to Deng Xiaoping, Mao was 70% good and 30% bad. Of course, if you were among the many millions of people who died because of his vindictiveness or his callous adventurism in social experimentation, from your perspective, he would have been 100% bad. Deng didn't die because of Mao. That said, it is a tribute to

Deng's magnanimous nature that he was able to conclude that Mao was only 30% bad, as Mao's impact on Deng and his family (Deng's son was reportedly paralyzed when he was pushed out a window by Mao's Red Guards during the Cultural Revolution) was bad enough to cause most people to despise Mao forever.

But perhaps the most vivid depiction of Chinese attitudes toward Mao came in early 2013, when Ruth and I went on a weekend outing at the Naked Retreat (a resort where guests are close to nature but not actually naked) at the foot of Moganshan, a small mountain about two hours' drive outside of Shanghai. We arrived on a Friday, and on Saturday, Ruth and I decided to hike the mountain. When we got there, we stopped to study a large map of the area to figure out where to go next. Our ability to read characters at that point was very weak. Fortunately, a van pulled up and a small family consisting of a mother in her late thirties, a father in his forties, and a 10-year-old son, popped out. They offered to help us. Because their English was as poor as our Chinese, communication was challenging. But they wanted to practice their English as much as we wanted to practice our Chinese. So, we spent the day together.

The family took us to lunch at a farmhouse restaurant, where we had about five different dishes, each based on bamboo. After lunch, we visited a villa that had belonged to Chiang Kai-shek, and another that had belonged to Mao. When they dropped us off at the Naked Retreat at the end of the day, Happy Liao (the father) told us that Mao was a god. His decisions may have resulted in the death of tens of millions of people, *but he united China*.

- **Authority**

Who makes decisions in China? On our visit to Qufu, I received a stern lecture that when the emperor (or the Party Secretary) makes a decision, it is passed on down through the ranks all the way into the individual family to the youngest child, step by step, level by level. In theory, China needs only one decision-maker—namely, the Party Secretary.

Conversely, everyone who has a decision to make pushes it up through the ranks. In theory, all decisions end up on the desk of the Party Secretary. Direction comes from above. That has significant ramifications. One of them, which can be very important in a business setting, is that you will never meet the ultimate decision-maker. After intense discussion, the Chinese side will always tell you that they'll have to "run it up the flagpole" and get back to you. This may take time. In some cases, it takes years. You'll be frustrated, and you'll want to meet the decision-maker in person. Good luck. Which introduces the corollary: If you're the decision-maker on your side of the negotiation, you should not be in the room with the negotiators. Your presence diminishes your "face." You should not be seen.

The fundamental Chinese belief is that the true decision-maker shouldn't be accessible. If you're accessible, you're not the real decision-maker. That person must be somewhere else—perhaps at your headquarters back in California!

- **Subordination of the individual to the group**

Gish Jen, an American writer of Chinese descent, calls the Asian identity the "flexi-self," a bendable Gumby that is closely entwined with family and community, while the Western identity is a "pit-self," independent minded and self-absorbed like an avocado.[12] Her point is that Asians subordinate their will and their needs to those of the body politic, and Westerners stubbornly defend their right to be heard, regardless of the needs or will of the group. I understand her point, and on the surface, it would appear to hold true. But my experience has been somewhat different.

The same employees who will begin every report by saying, "Under the guidance of our leader, Ken, and with the unmitigated support of my team, we were able to . . ." will tell me in private, unabashedly, that they're smarter than all the others, did the bulk of the work themselves, and deserve the biggest bonus.

This dichotomy reflects some major window dressing. The advertisement is "We Chinese are much humbler than you Americans. We always subordinate our will to the will of the group." In reality, this doesn't hold true at bonus time.

- **Deferred gratification**

  I believe that the ability to accept "deferred gratification" is a major cultural strength of the Chinese people. Many Chinese will commit themselves to a life of severely underpaid hard labor for the sake of future generations. This reflects the belief in "eating bitter" to ensure a better future for children and grandchildren. "Eating bitter" is honorable and viewed as a moral obligation of people who care about their family and about China.

  But this belief may be fading. In 2010 in China, the following quote became an online sensation: "I would rather cry in a BMW than smile on a bicycle." The person who uttered that sentence was a female contestant on a nationally televised quiz show responding to a question by an unemployed admirer who asked if she'd ride on the back of his bicycle on a date with him.

  I believe that this small statement and the attention it generated is a harbinger of the changes taking place in China as we speak.

- **Diet**

  You are what you eat. We see this same belief among Native Americans, or at least we did in bygone centuries. If you want to be courageous, eat the flesh (or any other part) of an animal that demonstrates courage. If you want to be virile, eat the part of an animal that symbolizes virility. A Chinese friend of mine received a dried moose penis as a gift. His wife felt that he needed a shot of virility. She made him a stew with the moose penis, and he ate it without knowing what it was. When he finished his meal, she told him what he'd eaten. I would have been horrified. Instead, he was delighted. Furthermore, he imagined his virility to be increasing. Who knows? Maybe it really was.

- **Baijiu**

First, if you're going to do business in China, you will of necessity become familiar with Baijiu, an extremely strong alcoholic beverage made from fermented sorghum or some other grain. Most "getting to know each other" sessions gravitate quickly toward imbibing together, often to the point of becoming extremely drunk.

This custom reflects two beliefs. First, "real men" can consume immense amounts of Baijiu and there is honor (rather than shame) in becoming "stink-drunk" in the process of building relationships.

And second, you can never trust a business partner who's not willing to get (extremely) drunk with you. If you want to be trusted, you'll need to sacrifice your liver.

- **China today**

Most Chinese today are proud of China. Very proud. Older people believe that Xi has brought China to the point where it doesn't have to dwell with shame on the Century of Humiliation. Most younger people are less focused on that era and are more concerned with China's success in these past several years in overtaking the West in general and the United States in particular . . . with respect to both wealth and power.

16.2 ATTITUDES TOWARD AMERICANS

Some of the most entrenched Chinese views about Americans is that we betrayed Mao by siding with the Nationalists. However, the books I've read suggest otherwise. Of particular note is *China 1945* by Richard Bernstein, a well-regarded journalist who studied Chinese under the famous Harvard professor John King Fairbank. Bernstein proved to my satisfaction that the Americans, led by George Marshall, the diplomat in charge, tried their best to stay neutral between the Nationalists and the Communists. Mao did his best to curry their favor, but he did so by lying (and I mean really blatantly lying).

In the 1944–1945 timeframe, Mao engineered several meetings with the American contingents, during which he flattered them by telling them that he greatly admired our founding fathers and that he intended to create a democracy in China modeled after ours. Of course, he had no such intention. By the fall of 1945, as the Soviets were pouring into Manchuria to claim the victory that the Americans had just won over the Japanese, Mao reunited with the Russians and started shooting at U.S. Marines as they escorted Japanese soldiers to the ships waiting to take them back to Japan. Mao was nothing if not treacherous. It was *he* who declared the Americans his enemies, not the other way around. That said, the schools in China have been successful for 70 years in getting the Chinese people to fervently believe this myth.

As long as I've been going to China (since 2000), mid-level government officials have been telling me that America is an enemy, and war with the United States is inevitable. Even Mr. Luo believed this. Based on my reading, I believe that this idea was a mantra under Mao. It has become even more of a mantra under Xi, and especially since former President Trump took office in 2016.

Today, in the early 2020s, many if not most people in China seem to believe that America is in an irreversible decline. Furthermore, they're convinced that Americans are angry and jealous of China's rise. Because they don't want to see China surpass the United States economically or militarily, Americans are anti-Chinese. The Chinese appear to be proud of this. It's clear that the Propaganda Department is doing its best to reinforce this view. Apparently, U.S. participation in the Century of Humiliation gives China the right to appropriate American technology with impunity.

Also, the Chinese, in general, believe (and perhaps rightly so) that America criticizes them for doing things that the United States itself does. For example, we criticize China for what it's done in Tibet, yet what we did to the Native Americans is not dissimilar. We criticize China for the way it interferes in the affairs of other countries, yet the United States has a long history of doing the same. With a little knowledge of history and a little imagination, anyone could build a much larger list of ways in which the United States (as the pot) calls the kettle (China) black. It's difficult to defend the United States. On the other hand, the kettle is indeed black.

However, I think there are three ways in which this kind of thinking is not very productive. First, if you've ever been in a relationship with another human being, you know that things never improve if either or—worse yet—both parties take this approach to solving problems. This technique is mere deflection. Second, we know that two wrongs never make a right. And third, the approach itself indicates an attitude that will never improve.

Despite the antagonistic beliefs described above, there's also an attitude of affection and admiration for Americans. In 2012, friends visited us in Shanghai with their daughter, who had spent the summer studying Chinese in China. We took them to Fuxing Park, where elderly men using large brushes paint characters with water on the sidewalks. The characters evaporate and disappear. Our friends' daughter amused the crowd by joining in the fun, painting her own. The bystanders seemed amazed by her prowess. People wanted to know where we were from. When we answered "*Meiguo*" (America), they responded with an enthusiastic thumbs up. "We love *Meiguo*," they said, smiling. "You bombed the Japanese."

Curiously, SPDB's Mr. Luo, a member of the CCP, also had a somewhat positive view of the American–Chinese relationship: that Americans and Chinese would work well together if their respective governments would only let them.

But some Chinese are so xenophobic that they'll pay extra money to avoid dealing with foreigners. An acquaintance, Xiao Hong, borrowed $50,000 (305,000 RMB) from friends and relatives for a real estate transaction. Then she asked for my help in securing a proper bank loan to repay her friends and neighbors after she'd completed the deal. Of course, our JV bank wouldn't make a loan of this sort, but I thought SPDB might, so I asked Mr. Liu for help. He made a phone call, and SPDB was ready to help Xiao Hong.

When her husband found out, he was incensed. He professed to hate foreigners, presumably including me. He refused to take the loan from SPDB and instead went to the Bank of China, where he paid a 10,000 RMB ($1,640) bribe to the branch head for an identical loan. Identical, I suppose, except that this loan cost him an additional 10,000 RMB.

Another example came from our dear, sweet maid, who believed that the Chinese have evolved further than Westerners. The evidence, she said, was conclusive: Chinese cook their vegetables, whereas many Westerners eat theirs raw, in the form of a salad. Eating raw vegetables, she maintained, is uncivilized.

Most of the Chinese I met believed to a moral certainty that America just wanted to keep China down to prevent the Chinese from surpassing them. That was the mantra in the Chinese press. Yet I never had a conversation with an American about how to "keep China down." That said, I've had many conversations with Americans about how to avoid being "kept down" by the Chinese government.

16.3 OVERSEAS CHINESE

There is a large population of overseas Chinese in the United States. They're concentrated in Flushing, New York, and in California. In fact, 25% of San Francisco's residents are Chinese. In 1990, the noted architect I.M. Pei, along with Henry Kissinger, founded the Committee of 100 with a dual mission of "promoting the full participation of all Chinese Americans in American society and acting as a public policy resource for the Chinese American community and advancing constructive dialogue and relationships between the peoples and leaders of the United States and Greater China."[13]

The 100 committee members now number closer to 130 and represent prominent Chinese Americans in business, government, academia, and the arts. I've found that they tend to be laser-focused on making money, but perhaps that's just the slice of the population I've come to know.

In my experience, Chinese Americans tend to be extremely conflicted in their loyalties. A case in point occurred with SVB. In the late 2000s, before we founded the JV and we only had our small office on Huaihai Road, I arrived in Shanghai one spring evening just in time to take part in our annual Chinese New Year's party. The staff was ready with the makings of a skit in which they wanted me to participate. The premise was this: two of us were medieval bankers from another country seeking the emperor's permission to establish a bank in China. Not being able to speak Chinese, and in a demonstration of our respect, we were at his feet, communicating with him through interpreters.

Every time we asked for permission, he would answer in Mandarin, saying "Absolutely no way!" The interpreter would then turn to us and translate his message as "The Emperor says that he needs more gifts before he can give you an answer." Of course, we were all dressed in medieval garb, and two of our female employees were standing behind the emperor, fanning him. This skit had been written entirely by our Chinese employees, and they all seemed to think it was hilarious.

A few months later, I attended SVB's annual sales conference in California, with well over 500 bankers in attendance. Unbeknownst to me, someone had gotten the bright idea of showing a video of this skit as comic relief between more serious speeches. Again, the audience seemed to think it was a great parody, because most people in the bank knew how difficult it had been for us to get a license to establish a bank in China.

The next day, my admin told me that one of the attorneys in our legal department wanted to see me. This fellow was a Chinese American who'd grown up in New York City. I'm not sure he'd ever been to China. In any case, he started out by telling me he was ashamed to be working in a bank led by a CEO who'd allow a skit like this one to be shown, much less to participate in it himself. He didn't just request an apology; he *demanded* one on the spot.

I was placed in a very strange position. I didn't, honestly, care a lot about his outrage—he was a relatively low-level lawyer, and we could live without him. I realized he was focused on how the United States and the West has humiliated China. I gave him other ideas to think about: namely, the skit was written by native Chinese people; they thought it was hilarious; and I didn't invent the concept. Eventually, I managed to smooth his feathers by offering the "I'm sorry you were upset" apology.

The odd addendum to this affair was his outrage about the skit's depiction of the treatment of Chinese women. Women are treated far worse by the CCP. Those who are single (and often childless: single women are not allowed a "reproduction permit," meaning that their children cannot receive birth certificates and the benefits that come with that[14]) are marginalized and discriminated against. Single women, for instance, are handicapped in the lottery to buy an apartment in Shanghai, and are derogatorily considered "surplus women" if they haven't married by age 27.[15] Yet these same people, as described earlier, tend to be the smartest and most educated!

I was also aware of a number of Chinese, both academics and entrepreneurs, who were born in China, educated in the United States, and then lived bifurcated lives shuttling between the two countries, often with Hong Kong thrown in. Many believed that the tensions between the United States and China were irreconcilable, and although both parties were at fault, they preferred to live in China. We Americans passively assume that anyone who had succeeded in the United States and had the option would prefer to live (and die) in our country. But it's simply not true, no matter how much we may want it to be.

NOTES

1. Statistics Times, "Gender Ratio," United Nations World Population Prospects 2019, January 16, 2021, https://statisticstimes.com/demographics/country/china-sex-ratio.php.
2. Mary Kay Magistad, "China's 'Leftover Women', Unmarried at 27," *BBC News*, February 21, 2013, https://www.bbc.com/news/magazine-21320560?zephr-modal-register. Sadly, this mismatch occurs in the West as well, but I don't hear about it as much.
3. Among other treatments of this topic, I would suggest Alison A. Kaufman, "Testimony Before the U.S.-China Economic and Security Review Commission Hearing: The 'Century of Humiliation' and China's National Narratives," USCC, March 10, 2011, https://www.uscc.gov/sites/default/files/3.10.11Kaufman.pdf.
4. S. Frederick Starr, *Xinjiang: China's Muslim Borderland*, (New York: M.E. Sharpe, 2004).
5. Hsiao-ting Lin, *Tibet and Nationalist China's Frontier: Intrigues and Ethnopolitics, 1928-49* (Vancouver: UBC Press, 2006), and Jianglin Li, *Tibet in Agony: Lhasa 1959* trans. by Susan Wilf (Cambridge, MA: Harvard University Press, 2016).
6. Young-tsu Wong, *China's Conquest of Taiwan in the Seventeenth Century: Victory at Full Moon* (Singapore: Springer, 2007), and Jean-Marie Henckaerts, ed., *The International Status of Taiwan in the New World Order: Legal and Political Considerations* (London: Kluwer Law International, 1996), 337.
7. Koya Jibiki, "Rejection of China's 'Nine-Dash Line' Spreads from Asia to Europe," *Nikkei Asia*, December 1, 2020, https://asia.nikkei.com/Politics/International-relations/South-China-Sea/Rejection-of-China-s-nine-dash-line-spreads-from-Asia-to-Europe.
8. Lee Lescaze, "Peking [sic] and Hanoi Teach Each Other a Lesson," *Washington Post*, March 18, 1979, https://www.washingtonpost.com/archive/opinions/1979/03/18/peking-and-hanoi-teach-each-other-a-lesson/bac0c6fb-8917-4c48-ac34-ab48d4084963.
9. Hsiao-ting, *Tibet and Nationalist China's Frontier*.

10. Hsiao-ting, *Tibet and Nationalist China's Frontier.*
11. BBC News, "Tibet Profile," August 25, 2023, https://www.bbc.com/news/world-asia-pacific-16689779.
12. See, for instance, Harvard Public Affairs & Communications, "'Baggage' Claims Gish Jen," *The Harvard Gazette*, April 4, 2017, https://news.harvard.edu/gazette/story/2017/04/gish-jen-at-harvard.
13. The Committee of 100, "About Us," n.d., https://www.committee100.org/mission-history.
14. BBC News, "China's Two-Child Policy: Single Mothers Left Out," November 2, 2015, https://www.bbc.com/news/world-asia-china-34695899.
15. Shuli Ren, "China Forgets Some Women Who Hold Up the Sky," *Bloomberg*, August 2, 2021, https://www.bloomberg.com/opinion/articles/2021-08-02/how-china-s-three-child-policy-affects-generations-of-independent-women.

CHAPTER SEVENTEEN

THE LIVES OF THE OTHER 93 PERCENT

The lives of the other 93% don't get as much attention as those of their CCP countrypeople, in part because they're less likely to interact with non-Chinese. We had a chance to get to know some of these delightful people, and I can relay a few stories.

In 2012, Ruth and I went to Huangshan (Yellow Mountain), a very popular destination for both foreign and Chinese tourists and one of China's most photographed attractions.

We hired a Chinese guide to accompany us to the top. She was in her late thirties and eager to share her story. She told us that when she was a child, her mother had gotten pregnant for a second time, this time with twins. The twins' "journey to Earth" was well underway when the police who enforced the one-child policy showed up with the mobile abortion clinic, forced their way into the house, and did their evil work. Her mother fell into a depression from which she never recovered, and the family ultimately fell apart.

Today, the birth rate in China has fallen well below the natural replacement rate, which is 2.1%, the minimum rate required to prevent the population from decreasing. Accordingly, the government is worried about having too few young workers to support the population of retirees. As a result, China scrapped the one-child policy in 2016 in favor of a two-child limit, which has failed to make an appreciable difference. In May 2021, Xi Jinping approved a policy that will allow couples to have up to three children. Whether this will change China's stubborn birth dearth is unclear: urban living costs are high and most Chinese adults have never experienced siblings.[1] So far, it does not appear to have helped.

While much is made of the Chinese work ethic—which is prodigious, except, it appears, among the youngest generation and many Party offspring—they still make time to have fun. My assistant Chrystal told me about a short vacation that she took with a woman whom she described as a cousin. It turns out that the woman wasn't really her cousin, but just a good friend. In China, people often refer to good friends as cousins, or (if they're older) as uncles or aunties. The two of them took their kids and checked into a hotel for a night. The kids fell asleep, and the two adults stayed up eating pig intestines, duck heads, and chicken feet, drinking beer, and sharing secrets until the wee hours. They went home the next day feeling happy and refreshed. How can you not find that charming?

Another charming aspect of life in Shanghai while we were there was the dancing in the streets. On hot summer evenings, people often gathered in the streets and danced. In my observation (which could be incorrect), this tradition started about the time we arrived, in 2011, with small groups of women, and involved mostly line dancing. As time went by, it evolved to include men as well, and then, subsequently, couples dancing. My wife, Ruth, and a few of her more adventuresome Western friends joined in.

It was fun to watch. I must say, our Chinese neighbors seemed bemused, at least initially. In time, they didn't even seem to notice. In my eyes, at least, people of different ethnicities all look the same when they're dancing.

After we'd returned to San Francisco in 2015 and Xi had begun to tighten his grip, I read that the government had prohibited the dancing, at first allowing only state-sanctioned dances and then, ultimately, none at all.

As happened with the dancing, the fortunes of individual people can rise and fall without explanation. The famous entrepreneur and blogger Kai-Fu Lee became the victim of a government-instigated smear campaign. Why? He had too many (some say over 50 million) followers on Weibo (the Chinese microblogging site), and he criticized the Chinese government for its (in his view at that time) inadequate support of technology start-ups.

Today, Kai-Fu writes only good things about China. His 2018 bestseller, *AI Super-Powers: China, Silicon Valley, and the New World Order*, predicts China's rise to preeminence. He's Taiwanese, was educated at Princeton, and has become unabashedly and somewhat one-sidedly pro-PRC.

Yet there are stories that break your heart. In the summer of 2014, I ran a training session on the SVB culture at our office in Hong Kong. At the start, everyone told a story about an adult who'd influenced them when they were very young.

Geoffrey told the group he'd never seen his biological parents. With his birth, they'd broken the one-child policy and couldn't afford to pay the fine. They chose to give him up, and—because he was a boy—they were able to sell him to his "adoptive" parents.

Another employee, Orchid, told us that she was her parents' first child. Because she was a girl and they were allowed only one child, they gave her to a childless relative to raise as her own. Sadly, the relative died when Orchid was five. Her biological parents took her back, but she was never allowed to call them "Mom" and "Dad" because they didn't want to get caught and pay the fine.

The human cost of the one-child policy is rarely discussed in China.

17.1 THE LIFE OF XIAO HONG

Our acquaintance Xiao Hong, who appeared in Chapter 16, probably led a life that was similar to many of the other 1.3 billion non-CCP members. I recount what I know of it here, as it's an example of the challenges and dreams of so many in this enormous country.

Xiao Hong was born in 1978 in a small village in Henan province. Her name bears explanation. Xiao is an endearment meaning "Little"—it's a bit like Lao Ding, for whom "Lao" was an endearment meaning "Old." "Hong" was Xiao Hong's first name, which translates as "red." Many children born in that period were named "Hong" to show dedication to the Party. Thus, her name translates as "Little Red." It fit, as she was the most petite woman I ever met.

In May 2014, Ruth and I traveled to Xiao Hong's home village with her and her six-year-old daughter, FangFang (many Chinese women have these repeated single-syllable names). Xiao Hong had grown up in a dirt-floor structure and as a child suffered from a chronic lack of adequate food and clothing. This malnutrition likely contributed to her tiny frame. Nevertheless, the river running through her village wasn't polluted then, and the countryside was, in her memory, still beautiful. When we saw it, the entire landscape had been ravaged by pollution, industrialization, and development.

Xiao Hong's father and stepmother (her birth mother passed away when she was a child) earned their living tending 30 goats. The house they lived in now has a concrete floor, a step up from the dirt floor of her childhood.

Xiao Hong's father, an affable and kind man in his early sixties wearing a military dress coat, greeted us at the door. God only knows where he got the coat, since he never served in the PLA, but he looked very nice in it and was obviously proud of it. Born in 1955 into a farming family, Xiao Hong's father had never been outside his village, except for a single trip, years earlier, to Zhengzhou, about 30 kilometers away. A number of years before, the government had confiscated his land to build a Hummer factory.

Xiao Hong gave us a tour of the village. The most striking things I noticed were: 1) the village was *very* poor, and 2) there was an entire courtyard devoted to dilapidated religious structures, including a small Buddhist temple, a small Daoist temple, an "animist" temple, and a small Christian church. This last was provided by the local CCP in deference to Xiao Hong's father, who turned to Christianity in his middle age and functioned as the leader of the village congregation. He was clearly both liked and respected, even by the local CCP.

We also saw the neighbor a couple of doors down the street. He and his wife lived in a broken-down hovel. Junk filled the yard, and the walls of the small structure were crumbling. His wife was puttering around in a very primitive kitchen, and the man was crouching in the trash-filled "yard" in front of his home. His story, as told to me by Xiao Hong, was heartrending.

When the man was in his twenties, with a wife and three small children, he was falsely accused of rape. For this he spent 40 years in solitary confinement. Only recently had the government concluded that he'd been falsely accused in a cover-up for someone else with *guanxi* with the local authorities. But 40 years in solitary had broken him. He appeared crazed, and Xiao Hong told me that at this point he was basically unintelligible. He died only a few weeks after we met him.

Xiao Hong's marriage was not ideal, and her in-laws were very unhappy with her. Not only had she produced a single child, but—worse yet—it was a girl. They had a plan: she would get pregnant again, fly to Hong Kong where the hospitals could determine the fetus's sex, and if the new baby was another girl, she would abort. Xiao Hong refused, further exacerbating the already terrible relationship she had with her husband's parents.

Xiao Hong's life also demonstrated the challenges of the *hukou* system. A word of background: everyone in China is born into a *hukou*. The system can be traced to the fifth century BCE but took its current form in 1958 under Mao.[2] It established the locale of a person, which was, for the most part, immutable. Wherever you were born became your *hukou* for life, and you were expected to live there forever. If you moved somewhere else, you would not have access to the same rights or social services that you would in your own *hukou*.

The system was designed to create stability. The government would always know where you were, and the government representatives in your *hukou* would know you. To change *hukou*s, you must petition the government, which may take years and isn't always successful. These days, many people migrate from the countryside to the cities to earn more money. This usually entails a trade-off between higher salaries and the costs of losing the rights and social services to which they and their families were entitled in their *hukou*.

For example, Xiao Hong's *hukou* was her village. When she was 18, the government granted her a temporary *hukou* to attend university in Zhengzhou. Later, she moved to Shanghai to attend Shanghai University in that city's Baoshen District, where she received another temporary *hukou*.

After graduation, she moved to the Changning District in Shanghai. Again, the government gave her a special *hukou* in Changning for university graduates who rent. A few years later, she bought a flat in the neighboring district of Jiading. To do this, her employer wrote a special letter for her to present to the government. Once in Jiading, Xiao Hong wanted her daughter, FangFang, to enroll in school in Changning, where she thought the schools were better. But since her apartment and her *hukou* were in Jiading, that's where FangFang went to school.

Meanwhile, her husband's *hukou* was still in their village, because to get a *hukou* in Shanghai (if you weren't born there), you needed either to hold a master's degree from a university in Shanghai or to be married for at least seven years to someone with a Shanghai *hukou*. Although Xiao Hong had her master's from Shanghai University, that only covered her. Because she and her husband had been married for fewer than seven years, he couldn't piggyback on her Shanghai *hukou*.

In 2011, Xiao Hong's husband decided to get his own master's degree. He wanted to qualify for a Shanghai *hukou* on his own rather than rely on her. For his university, he chose a substandard school that promised to get him a *hukou* in Shanghai, rather than a much better school that would *not* promise the *hukou*. He graduated and got a *hukou* in Shanghai's Jiading district, on his own merit. Xiao Hong decided to buy a new apartment in Putuo (yet another district in Shanghai), because she felt the schools there were better. Now she needed a *hukou* in Putuo. Her husband didn't care about his daughter's education because she was not a boy, but he "let" Xiao Hong pursue the project on her own.

To buy the new apartment in Putuo, Xiao Hong needed to do a number of things. First, to make the down payment on the Putuo apartment, she had to sell the apartment in Jiading. She found a buyer who put up earnest money, but then the prospective buyers changed their minds and wanted the money returned. Xiao Hong now held the money and refused to return it. Fair is fair, she said.

But her relatives and neighbors felt that Xiao Hong herself was being unfair and pressured her to return the cash. Then she was in a real jam. Because she'd failed to sell the first house in Jiading, the new house in Putuo was considered a second residence and carried a higher interest rate. There was only one convenient solution: she and her husband got divorced. Of course, it was only a "fake" divorce. Her husband got the house in Jiading, which became his primary house, and she took the house in Putuo, now *her* primary house. Thus, she qualified for the lower interest rate.

But there were further complications. The school authorities in Putuo said that FangFang could not attend school there because her *hukou* was in Jiading. In the eyes of the government, FangFang's *hukou* was her father's, not her mother's. The bank then told Xiao Hong that she could not pay off the old loan on the Jiading house until she gave up her Jiading *hukou*, but the *hukou* office in Putuo said she couldn't apply for a *hukou* in Putuo until she'd paid off the loan on the Putuo apartment. This she couldn't do until her husband moved out of the Jiading place and she could sell that.

And so it goes. Chinese people, at least those without sufficient *guanxi*, spend their days trying to solve these types of puzzles.

17.2   NON-CHINESE LIVING IN CHINA

Early in our stay in Shanghai, we met Betty Barr, who was in her early eighties. The daughter of missionaries—her father from Scotland and her mother from Texas—she'd been born in Shanghai in 1933. When the Japanese invaded and ultimately put all the Americans into prison camps, she and her parents were incarcerated as well. By the time we met her, she'd spent more than half of her life in China. She was married to George Wang, who was both Chinese and a Party member.

Betty was remarkable. What I found most interesting, notwithstanding her heartfelt dedication to China and the many ways in which she'd demonstrated it, was that although the Chinese had made her an honorary citizen of Shanghai, they refused to grant her Chinese citizenship because she was not "Chinese." If you're not *born* Chinese, you can never *become* Chinese. And yet, to this day, a Chinese woman who's pregnant with a Chinese child can fly to California, give birth, and return to China with a baby who has an American passport.

17.3 STRANGE THINGS THAT HAPPEN

Throughout our residence in Shanghai, strange things happened that were never explained. Only long after the fact or never did we learn why or how certain things occurred. It was strange, until it just wasn't.

In mid-2013, 15,000 pigs were found dead in the Yangtze River. I only learned 10 years later, and from an unofficial source, where they came from. Apparently, they were discarded by swine raisers because the pigs had contracted porcine circovirus (swine flu). The farmers were compelled to cull their herds but no one told them what to do with the corpses, which were unsafe to eat—so the bodies were dumped in the river. This situation is a classic example of the CCP's approach to governing: mandates are issued but there is no guidance about how to implement them nor are resources provided to follow through. Such missteps occur frequently within Party verticals, whether federal, provincial, district-wide, or even on a city basis.[3] At the time of the "river of dead pigs," I heard of no uproar or investigation. If there was one, it was quickly suppressed.

I list a few of the other strange things that happened without much explanation or official inquiry:

Children were kidnapped and left in fields blinded because the corneas had been cut out of their eyes to sell in the black-market organ trade. This event actually did cause a significant uproar (as uproars go in China). Of less concern seems to be the widespread and state-sanctioned practice of removing and selling the organs from prisoners before their executions.[4]

Newspapers in China reported that wealthy Chinese were buying human milk from women nursing infants. It was widely believed, at the time, that ingesting human milk had a rejuvenating effect on the adult body, so demand was driving up prices, and the government was concerned that actual infants were being deprived of nutrition.[5]

Just after we'd arrived, there was a significant train accident near our apartment. There was never any explanation or compensation that we heard of; rather, the government brought in heavy equipment and buried the train.

No questions are asked or answered, people don't understand why these events occur and they gradually drift off in the direction of not worrying about it.

NOTES

1. Stephen McDonell, "China allows three children in major policy shift," *BBC*, May 31, 2021, https://www.bbc.com/news/world-asia-china-57303592.
2. Fei-Ling Wang, "China's Household Registration (*Hukou*) System: Discrimination and Reform," Statement to the Congressional Executive Commission on China, September 2, 2005, https://www.cecc.gov/sites/chinacommission.house .gov/files/documents/roundtables/2005/CECC%20Roundtable%20Testi mony%20-%20Fei-Ling%20Wang%20-%209.2.05.pdf.
3. A recent example of such a mandate-without-implementation is the reversal of the COVID lockdown policy, which was abandoned without guidance for vaccination or safeguards for the vulnerable. As a result, a lot of people died—exactly how many will likely never be known because the government stopped keeping count. (The Economist, "Will We Ever Know How Many People Died of Covid-19 in China?" February 2, 2023, https://www.economist.com/china/2023/02/02/ will-we-ever-know-how-many-people-died-of-covid-19-in-china.)
4. Jiayang Fan, "Can China Stop Organ Trafficking?" *The New Yorker*, January 10, 2014, https://www.newyorker.com/news/news-desk/can-china-stop-organ-trafficking.
5. Chinese newspapers cited in BBC News from Elsewhere, "China: Wealthy 'Drink Human Breast Milk,'" *BBC News*, July 3, 2013, https://www.bbc.com/ news/blogs-news-from-elsewhere-23161765.

CHAPTER EIGHTEEN

CONCLUSION

SEEKING TRUTH
FROM FACTS,
MAKING SENSE
OF IT ALL, AND
TRYING TO PREDICT
THE FUTURE

Eight years have gone by since Ruth and I came back to San Francisco from China. We were so taken with our experiences there that we've had a hard time "getting them out of our systems." Since our return, we've tried to learn as much as we could, both about China and about the mistakes we made there. Having devoted four years to trying to build a bank in China, while "seeking truth from facts" (as Deng would say), with correspondingly little time to reflect, we've spent most of our time back home trying to figure out what various members of the CCP had intended when they urged us in 2008, 2009, and 2010 to come and join them in building a JV bank.

To that end, I became involved in a number of organizations. Susan Shirk at the University of California at San Diego asked me to join her board of advisors at the 21st Century China Center, where I served as chair for a time. Jay Xu, the president of the Asian Art Museum in San Francisco, invited me on his board as well, and then promoted me to treasurer. Jack Wadsworth, formerly the head of Morgan Stanley's activities in Asia, recruited me to succeed him as chair of the Asia Society in Northern California.

I grabbed every chance to meet with "China Experts." I wanted to learn everything I could from people who knew more about China than I did, and—more importantly—had studied it from a different angle and had had more time to reflect. And, of course, I accepted SVB's invitation to remain as its representative on the board of the JV for six more years, the maximum allowed by the Chinese regulators. This enabled me to keep my oar in the water, visiting China quarterly and staying for about two weeks each time.

In addition, I read, whenever I had a spare moment. In these past eight years, there has been a constant flow of new books on China. A generation of Old China Hands has begun to fade, replaced by a whole new generation of young scholars, government officials, think tankers, and China watchers, many of whom were barely known in the China expert circles when we arrived there in early 2011. They now appear regularly on panels and in discussion groups, and in many cases set the tone with a whole new view of the CCP. From my perspective, these new experts are less sentimental and more objective than their predecessors. They never had a love affair with China and therefore don't feel jilted. In this final chapter, I refer to a number of their books that helped me interpret my experiences on the ground while we built the bank in China "in collaboration" with the CCP.

From today's vantage point, I firmly believe we were (and are still) being played.

Every time I think about my experience in China, Mel Gibson's 2004 epic *The Passion of the Christ* comes to mind. I'm not particularly religious in a conventional sense, but I saw the film on its release and found it extremely graphic and emotionally engaging. By the time the cross arrives at Golgotha (the actual site of the crucifixion), many viewers are thoroughly exhausted and hope that the film will end soon. I can't get the film out of my mind and find myself haunted by the parallels to my efforts in China, particularly the stations of the cross. In the Catholic tradition, the stations of the cross are a 14-step devotional sequence that commemorates specific events in Jesus Christ's last day of life. The last of these has the body laid in the tomb. There is no sense of "happily ever after."

In my case, I've identified eight discrete stations that correspond to my experience in setting up the JV bank.

Station 1 (kissing frogs): For seven years, from 2000 till 2007, we wandered around China meeting as many people as we could, trying to interest them in our bank. We were Silicon Valley Bank, the only commercial bank in the whole world exclusively dedicated to financing the creation and development and, ultimately, commercialization of technology. We felt compelled to be in China by two beliefs that have, over time, proven to be correct: 1) technology is a global phenomenon, and 2) China would eventually become a leader. The entrepreneurs we kissed were largely polite, the government officials less so. We were determined. We persevered.

Station 2 (finding a prince): Finally, in 2007, we found a prince: Party Secretary Ding, the leader of the Yangpu District in Shanghai. He was the first government official to embrace us, literally. Every time we met with him, he gave me a monstrous bear hug. A few years later when I started to study Chinese formally, one of the chapters in my textbook was entitled "Chinese Don't Like to Hug." This did not apply to Lao Ding. Apparently, he *loved* to hug. On a winter day in 2008, our driver pulled up into the courtyard at Lao Ding's administration's suite of offices in Yangpu to find him, along with 10 members of his team, all lined up on the front steps with outstretched arms, ready to hug us the minute we stepped out of the van.

Lao Ding had found what he was looking for: the bank that would teach him how to finance start-ups so that he could transform the economy of his old-fashioned rust-belt manufacturing district into a marvel of modern technology. We were the one, and he wanted us. In fact, he liked us so much that he "borrowed" our business model when we weren't paying attention and tried it out at the Shanghai Rural Commercial Bank. That experiment was successful enough that he gave us an award for being a top "innovation advisor for Yangpu." And then he began introducing us to the government officials who could arrange for us to obtain a license to operate in China.

Station 3 ("You are the best bank in the whole world."): Lao Ding introduced us to Yu Zhengsheng, then Party Secretary of all Shanghai, and later a member of the Standing Committee—in other words, one of the most powerful people in China. Yu knew just how to flatter us, saying: "Our researchers have studied all the banks in the entire world, and yours is the most impressive, even more impressive than Goldman Sachs or Morgan Stanley. We need you here in China." Imagine how important I—a guy who grew up in Flint, Michigan—felt upon hearing that.

Station 4 ("Don't worry, 1 will handle the regulators for you."): With Yu paving the way for us, getting to know the regulators was a piece of cake. They were crusty and skeptical, but their resistance was within the allowed parameters. They knew that, in the end, if Yu wanted us to have a license, they would probably have to comply. Of course, they had objections, which—for the most part—were well-founded. We were naive. We didn't understand or appreciate the fact that the Chinese system was so different from our own that it might be impossible to apply our business model successfully in China. Furthermore, other province-level Party Secretaries wanted licenses for their favorite foreign banks, and there were only so many of these licenses to go around.

Actually, as we discerned over time, Silicon Valley Bank ended up being the first foreign *commercial* bank in the history of the CCP to be given a license to enter into a joint venture with a Chinese commercial bank. In retrospect, I believe that the regulators were trying to protect us from our own naiveté and from Yu's enthusiasm.

Station 5 ("Did we mention you'll need a joint venture partner?"): That's the law: to obtain a license to found a new bank in China, you must have a JV partner. The ostensible reason is stated in the following way, and with some justification: "You need a JV partner because China is different, and as such, risky for those unfamiliar with it. Therefore, to make sure you can succeed, you will need a partner."

The logic is sound, and the reasoning is correct. Chinese banks are not at all the same as U.S. banks, and the context within which they operate is not at all the same as the context within which U.S. banks operate. Chinese capitalism is not at all the same as U.S. capitalism, and Chinese banks work totally differently from the way U.S. banks work. The only thing they have in common is the nomenclature: banks, money, loans, and so on. But these words mean something totally different in China, as we discussed in the section on Chinese banking and the economy. In any case, you *do* need a Chinese partner. However, the ostensible reason and the actual reason are somewhat different. While the ostensible reason is true, the real reason is this: China wants to learn from the foreign banks, and it's easier to learn from them if China, in effect, owns them through the structure of a joint venture.

One other important point here: I went to China thinking that it would be important for us to own more than the 20% that the law allowed a foreign bank to own. But I was wrong on both counts. No matter what the law said, if you pushed hard enough and if you had credible leverage (as in: "If I don't get more, I'm leaving"—of course, assuming they don't want you to leave), you could get more. In fact, we got 50%. But—guess what—it doesn't really matter what percentage you own. In the end, your JV is in China, the Chinese government rules China, and the CCP rules the Chinese government.

Station 6 ("You're all set, except one small thing . . ."): There's always one small thing. In our case, that one small thing was this: there was a law in China that said that if you're a foreign bank and you're a partner in a JV with a Chinese bank, that JV bank may not use Chinese currency for the first three years of its existence. Again, there's an ostensible reason, which is real enough; and there's an actual reason, which is even more important than the ostensible one because it's the *operative* one. Much like the ostensible reason in Station 5, the ostensible reason here is: China is very different from the United States, and therefore it is very risky for you because you don't understand it, and perhaps never will. Therefore, for the first three years or so, you may not use Chinese currency, which means you won't be able to do business and therefore you'll avoid getting yourself into trouble. It's for your own good, after all! And the real reason: We (the Chinese) want to learn from you, so we want you to spend the first three years teaching us so that as soon as you can actually do business, we (the Chinese) can immediately begin competing against you, using those aspects of your business model we like most.

Station 7 ("Don't worry about not being able to do business for the first three years. You can spend your time teaching us."): And indeed, during those first three years we were constantly under pressure to spend our time teaching others—the Bank of Beijing, a brand-new bank in Beijing's Z Park, China Merchants Bank, various SPDB branches around the country, the Bank of Hangzhou, and so on. Furthermore, knowing that we would not be able to do business if we couldn't use RMB, the Shanghai Municipal Government gave us a subsidy every year—not enough for us to show a profit, but enough to prevent us from entertaining the notion of just giving up and returning home.

Station 8 ("We are so happy that the three years are up and that you can now begin using Chinese currency. There's just one other little thing . . ."): At about the three-year mark, representatives of the Shanghai Municipal Government came to us to congratulate us and tell us how happy they were that the three years were almost up and that we could now begin using Chinese currency. But, of course, there was "just one other little thing." They admired our business model so much that they'd decided to open *a bank of their own*, that did the exact same thing. Would I mind spending some time with the management team of the new bank helping them better understand some aspects of our business model that had eluded them in the past, just to make sure they got it right? They asked me this without even blushing.

So, in summary, I went to China representing an American bank, filled with goodwill and optimism, intending to build a brand-new bank with a partner assigned to me by the CCP. By the time I moved back to the United States four years later, I felt *supremely exploited.* In addition, I now believe that the outcome—meaning how well our JV will do over time—is largely determined by the CCP, not so much by our own hard work (although that helps, I'm sure) and not by market forces. And finally, I'm somewhat jaded about how it will all come out in the end.

I believe that I was "guided" along the way by a secret team of 10 or 12 people who were in regular communication with each other, and who all appeared to be reasonably well-disposed toward both me and the bank I was representing.

And yet, although I feel shafted, so to speak, I'm not bitter. I like the people who comprised my secret team. In fact, I enjoyed the vast majority of the many people I met in China. The people were just fine, both the 7% in the Party and the 93% not in the Party. Overall, as I've mentioned, both Ruth and I feel that our four years in China were the most interesting and rewarding of our entire lives.

18.1 HOW WESTERN COMPANIES FAIL IN CHINA

I perceive three major themes in SVB's experience that explain why Western companies fail in China. Looking back through the book, they're pretty obvious, but since I was caught in the bear trap, I didn't see them. In short, China succeeds by:

1. **Deceit, manipulation, and leverage:** These approaches stem directly from both *The Art of War,* China's Bible for negotiation, and the nuanced understanding of *guanxi. The Art of War* recommends deceit and manipulation rather than outright confrontation as a strategy to win any "battle," whether it be military or economic competition. *Guanxi* emphasizes the importance of doing business with people whom you know and have leverage with. If that

leverage shifts, the balance of power shifts too and the relationship will immediately be rebalanced. You see this dynamic even in marriages—the sense of which partner is more important will shift depending on who earns more or needs more support.

2. **Engineering the human soul:** In a powerful and insightful essay, John Garnaut traced the influence of Stalin on Mao and then Xi.[1] Stalin's goal was to engineer the human soul, recreating citizens to be the perfect servants of the state. Stalin failed in this effort because he lacked absolute control of the populace—*samizdat* literature, underground projects, and fundamental human idealism and altruism were too powerful. But Xi has artificial intelligence at his disposal, along with his social credit system. How long can someone resist if they and their family become homeless, jobless, penniless, and barred from educational opportunities? Until the recent protests against the Zero COVID policy, I had thought Xi was well on his way to achieving his goal, especially given his recent elevation as "President for Life" surrounded by a politburo of yes-men.

3. **Through the looking glass:** There is a quality of reality distortion in dealing with China. First, the language is impenetrable, adding an inevitable layer of uncertainty in any interchange. Second, the basic cultural assumptions are fundamentally different between the United States and China, even with respect to business. That the duties and day-to-day involvement denoted by the titles "CEO" and "chairman" would be completely inverted is stunning. Both parties to the JV bank were completely delighted with what turned out to be a hellish misunderstanding that was *so fundamental that neither of us thought to check that our assumptions were shared.* Nor was this the only such entanglement: William misunderstood how company cars should be used; ostensible agreements disappear into thin air; counterparties with whom one has established a good working relationship get reassigned; rules are waived and new ones imposed. Reality is a concept

that gets redefined on a daily basis and the ground is forever shifting under one's feet.

As I reflected, I started wondering whether these three themes were cunningly used to exhaust the Western business leader. After discovering that a point you'd thought had been resolved comes out for renegotiation again, it's tempting to just give up in hopes of moving on. Don't. You won't move on and you will have lost *guanxi*.

I feel that we were enticed into the wide end of a funnel like pigs in a slaughterhouse and then guided, greased up, and shoved slowly down that funnel into the narrow end, the outcome of which was both predetermined and predictable.

I've come to believe that good people can become members of organizations that do not have virtuous goals. A malevolent organization can manipulate good people into doing things that betray their own personal value systems, and if that happens often enough, those same good individuals can slowly become inured to the malevolent nature of what they're doing in the context of the organization.

How does China transport an organization like the one I represented from the wide end of the funnel to the narrow end and then out the bottom, rendering it almost unrecognizable? At the organizational level, it depends largely on three mechanisms:

1. A confusing plethora of regulations and laws, applied selectively to achieve certain ends: The ends are determined by the Party leadership, and the selection and application of the laws and regulations are left to the secret team. The secret team is motivated by the desire for promotion, money, and power, coupled with a fear of ostracism and/or reprisal. In other words, be they tigers or flies (well-known or insignificant), none wants to become the victim of an anticorruption campaign.

2. A license for every activity and no activity without a license: The secret team, acting in accordance with the goals set for it by the Party leadership, will choose to either grant or deny licenses in a way that helps to ensure a result consistent with the leadership's intention. Thus, we were denied a license for the most critical element of our business model—lending to VC firms—because having to rent it from SPDB allowed them to control us.

3. More recently, the mandatory installation of a Party Committee: Since Xi came to power, every foreign and "private" company is required to have a Party Committee. To the extent that the secret team falls short or needs assistance, the Party Committee can provide a "belt and suspenders"-style backstop by issuing "recommendations" that the Chinese portion of the board insists on implementing.

As an aside, in discussion with a friend who's a partner in one of the Big Four U.S. accounting firms, I learned that since Xi has been in power, Party Committees have begun to have influence in the United States, not just in China. At this particular accounting firm (and I assume at the other big three as well), the Party Committee has stipulated the following: if an American partner is meeting with an American client to discuss the possibility of doing business in China, even if the meeting takes place on American soil, a member of the CCP must be in the room to help portray a positive view of China. This was shared with me on condition of anonymity.

You may wonder what the CCP is trying to accomplish. That question could be addressed on two different levels, that of the individual company and that of the world at large. I'm not sure I'm equipped to address the second, but I do have a theory regarding the first.

I think the answer was given to me openly and plainly during my visits to the Party School in Beijing. You may recall that at the conclusion of my speeches about our bank at the Party School, I always got the same enthusiastic response: "Your bank is terrific. We want one of our own." And when I pointed out that they already had one and it was ours (meaning that they already owned half of it—all the employees are PRC citizens, and all of the clients are PRC tech companies)—they always responded in the same way: "Yes, yes, we know, but we want one of *our own*."

If you were in that situation and you wanted one of your own, how would you go about it? I don't even have to tell you. The CCP has already written the playbook, and I've just described it to you in as much detail as I can convey.

But lest you think my experience is unique, let me describe what happened to Siemens Gamesa (Gamesa). Gamesa is a technology company founded in Spain in 1976. In 1994, it created a subsidiary focused on producing cutting-edge wind turbines. Sometime thereafter, it decided to enter China. By 2005, Gamesa held a third of the market there. Then the CCP introduced Notice 1204, requiring that 70% of the value of equipment used in Chinese windfarms must be manufactured by Chinese companies. Almost immediately, the relevant Chinese suppliers emerged. In time, the various Chinese suppliers banded together to create a company to compete against Gamesa. Now, Chinese companies control the bulk of the market, but Gamesa is unwilling to complain and claims it's happy even with 3% of the market. Industry observers allege that Gamesa is scared and scarred. In late 2022, after Gamesa suffered its third year of losses, Siemens Energy took full control of the unit, hoping to better address both cost and supply chain issues confronting the entire industry and component failures resulting from turbines that were rushed to market. The year before, the China division had signed an MoU to license its technology to a Chinese firm, even as worldwide competition from low-cost Chinese products was decimating the European wind turbine industry.[2]

So, why did I write this book and what did I want to accomplish by publishing it, other than just venting my spleen?

First, as much as I would like to withdraw, disengage, and lick my wounds, I don't believe that total disengagement is either possible or wise. I am sure that we could learn to live without importing so many of our consumer products from China. But, as we all know at this point, the issue is much more complicated than that glib statement would make it appear. Like it or not, the world has become much more interdependent than it was when I was born. Supply chains are extremely complex, and all countries, regardless of their political systems, are much more dependent on each other than has ever been true in the history of mankind. And, given the rapid advancements in our technological knowhow in the past 75 years, the ability of almost all countries to interfere in each other's affairs, coupled with the ever-present temptation to do so, has reached a point of no return. Finally, many of our largest and most threatening problems, such as environmental degradation and pandemic diseases, are inherently global in nature. They cannot be localized.

Sadly, there is no turning back. Total disengagement is impossible. We have no choice. Engage we must.

In short, the continued existence of a rules-based international order depends on a better relationship with China. Ironically (or, perhaps, not so ironically), this heightened level of dependence appears just as China is appearing to behave ever more truculently. The need for cooperation has never been greater, and China appears to be less willing to cooperate than ever before.

If anything, China appears to be going in the opposite direction. Instead of trying to mend fences, China is burning them down. Put succinctly, China is hinting at divorce and—worse yet—refusing marriage counseling.

It appears to me that the relationship between China and the United States is at another historic low point. When I compare our relationship today, under Xi (and Biden), it seems much worse than it did when we initially lived in China, under Hu (and the younger Bush). True, I would argue that the CCP's attitude toward the United States has always been gratuitously confrontational, and in that sense nothing has changed since 1949. But the attempt that China made under Deng, Jiang, and Hu to hide its animosity has all but disappeared under Xi. Just read any one of the speeches made by Wang Yi, foreign minister of the PRC, in the past couple of years. He sounds angry. Unmitigatedly angry. He leaves not even the smallest opening for rapprochement. He hates us. He wants *out* of the relationship.

Internally, the CCP has become more controlling than ever, I believe. Of course, the level of control possible today, using advanced technologies such as facial recognition, is much higher than ever in the past. Ironically, on a Saturday in March 2023, I was talking with friends in China on the phone. It was their Sunday noon, and they were in the process of leaving their apartment building to go out to lunch to celebrate their teenage son's birthday with their in-laws. When I got up on Sunday, I read my text messages as usual. Turns out, when my friends in China returned after lunch, their entire apartment building was in lockdown because a single case of COVID had emerged while they were out. They had to find somewhere else to stay. Since then, they have told me, when they awaken in the morning they never know if they'll be locked in, and when they return from work in the evening, they never know if they'll be locked out. As I write this, young people all over China are being arrested for protesting these circumstances and the Zero COVID policy has been relaxed, but the fate of millions of unvaccinated Chinese is uncertain. I wonder what happens next with the efforts to engineer the souls of 1.4 billion people.

Under Xi, China's foreign service has assumed a new tone, called "wolf warrior" diplomacy as I described earlier. The open and deeply antagonistic attitude announced in my dinner with the Chinese general counsel is probably consistent with the CCP's internal stance since 1949. But until recently, the diplomatic corps would have at least tried to appear civil. One of the most interesting books I have read in the past couple of years is *China's Civilian Army: The Making of Wolf Warrior Diplomacy* by Peter

Martin.[3] Martin describes the origin of China's foreign service in 1949. Set up by Zhou Enlai, it has been guided by the same set of rules for 73 years now, including, in effect: "Never admit to a mistake, always blame the other country." Deceit, manipulation, and leverage in play.

Also in 2021, another youngish scholar, Rush Doshi, wrote *The Long Game*, an insightful book about the CCP.[4] Doshi underscores the Party's lifelong commitment to Leninism: the CCP has always sought to control *all* aspects of life in China. Doshi cites Xi's echoes of Mao ("Party, government, military, civilian and academic, north, south, east, west, and center, the Party leads everything"[5]), asserting that Xi has the same worldview. Xi is no exception to Mao, and he is doing his best to engineer the human soul.

Shortly before Doshi's book appeared, another youngish scholar/ journalist/government official, John Garnaut, spoke at a seminar of Australian government officials, entitled "Engineers of the Soul: What Australia Needs to Know About Ideology in Xi Jinping's China" (subsequently reprinted in Bill Bishop's newsletter, *Sinocism*, on January 16, 2019). Here, he describes Mao's devotion to Stalin's philosophy as expressed in his *Short Course on the History of the Bolsheviks*, published in 1938. In this book, Stalin talks about himself and the Party as "engineers of the human soul." Mao saw himself in the same light, and—to all appearances—so does Xi.

David Barboza's weekly online magazine, *The Wire China*, recently published an interview with Teng Biao, a well-known human rights attorney, formerly in China and currently living in exile in the United States, with no prospects of ever being allowed to return to China. According to Teng Biao:

> The Chinese government has no tolerance for troublemakers. My passport was confiscated. My legal license was revoked, I was banned from teaching and eventually fired by Peking University. I was frequently put under house arrest. I was kidnapped and detained three times by the secret police. I was physically and

mentally tortured. My family members were targeted. My wife and daughters were banned from leaving China after I arrived in the United States in 2014. They were used by the Chinese government as hostages to punish and silence me.[6]

Many protestors, journalists, and other critics of the CCP have suffered a similar fate under Xi.

So I wonder. Xi exhibits a desire for more and more control over people within China, and his attitude toward the West, and in particular the United States, seems to be one of extreme hatred. He accepts blame for nothing that has gone wrong in our relationship; he blames us for absolutely everything and refuses to even consider rapprochement. Are his ambitions limited to within China? We don't know.

But we do know this. Contrary to international norms, he claims large portions of the South China Sea and the East China Sea; he seeks to manage and, in some cases, to own ports in countries around the world; he initiates border disputes with India and is taking over (by eminent domain) parts of Bhutan (no country on Earth is as unassuming and harmless as Bhutan). We know that the "United Front"—CCP-controlled or -influenced networks—is very active in many Western countries, including the United States, and seeks to influence many of our politicians and government officials.[7] What are Xi's intentions, ultimately? What will satisfy his ambition? For more on this topic, consider reading *Hidden Hand: Exposing How the Chinese Communist Party Is Reshaping the World* by Clive Hamilton and Mareike Ohlberg, published in 2021.[8]

In my view, the current situation is potentially threatening, and I am worried about whether we will be able to address it effectively. The older generation of China experts are, in my view, compromised. They fell in love with China, and like most people who are in love, they tend to see the object of their affection as they wished it were, not as it truly is. Now that Xi has decided to make it painfully obvious that China never was in love with us, and certainly has never intended to "grow up to be just like us," the Old China Hands are acting like jilted lovers. The business community, on the other hand, has for decades been enthusiastic about China, seeing there a vast market in which they could make billions of dollars. That enthusiasm itself exposes us to risk—as Lenin supposedly said, "The capitalists will sell us the rope we use to hang them."

Some Western companies have succeeded in China, but only to the extent that the CCP has allowed them to, and others have failed, precisely because the CCP has ordained that result. But they are disinclined to admit it, partially out of pride and partially because they fear retribution. The CCP has trained us to self-censor and done so in a way all the more powerful because it is vague. As described back in 2002 by Princeton sinologist Perry Link, "the Chinese government's censorial authority . . . has resembled not so much a man-eating tiger or fire-snorting dragon as a giant anaconda coiled in an overhead chandelier. Normally the great snake doesn't move. It doesn't have to."[9]

And yet, there are other factors as well. As Alex Joske (also part of the newer generation) points out in his recent book, *Spies and Lies*,[10] the CCP has done a brilliant job of propagating the myth of "China's Peaceful Rise." This phrase refers to the idea that China's rise does not have to be viewed as threatening. China will be happy to rise peacefully. However, the whole concept is predicated on our letting the Chinese government have its own way, with Taiwan, Tibet, the Uyghurs, the South China Sea and the East China Sea, and so forth. In other words, if we let China have its way about everything, it will rise peacefully; but if we don't . . . the onus is on us. If China's rise is not peaceful, it is our fault, and ours alone, not China's.

Another element that Joske mentions is "The Access Culture." All of us in the West want to succeed in China. We want to "crack the code." Knowing this, the CCP uses our ambitions to its own advantage. It goes like this: "Ken, you are one of the smartest Westerners we have ever encountered. And your bank is the most important bank in the world. More important than Goldman Sachs or Morgan Stanley. We want you here. We'll pave the way for you."

Most of us fall for that. We don't realize that a parallel meeting is taking place down the hall with Goldman, and another with Morgan Stanley, in which *each* is being told the same thing, following the time-honored strategy of deceit, manipulation, and leverage. Soon the CCP is offering each of us access to high-level people who can help us accomplish our goals. These are important people. So important that other Westerners don't ever get access to them. But we do. Because we are special. These important people like us because we see things the way they want us to, or at least we pretend we do. The problem is that the victims of this kind of manipulation often find themselves getting in deeper and deeper over time. Soon they are accepting special bonuses and sometimes other favors as well. At the very least, we learn too late that we've fallen down the rabbit hole into Looking Glass land, where things aren't as we thought.

Eventually they reach a point of no return. And then another very human mechanism kicks in: cognitive dissonance, which we all learned in Psychology 101. When you find yourself in turmoil with two conflicting circumstances, you rationalize one of them to bring it in line with the other one, to eliminate the dissonance. In other words, you begin to believe in the ultimate goodness of the CCP.

And soon, you are a China apologist.

While all of this is happening, America itself is slowly deteriorating. Our two parties can't get along well enough to govern. Extremists are attempting to dismantle our democratic institutions. Our infrastructure is crumbling from inattention. We are degrading the environment. And we're seemingly powerless to prevent mass shootings. Instead, we're all arming up in a futile attempt for protection, ironically, from ourselves.

This is why I want to publish this book. I want businesspeople to know in advance what is likely to happen when they take their company to China. And, in addition, I want them to understand what's likely to happen within the context of the larger situation—namely the relationship between the United States and China, between democracy and Leninism.

Friends and others have warned me that I may face repercussions. I understand. I want to be on the right side of history, regardless. I wouldn't want to live in a world dominated by the Chinese Communist Party. To envision what that might be like, I turn to an article in *The Atlantic* written on October 5, 2020, by Michael Schuman, a journalist who covers Asia for a number of well-respected periodicals, and who is thought by many to be somewhat of a "China expert." The article in question is called "What Happens When China Leads the World."[11] He predicted that:

- China will not be a pacifist power.
- China will insist on its own world order.
- China will export its values.
- China only tolerates relationships it can dominate.

My guess is that Schuman is right. And I'm certain that I don't want to live in that world, and I don't want my grandchildren to, either. Or you and yours.

NOTES

1. John Garnaut, "Engineers of the Soul: What Australia Needs to Know About Ideology in Xi Jinping's China" (subsequently reprinted in Bill Bishop's newsletter, *Sinocism*, on January 16, 2019).
2. Keith Bradsher, "To Conquer Wind Power, China Writes the Rules," *New York Times*, December 14, 2010, https://www.nytimes.com/2010/12/15/business/global/15chinawind.html; Thomas Gualtieri and Wilfried Eckl-Dorna, "Siemens Energy's Troubled Wind Takeover Haunts Green Push," *Bloomberg*, December 19, 2022, https://www.bloomberg.com/news/articles/2022-12-19/siemens-energy-will-fully-own-gamesa-with-a-tough-task-to-get-to-profitability; and Siemens Gamesa, "Forging Ahead in China: Siemens Gamesa Signs MoU to License 11 MW Direct Drive Offshore Technology to China Energy United Power." Press release, November 5, 2021, https://www.siemensgamesa.com/en-int/newsroom/2021/11/siemens-gamesa-mou-license-11-mw-technology-china.

3. Peter Martin, *China's Civilian Army: The Making of Wolf Warrior Diplomacy* (Oxford: Oxford University Press, 2021).
4. Rush Doshi, *The Long Game: China's Grand Strategy to Displace American Order* (Oxford: Oxford University Press, 2021).
5. Xi's speech opening Congress in 2017, cited in Christian Shepherd, "China's Neo-Maoists Welcome Xi's New Era, But Say He Is Not the New Mao," Reuters, October 27, 2017, https://www.reuters.com/article/us-china-congress-maoists/chinas-neo-maoists-welcome-xis-new-era-but-say-he-is-not-the-new-mao-idUSKBN1CX005.
6. Scott Savitt, "Teng Biao on Fascism with CCP Characteristics," *The Wire China*, November 13, 2022, https://www.thewirechina.com/2022/11/13/teng-biao-on-fascism-with-ccp-characteristics.
7. Bethany Allen, in her stunning book *Beijing Rules* (New York: Harper Collins, 2023), gives many examples of the extent to which the United Front is active in the United States.
8. Clive Hamilton and Mareike Ohlberg, *Hidden Hand: Exposing How the Chinese Communist Party Is Reshaping the World* (London: Oneworld, 2021).
9. Perry Link, "China: The Anaconda in the Chandelier," *The New York Review*, April 11, 2022, https://www.nybooks.com/articles/2002/04/11/china-the-anaconda-in-the-chandelier.
10. Alex Joske, *Spies and Lies: How China's Greatest Covert Operations Fooled the World* (Berkeley: Hardie Grant, 2022).
11. Michael Schuman, "What Happens When China Leads the World," *The Atlantic*, October 5, 2020, https://www.theatlantic.com/international/archive/2020/10/what-kind-superpower-will-china-be/616580.

PART V

FOUR YEARS OF LESSONS, CONDENSED

In the previous account, I've described a host of lessons in narrative form. For ease of reference, I've distilled them below.

1. Unlike in America, **in China there's no substantive difference between state owned and privately owned companies.** If it's large enough to have an impact, the government will notice and will seek to control it, either through regulation or actual ownership.

2. Unlike in the West, **Party, government, and big business are fundamentally the same thing.** This is very difficult for Westerners to internalize. We've all spent a lifetime thinking about these three things as distinctly different.

3. **Chinese thinking is primarily informed by** *The Art of War*, Buddhism, Confucianism, Daoism, and Stalin's version of Marxism. *The Art of War* teaches how to win without fighting, but rather, through deceit and manipulation. Confucianism is important, but second to *The Art of War*. And China is, beyond a shadow of a doubt, a Leninist state.

4. **The guiding principle in the West is rule of law; the guiding principle in China is leverage.**

5. **China is a *quid-pro-quo* society.** You must give to get. My advice: Give only a little, and as little as possible until you get—then give a little more. Baby steps are safer than giant steps, to ensure an even exchange. The Chinese government won't keep promises unless it is to their advantage. Therefore, make sure that only a small amount of time elapses between what you do and what they're supposed to do in return.

6. **Stay close to the government.** Ingratiate yourself by helping government officials achieve their KPIs, thus helping them get promoted.

7. **If you succeed in China, it's because the government allowed you to.** The government can ignore you, prevent you from succeeding, or cause you to succeed. They will ignore you if you're small and have nothing (IP or a business model, for example) that they want. They'll prevent you from succeeding if you don't help them. You will succeed if you do help them. Therefore, if you want to succeed, you will provide a conference speaker when they ask you to, you will contribute to a discussion of best practices when they ask you to, and you will attend a gathering if they want you to.

8. The West is driven by Wall Street's demands for quarterly return on equity (ROE). **China is driven by strategy . . . and corruption.**

9. **The Chinese are concerned with *guanxi*, learning, growth, ownership, prestige, leverage, power, and winning *in the long run*.**

10. **The Chinese don't distinguish between debt and equity.** Nor are they focused on ROE.

11. **"Face" is of utmost importance.** This goes beyond not embarrassing others, but focuses on showing them respect in public settings. When Trump criticized China in public, he forced Xi to dig in his heels and refuse to cooperate. In other words, Trump prevented Xi from doing what Trump wanted Xi to do.

12. **In China, people are generally fine with breaking the rules, as long as they're not caught.** But they are terrified of being caught because, above all, they fear the public shame that comes with discovery and punishment by the Party.

13. **The Chinese people place a higher value on stability than on freedom of speech.** In the months leading up to the Tiananmen Square debacle in June of 1989, Deng several times said things that foreshadowed his decision to use force to remove the protesters. For example, in March: "China cannot afford any disorder. . . We have to send out a signal that China will tolerate no disturbances." And a month before, in February: "The need for stability overwhelms everything else."

14. **State capitalism is dominant;** free markets are not—even though they may be preferable. State capitalism is not capitalism. Everything is controlled by the state.

15. **Virtually all Chinese, no matter how open-minded or progressive, are imbued with certain basic beliefs:**
    - Theirs is and always has been the most advanced civilization on Earth.
    - The Western world has been picking on them since 1839.
    - The West wants to hold China down.
    - China has never invaded another country or attempted to influence the internal affairs of another country.
    - Foreigners are barbarians.

- Ninety-five percent of the people in China are pure-bred Chinese.
- Even though between 20 and 40 million people perished under Mao, he was fundamentally an excellent ruler.
- They are Chinese and are therefore different and always will be. That "essence" is immutable.
- Foreigners are not as culturally sophisticated as the Chinese, no matter where they come from.
- The state *must* come before the individual, but not necessarily the family.

16. **It makes no difference what percentage of ownership Westerners negotiate** in their joint ventures in China. In the end, China rules.

17. **Laws and regulations play a different role in China than in the United States.** Whereas ours are relatively non-negotiable, theirs appear to be negotiable. The government can decide to apply rules to one company and not to another, to reward one that's been helpful or punish those that haven't been. For example: Our bank desperately needs the custodial license to bank start-ups. We have applied for it many times, to no avail. For a while we thought it was because we are a "foreign bank" (although we are 50 percent owned by the Chinese government, all of our employees are Chinese, and all of our customers are Chinese). But recently, the government granted that same license to Citibank. Turns out Citi had done something that the Chinese government very much appreciated. My current interpretation is that the license was a reward. In addition, the government currently appears to be very helpful to Goldman Sachs, because (I believe) Goldman can help China in ways that China wants and that other banks can't.

18. **The Chinese innovate as well as Westerners, although not in the same way.** Their process is different (less planning, more trial

and error); and their goal is different—move around *any* obstacle, usually regulatory; whereas in the West, innovation is more associated with scientific invention. Make no mistake, however, the Chinese *can* also innovate in terms of scientific invention . . . and just as well as Westerners.

19. **China is obsessed with hierarchy.** If two seemingly equal entities in the same category are together, they'll spend all their time trying to figure out which of the two is taller, richer, more powerful, and so on. The Chinese find it difficult to conceive of separate but equal. That's why they don't believe that China can rise unless the U.S. falls.

20. **The building blocks of Chinese society are warring families and the CCP.** The warring families often set aside their differences in deference to the CCP, but these families control the country and thus enrich themselves. The overall mechanism works as follows: The CCP grants business concessions to families, which get 70 percent of the profits, while the CCP gets 30 percent.[1]

21. **Nepotism and conflict of interest in China are not crimes.** They are foundational.

22. **The most important leaders of the Chinese Communist Party (Mao and Xi) have had global aspirations.** The focus is on continuous revolution within the Party to avoid reversion to bourgeois decadence. Only through global aspirations, enhanced by fear and propaganda, can the Party reach that goal. This is the essence of dialectical thinking as practiced by Marx, and both Mao and Xi are Marxists. The future holds more Maos and Xis.

23. **The CCP wants its members to prioritize their allegiance to it over their allegiance to family, morality, and independent thought.**

24. **The Chinese believe that the basis for nationhood is common "racial" ancestry.** This philosophy has numerous ramifications

that Westerners might not anticipate. It means that all Chinese, Korean, Japanese, and so on, should be part of the same country, and that nobody else should be part of that country. Presumably all Caucasians should band together in a single country as well.

25. **The dynasties have always benefited from having an outside enemy.** The people's fear of the outside enemy increases their allegiance to the emperor. Dynasties have usually ended by rebellion from within. In only a few cases have dynasties ended because of an attack by the outside enemy. The two most notable of these are the invasion of the Mongols (ending the Song dynasty in 1271) and the invasion of the Manchus (ending the Ming dynasty in 1636). Since "the Liberation" in 1949, the U.S. has been that outside enemy.

26. China is fond of talking about "friends," but what it's really seeking in the community of nations is respect; should that fail, **China will settle for fear.**

27. **The most important determinants of success in China are *guanxi* and leverage.** The most successful foreign companies in China have worked hard to develop *guanxi* with government officials, and to create and constantly extend their leverage.

28. **The aspect of China that is least recognized and understood by Westerners is the role of the Party.** In 2017, Xi quoted Mao in an address to the 19th Party Congress, saying, "'Government, military, society, and schools, north, south, east and west—the Party rules everything."[2] It's true.

29. **China has no intention of becoming "like us."** That was an illusion propagated by well-meaning Old China Hands. China is not trying to create a "level playing field." It is trying to create one that is steep enough to give themselves the "home court advantage" and level enough that we can attempt to convince ourselves that appeasement is the best course of action.

30. **China is skilled at integrating an "invading" company so well that it becomes, in many ways, a Chinese company,** serving China to a greater extent than its country of origin. After all, remember that China integrated the Mongol invaders in the thirteenth century and the Manchu invaders in the seventeenth. In some ways, Apple might be said to be gravitating in that direction.

31. **We must engage with China; decoupling won't work.** We must confront China on issues that are important to us (such as market access and a level playing field), but we should do so behind closed doors. We should praise China in public for its many accomplishments. We should work together with China to solve common (global) problems (global warming, global terrorism, nuclear proliferation, and so on). Above all, we should follow the mantra of Teddy Roosevelt: "Speak softly and carry a big stick."

32. **We cannot change China.** For those who doubt this, I would suggest that you spend some time reading the famous sinologist Jonathan Spence, especially his book *To Change China*. For hundreds of years, Spence asserts, Westerners have tried to change China, to no avail. China has changed *them*. Only China can change China.

NOTES

1. An example of this is detailed in Desmond Shum's *Red Roulette: An Insider's Story of Wealth, Power, Corruption, and Vengeance in Today's China* (New York: Scribner, 2021).
2. Clive Hamilton and Mareike Ohlberg, *Hidden Hand: Exposing How the Chinese Communist Party Is Reshaping the World* (London: Oneworld Publications, 2021): 15.

EPILOGUE

And then on March 9, 2023, the Federal Deposit Insurance Corporation (FDIC) took over SVB after a run on the bank. Although I had been long relieved of my managerial duties there, it was sad and upsetting. I thought that, given the connection between SVB and the subject matter of this book, readers might want to know any insights I might have into that event. What follows is a compilation of third-party accounts, rather than any sort of "inside scoop" as I truly am past the stage of having any.[1]

As Ernest Hemingway described personal bankruptcy, SVB's decline happened "first slowly and then all at once."[2] According to Nobel laureate Douglas Diamond of the University of Chicago's Booth School of Business, banks are inherently fragile[3]—and SVB more than many. I explain in this book that SVB's model involved banking start-ups, which raise a lot of money and deposit it with us, gradually drawing down the principal until they raise another round. Thus, SVB always had a very liquid model and wrestled with the challenge of finding places to invest the capital that would generate reasonable returns while keeping it accessible to our depositors.

The VC boom of the early 2020s and then its reversal set up a "perfect storm" of sorts. Government stimulus programs and low interest rates meant there was a lot of money seeking any non-zero return. A torrent of capital poured into venture capital start-ups, which deposited it in SVB. SVB invested it in bonds and long-term Treasury bills, which offered both safety and interest rates that were slightly above the prevailing dismal levels. This was an unprotected bet that interest rates would stay low, which proved to be incorrect.

SVB thus found itself with cash tied up in long-dated vehicles, mostly bonds, when its clients needed it in the short run as interest rates rose and VC financing tightened. To meet these demands, SVB had to sell the bonds at a loss, which shook client confidence. The venture capitalist community, which SVB had backed for its 40 years, sounded the alarm and sent its companies to withdraw their capital. In 48 hours, $42 billion, about 20% of the bank's assets, was withdrawn. As always happens, the value of the securities in which SVB held this money dropped precipitously just when it needed access to them. Ironically, the bank banking innovation was done in by the oldest bank killer in history: the rumor-fueled run.[4]

The nature of SVB's client base further augmented the fears. At the time, the FDIC insured deposits up to $250,000 held by individuals in any one bank. Only 7% of SVB's clients qualified for that insurance. The start-ups that held larger balances were, obviously, counting on them for payroll and the specter of a widespread crash throughout that community made government intervention more critical.

This introduced the second and final nail in SVB's coffin. The regulators had always regarded SVB as a sort of bumblebee, a creature that wasn't designed to fly (or be a bank) but managed to do so anyway. They never completely believed in SVB's reliance on an equity infusion or sale of IP as its belt-and-suspenders means of repayment. Perhaps cynically, I see their willingness to let the bank collapse as the regulators' final thumb of the nose to SVB and its innovative model.

At 9 a.m. Pacific time on Friday, March 10, the SEC halted trading in SVB's stock after a 63% pre-market plunge.[5] The California Department of Financial Protection and Innovation closed the bank and appointed the FDIC its receiver. The FDIC and the U.S. government hoped someone would buy the entire entity, as happened with HSBC's acquisition of SVB's UK branch for £1 ($1.22).[6] In the United States, though, the complexity of SVB's model and, possibly, the competitive strategies of other financial entities worked against this goal. On Monday, March 13, SVB reopened as a so-called "bridge bank," the Deposit Insurance National Bank of Santa Clara (DINB) and news reports suggested that several large private equity funds, including Blackstone, Apollo, and KKR, were looking to purchase elements of SVB's portfolio. By later in the week, calmer heads were wondering how to plug the hole in the VC ecosystem left by SVB's demise. On March 27, First Citizens Bank announced it had agreed to purchase the entirety of SVB.

Did SVB's management team make mistakes? Absolutely. Were they asleep at the risk management switch? Completely. But I'm convinced that a gaping hole in the VC ecosystem, in part of its own making, will soon emerge. No one ever had to think of the VC industry without SVB because SVB has always been there. No more.

Tim Hardin, the head of credit for the JV bank at its start, and I were in touch on Friday, March 10, as the news unfolded. Our overwhelming emotion was sadness. It was a great organization, doing important work in the innovation community. And now it's not there and even its acquirer doesn't have SVB's commitment to and experience in that role. In addition, I fear an acceleration of the trend where Chinese companies acquire U.S. innovation for pennies on the dollar because the United States is too shortsighted to fund the truly moonshot companies. I described this with A123 Batteries, MiaSolé, and Icon Aircraft in this book. I had hoped the list would stop there.

And what happened to SSVB? Oddly enough, nothing, at least nothing yet, three months after SVB failed and as I write this. It's sort of in stasis.

The CCP hasn't announced it would take over the other half and no one else has stepped forward to do so. I suspect that eventually the CCP will absorb the half of the JV they don't own. Perhaps they'll fold it into Huarui Bank, the all-Chinese technology-lending bank that uses the JV's model. As it stands, though, SSVB is no longer a joint venture. It's all theirs. The CCP owns not just the bed, but the blankets, the frame, the pillows, the mattress, and the dust ruffle as well.

NOTES

1. To keep dates, times, and figures straight, I consulted a number of external sources for this piece. Much of the detail comes from Dan Primack's piece, "The Week That Killed Silicon Valley Bank," *Axios*, March 14, 2023, https://www.axios.com/2023/03/14/week-that-killed-silicon-valley-bank.
2. Ernest Hemingway, *The Sun Also Rises* (New York: Scribner, 1926).
3. Shawn Tully, "The Economist Who Won the Nobel for His Work on Bank Runs Breaks Down SVB's Collapse—and His Fears over What's Next," *Fortune*, March 15, 2023, https://fortune.com/2023/03/15/economist-douglas-diamond-silicon-valley-bank-collapse.
4. Diamond, the Nobel laureate, has also said that it's irrational to start a run on a bank. Once a run has started, though, it's irrational not to participate in it.
5. PYMNTS, "SVB Financial Group Share Trading Halted After 68% Premarket Plunge," March 10, 2023, https://www.pymnts.com/news/banking/2023/svb-financial-group-share-trading-halted-after-68percent-premarket-plunge.
6. HSBC, "HSBC Acquires Silicon Valley Bank UK Limited." Press release, March 13, 2023. Exchange rate from Yahoo!Finance, accessed March 10, 2023.

REFERENCES

I've read well over 100 books on China over the past 10 years. I consider these the most informative:

The Art of War by Sun Tzu is more important than any other book I've ever read in terms of understanding China.

The Beautiful Country and the Middle Kingdom: America and China, 1776 to the Present by John Pomfret offers a history of the relationship between China and the United States, beginning with the first encounter in 1784 and taking the reader up to the present.

Beijing Rules: How China Weaponized Its Economy to Confront the World by Bethany Allen provides a broader context for my specific experience with SVB.

China 1945: Mao's Revolution and America's Fateful Choice by Richard Bernstein helps us understand how the United States and Mao went their separate ways (my favorite book).

China's Civilian Army: The Making of Wolf Warrior Diplomacy by Peter Martin describes China's rise to its current status as a global superpower through its diplomatic corps.

Chinese Commercial Negotiating Style by Lucian Pye is a classic, still relevant today.

"Engineers of the Soul: What Australia Needs to Know About Ideology in Xi Jinping's China" by John Garnaut is a speech given for the Asian Strategic and Economic Seminar Series in 2017 that spectacularly recounts the Stalinist roots of Xi Jinping's thought. It was reprinted under the same title in *Sinocism*, January 17, 2019. https://sinocism.com/p/engineers-of-the-soul-ideology-in. It's worth the challenge of finding it.

Hidden Hand: Exposing How the Chinese Communist Party Is Reshaping the World by Clive Hamilton and Mareike Ohlberg describes how the CCP is seeking to expand its influence around the world.

The Long Game: China's Grand Strategy to Displace American Order by Rush Doshi underscores the Party's long-term commitment to Leninism.

One Billion Customers: Lessons from the Front Lines of Doing Business in China by James L. McGregor (no relation to Richard) is a guide to doing business in China.

Red Roulette: An Insider's Story of Wealth, Power, Corruption, and Vengeance in Today's China by Desmond Shum describes the stunning rise of Shum and his wife to the highest levels of wealth and power in China and their subsequent fall from favor.

The Party: The Secret World of China's Communist Rulers by Richard McGregor describes how the CCP works.

The Political Thought of Xi Jinping by Olivia Cheung and Steve Tsang, published in 2024, gives important context for Xi's words and contrasts them against the policy implementations.

The Private Life of Chairman Mao by Li Zhisui (one of Mao's personal physicians) purports to tell the "real" story of Mao.

A Short History of Chinese Philosophy by Fung Yu-Lan serves as an "intellectual history" of China. Warning: tough to get through.

The Story of China: The Epic History of a World Power from the Middle Kingdom to Mao and the China Dream by Michael Wood was published in 2020 and grounds China's rise in its history.

The Third Revolution: Xi Jinping and the New Chinese State by Elizabeth C. Economy explores China's progress and the tensions it confronts since Xi Jinping's accession to power.

To Change China: Western Advisors in China by Jonathan Spence examines a collection of Westerners from missionaries and teachers to soldiers and engineers who sought to change China and failed.

Wild Swans: Three Daughters of China by Jung Chang, a Chinese history of the past century through the eyes of three generations of the same family (not only useful, but really fun to read).

BIBLIOGRAPHY

Allen, Bethany. *Beijing Rules: How China Weaponized Its Economy to Confront the World*. Harper Collins, 2023.

Areddy, James T. "China's Culture of Secrecy Brands Research as Spying." *Wall Street Journal*, December 1, 2010. https://www.wsj.com/articles/SB100014 24052748704584804575644470575141314.

AVCA. "The 2002 Guide to Venture Capital in Asia." *Asian Venture Capital Journal*, October 2001.

Barboza, David. "Billions in Hidden Riches for Family of Chinese Leader." *New York Times*, October 25, 2012. https://www.nytimes.com/2012/10/26/business/global/family-of-wen-jiabao-holds-a-hidden-fortune-in-china.html.

BBC News. "China Frees Wife of UK GSK Investigator Peter Humphrey," June 11, 2015. https://www.bbc.com/news/world-asia-china-33090372.

BBC News. "China's Two-Child policy: Single Mothers Left Out." November 2, 2015. https://www.bbc.com/news/world-asia-china-34695899.

BBC News. "Tibet Profile." *BBC News*, August 25, 2023. https://www.bbc.com/news/world-asia-pacific-16689779.

BBC News from Elsewhere, "China: Wealthy 'Drink Human Breast Milk,'" BBC News, July 3, 2013. https://www.bbc.com/news/blogs-news-from-elsewhere-23161765.

BBC Newsround. "Hong Kong Protests: What Is the 'Umbrella Movement'?" September 28, 2019. https://www.bbc.co.uk/newsround/49862757.

Buckley, Chris. "China Takes Aim at Western Ideas." *New York Times*, August 19, 2013. https://www.nytimes.com/2013/08/20/world/asia/chinas-new-leadership-takes-hard-line-in-secret-memo.html.

Bradsher, Keith. "To Conquer Wind Power, China Writes the Rules." *New York Times,* December 14, 2010. https://www.nytimes.com/2010/12/15/business/global/15chinawind.html.

Canales, Katie, and Aaron Mok. "China's 'Social Credit' System Ranks Citizens and Punishes Them with Throttled Internet Speeds and Flight Bans if the Communist Party Deems Them Untrustworthy." *Business Insider,* updated November 28, 2022. https://www.businessinsider.com/china-social-credit-system-punishments-and-rewards-explained-2018-4.

China Copyright and Media. "Planning Outline for the Construction of a Social Credit System (2014–2020)." April 25, 2015. https://chinacopyrightandmedia.wordpress.com/2014/06/14/planning-outline-for-the-construction-of-a-social-credit-system-2014-2020.

Cleveland Clinic Health Library, "Stockholm Syndrome," February 14, 2022. https://my.clevelandclinic.org/health/diseases/22387-stockholm-syndrome.

Clissold, Tim. *Chinese Rules: Mao's Dog, Deng's Cat, and Five Timeless Lessons from the Front Lines in China.* Harper Collins, 2014.

Clissold, Tim. *Mr. China.* Harper Collins, 2006.

Collins, Jim. *Good to Great.* Harper Business, 2011.

Doshi, Rush. *The Long Game: China's Grand Strategy to Displace American Order.* Oxford University Press, 2021.

Dunn, Michael J. *American Wheels, Chinese Roads: The Story of General Motors in China.* John Wiley & Sons, 2011.

Dunne, Michael. "The Sudden Death of Detroit in China." The Dunne Insights Newsletter, March 12, 2024. https://newsletter.dunneinsights.com/p/the-sudden-death-of-detroit-in-china?utm_campaign=email-half-post&r=ck&utm_source=substack&utm_medium=email.

Dunne, Michael. "Why Everyone Except Tesla Should be Terrified of BYD." The Dunne Insights Newsletter, January 2, 2024. https://www.businessinsider.com/china-auto-sales-automakers-ford-gm-making-losing-market-share-2023-4.

Erchi, Zhang, Qu Yunxu, and Guo Yingzhe. "In Depth: How SoftBank Wrested Back Control of Arm China." *Nikkei Asia,* July 5, 2022. https://asia.nikkei.com/Spotlight/Caixin/In-Depth-How-SoftBank-wrested-back-control-of-Arm-China.

Fan, Jiayang. "Can China Stop Organ Trafficking?" *The New Yorker,* January 10, 2014. https://www.newyorker.com/news/news-desk/can-china-stop-organ-trafficking.

Federal Reserve Bank of New York. "Quarterly Trends for Consolidated U.S. Banking Organizations First Quarter 2022." https://www.newyorkfed.org/medialibrary/media/research/banking_research/quarterlytrends2022q1.pdf?la=en.

Finnegan, Conor. "U.S. Forces Five Chinese Media Outlets to Register as Foreign Missions." *ABC News*, February 18, 2020. https://abcnews.go.com/Politics/us-forces-chinese-media-outlets-register-foreign-missions/story?id=69054342.

Fish, Isaac Stone. "Hu Jintao on China Losing the Culture Wars." *Foreign Policy*, January 3, 2012. https://foreignpolicy.com/2012/01/03/hu-jintao-on-china-losing-the-culture-wars.

Frank, Annaliese. "Battery Maker 123 Systems to Lay off 42 as It Steps Back from Manufacturing Work in Michigan." *Plastics News*, August 8, 2019. https://www.plasticsnews.com/news/battery-maker-a123-systems-lay-42-it-steps-back-manufacturing-work-michigan.

Freymann, Eyck. "Climate Changers." *The Wire China*, December 18, 2022. https://www.thewirechina.com/2022/12/18/u-s-china-geoengineering.

Gao, Charlotte. "The CCP Vows to 'Lead Everything' Once Again." *The Diplomat*, October 28, 2017. https://thediplomat.com/2017/10/the-ccp-vows-to-lead-everything-once-again.

Gara, Antoine. "JPMorgan Agrees to Pay $264 Million Fine for 'Sons and Daughters' Hiring Program in China." *Forbes*, November 17, 2016. https://www.forbes.com/sites/antoinegara/2016/11/17/jpmorgan-agrees-to-pay-264-million-fine-for-sons-and-daughters-hiring-program-in-china/?sh=1459ee8e5688.

Garnaut, John. "Engineers of the Soul: What Australia Needs to Know About Ideology in Xi Jinping's China." Speech to Asian Strategic and Economic Seminar Series, 2017. Reprinted under the same title in *Sinocism*, January 17, 2019. https://sinocism.com/p/engineers-of-the-soul-ideology-in.

Gracie, Carrie. "Investigator Peter Humphrey Warns Over GSK China Ordeal." *BBC News*, July 10, 2015. https://www.bbc.com/news/world-asia-china-33490446.

Gualtieri, Thomas and Wilfried Eckl-Dorna. "Siemens Energy's Troubled Wind Takeover Haunts Green Push." *Bloomberg*, December 19, 2022. https://www.bloomberg.com/news/articles/2022-12-19/siemens-energy-will-fully-own-gamesa-with-a-tough-task-to-get-to-profitability.

Halpern, Neil A., and Kay See Tan. "United States Resource Availability for COVID-19." Society of Critical Care Medicine blog, March 13, 2020. https://www.sccm.org/Blog/March-2020/United-States-Resource-Availability-for-COVID-19.

Hamilton, Clive, and Mareike Ohlberg. *Hidden Hand: Exposing How the Chinese Communist Party Is Reshaping the World*. Oneworld, 2021.

Hardymon, Felda, and Ann Leamon. "Silicon Valley Bank." *Harvard Business School Case No. 800–332*. Harvard Business Press, 2000.

Hardymon, Felda, Josh Lerner, and Ann Leamon. "Chengwei Ventures and the hdt* Investment." *Harvard Business School Case No. 802–089.* Harvard Business Press, 2002.

Harvard Public Affairs & Communications. "'Baggage' claimed Gish Jen." *The Harvard Gazette,* April 4, 2017. https://news.harvard.edu/gazette/story/2017/04/gish-jen-at-harvard.

Headley, Tyler Y. and Cole Tanigawa-Lau. "Why Did Hong Kong's Umbrella Movement Fail?" *The Diplomat,* April 6, 2016. https://thediplomat.com/2016/04/why-did-hong-kongs-umbrella-movement-fail.

Hemingway, Ernest. *The Sun Also Rises.* Scribner, 1926.

Henckaerts, Jean-Marie, ed. The International Status of Taiwan in the New World Order: Legal and Political Considerations. Kluwer Law International, 1996.

Hsiao-hwa, Hsia. "'Hurting the feelings of the Chinese people' could be punished by jail time." *Radio Free Asia,* September 7, 2023. https://www.rfa.org/english/news/china/china-hurt-feelings-09072023123314.html.

HSBC. "HSBC Acquires Silicon Valley Bank UK Limited." HSBC.com press release, March 13, 2023.

Humphrey, Peter. "'I Was Locked in a Steel Cage': Peter Humphrey on His Life Inside a Chinese Prison." *Financial Times,* February 15, 2018. https://www.ft.com/content/db8b9e36-1119-11e8-940e-08320fc2a277.

Jibiki, Koya. "Rejection of China's 'Nine-Dash Line' Spreads from Asia to Europe." *Nikkei Asia,* December 1, 2020. https://asia.nikkei.com/Politics/International-relations/South-China-Sea/Rejection-of-China-s-nine-dash-line-spreads-from-Asia-to-Europe.

Jin, Keyu. *The New China Playbook: Beyond Socialism and Capitalism.* Viking, 2023.

Jordan, George Racey. Freestanding quotation. *The Commonwealth: Official Journal of the Commonwealth Club of California* 31, no. 44 (1955).

Joske, Alex. *Spies and Lies: How China's Greatest Covert Operations Fooled the World.* Hardie Grant, 2022.

Kaufman, Alison A. "Testimony before the U.S.-China Economic and Security Review Commission Hearing: The 'Century of Humiliation' and China's National Narratives." *USCC,* March 10, 2011. https://www.uscc.gov/sites/default/files/3.10.11Kaufman.pdf.

Kobie, Nicole. "The Complicated Truth About China's Social Credit System." *Wired,* July 6, 2019. https://www.wired.co.uk/article/china-social-credit-system-explained.

Lerner, Josh, and Ann Leamon. *Venture Capital, Private Equity, and the Financing of Entrepreneurship,* 2nd ed. John Wiley & Sons, 2023.

Lescaze, Lee. "Peking [sic] and Hanoi Teach Each Other a Lesson." *Washington Post*, March 18, 1979. https://www.washingtonpostz.com/archive/opinions/1979/03/18/peking-and-hanoi-teach-each-other-a-lesson/bac0c6fb-8917-4c48-ac34-ab48d4084963.

Li, Jianglin. *Tibet in Agony: Lhasa 1959*. Translated by Susan Wilf. Harvard University Press, 2016.

Lin, Hsiao-ting. *Tibet and Nationalist China's Frontier: Intrigues and Ethnopolitics, 1928–49*. University of British Columbia Press, 2011.

Link, Perry. "A Fallen Artist in Mao's China." *New York Review of Books*, December 7, 2023.

Link, Perry. "China: The Anaconda in the Chandelier." *The New York Review*, April 11, 2022. https://www.nybooks.com/articles/2002/04/11/china-the-anaconda-in-the-chandelier.

Magistad, Mary Kay. "China's 'Leftover Women', Unmarried at 27." *BBC News*, February 21, 2013. https://www.bbc.com/news/magazine-21320560?zephr-modal-register.

Martin, Peter. *China's Civilian Army: The Making of Wolf Warrior Diplomacy*. Oxford University Press, 2021.

McDonell, Stephen. "China allows three children in major policy shift," *BBC*, May 31, 2021. https://www.bbc.com/news/world-asia-china-57303592.

McGregor, James L. *One Billion Customers*. Free Press, 2005.

O, Meemi. "Comparing China's Largest Banks." *Investor Insights Asia*, December 7, 2023. https://www.investorinsights.asia/post/comparing-china-s-largest-banks.

O'Keeffe, Kate. "U.S., Chinese Investors Feud over Startup Icon Aircraft During National Security Review of Deal." *Wall Street Journal*, February 8, 2022. https://www.wsj.com/articles/u-s-chinese-investors-feud-over-startup-icon-aircraft-during-national-security-review-of-deal-11644340248.

Ong, Ryan. "The Third Plenum of the 18th Chinese Communist Party Congress: A Primer." *China Business Review*, September 16, 2013. https://www.chinabusinessreview.com/the-third-plenum-of-the-18th-chinese-communist-party-congress-a-primer.

Phua, Jason et al. "Critical Care Bed Capacity in Asian Countries and Regions." *Critical Care Medicine*, 48, no. 5 (January 2020): 654–62.

Popper, Nathaniel. "Silicon Valley Bank Strengthens Its Roots." *New York Times*, April 1, 2015. https://www.nytimes.com/2015/04/02/business/dealbook/silicon-valley-bank-strengthens-its-roots.html.

Primack, Dan. "The Week That Killed Silicon Valley Bank." *Axios.com*, March 14, 2023. https://www.axios.com/2023/03/14/week-that-killed-silicon-valley-bank.

Pye, Lucian. "Chinese Commercial Negotiating Style." Rand Corporation, January 1982, R-2837-AF. https://www.rand.org/content/dam/rand/pubs/reports/2007/R2837.pdf.

PYMNTS.com. "SVB Financial Group Share Trading Halted After 68% Premarket Plunge." March 10, 2023. https://www.pymnts.com/news/banking/2023/svb-financial-group-share-trading-halted-after-68percent-premarket-plunge.

Qiu, Benjamin. "China Prepares to Crack Down on 'Hurt Feelings.'" *Wall Steet Journal*, September 25, 2023.

Ramzy, Austin. "9 Hong Kong Democracy Advocates Convicted for Role in 2014 Protests." *New York Times*, April 8, 2019. https://www.nytimes.com/2019/04/08/world/asia/hong-kong-umbrella-revolution-occupy-central.html.

Ren, Shuli. "China Forgets Some Women Who Hold Up the Sky." *Bloomberg*, August 2, 2021. https://www.bloomberg.com/opinion/articles/2021-08-02/how-china-s-three-child-policy-affects-generations-of-independent-women.

Rose, Steve. "The Eight Hundred: How China's Blockbusters Became a New Political Battleground." *The Guardian*, September 18, 2020. https://www.theguardian.com/film/2020/sep/18/the-eight-hundred-how-chinas-blockbusters-became-a-new-political-battleground.

Russell, Bertrand. *The Problem of China*. George Allen & Unwin, 1922.

Savitt, Scott. "Teng Biao on Fascism with CCP Characteristics." *The Wire China*, November 13, 2022. https://www.thewirechina.com/2022/11/13/teng-biao-on-fascism-with-ccp-characteristics.

Schoenhals, Michael. "Elite Information in China." *Problems in Communism*, 34, September–October 1985.

Schuman, Michael. "What Happens When China Leads the World." *The Atlantic*, October 2020. https://www.theatlantic.com/international/archive/2020/10/what-kind-superpower-will-china-be/616580.

Shanghai Pudong Development Bank. "SPDB HK Bank Opens, Marking a Substantial Step towards the Bank's Go-global Strategy." Press release, June 8, 2011. https://www.acnnewswire.com/press-release/english/6747/spdb-hk-branch-opens,-marking-a-substantial-step-towards-the-bank's-go-global-strategy.

Shepherd, Christian. "China's Neo-Maoists Welcome Xi's New Era, But Say He Is Not the New Mao." Reuters, October 27, 2017. https://www.reuters.com/article/us-china-congress-maoists/chinas-neo-maoists-welcome-xis-new-era-but-say-he-is-not-the-new-mao-idUSKBN1CX005.

Shum, Desmond. *Red Roulette: An Insider's Story of Wealth, Power, Corruption, and Vengeance in Today's China*. Scribner, 2021.

Siemens Gamesa. "Forging Ahead in China: Siemens Gamesa Signs MoU to License 11 MW Direct Drive Offshore Technology to China Energy United Power." Press release, November 2021. https://www.siemensgamesa.com/en-int/newsroom/2021/11/siemens-gamesa-mou-license-11-mw-technology-china.

Silicon Valley Bank. "Facts at a Glance." https://www.svb.com/newsroom/facts-at-a-glance.

Silicon Valley Bank. "Silicon Valley Bank Leads Delegation of Venture Capitalists on Educational and Networking Trip to Beijing and Shanghai." Press release, June 14, 2004. https://www.svb.com/news/company-news/silicon-valley-bank-leads-delegation-of-venture-capitalists-on-educational-and-networking-trip-to-beijing-and-shanghai.

Song, Yongyi. "Chronology of Mass Killings During the Chinese Cultural Revolution (1966–1976)." *SciencesPo*, August 25, 2011. https://www.sciencespo.fr/mass-violence-war-massacre-resistance/en/document/chronology-mass-killings-during-chinese-cultural-revolution-1966-1976.html.

Spence, Jonathan. *The Search for Modern China*, 3rd Edition. W.W. Norton, 2012.

Starr, S. Frederick. *Xinjiang: China's Muslim Borderland*. M.E. Sharpe, 2004.

Statistics Times, "Gender Ratio," United Nations World Population Prospects 2019, January 16, 2021. https://statisticstimes.com/demographics/country/china-sex-ratio.php.

Stent, James. *China's Banking Transformation: The Untold Story*. Oxford University Press, 2017.

The Committee of 100. "About Us." n.d. https://www.committee100.org/mission-history.

The Economist. "An Obsession with Control Is Making China Weaker but More Dangerous." October 13, 2022. https://www.economist.com/leaders/2022/10/13/an-obsession-with-control-is-making-china-weaker-but-more-dangerous.

The Economist. "Why Sequoia Capital Is Sawing Off Its Chinese Branch." June 8, 2023. https://www.economist.com/business/2023/06/08/why-sequoia-capital-is-sawing-off-its-chinese-branch.

The Economist. "Will We Ever Know How Many People Died of Covid-19 in China?" *The Economist*, February 2, 2023. https://www.economist.com/china/2023/02/02/will-we-ever-know-how-many-people-died-of-covid-19-in-china.

The National Bureau of Asian Research. "Update to The Report of the Commission on the Theft of American Intellectual Property." February 2017. http://ipcommission.org/report/IP_Commission_Report_Update_2017.pdf.

Tobon, John F., "Chinese Communist Party Members Move Money in Plain Sight, Threatening Security." *Defense Forum*, March 24, 2022. https://ipdefenseforum.com/2022/03/black-market-foreign-exchange.

Tully, Shawn. "The Economist Who Won the Nobel for His Work on Bank Runs Breaks Down SVB's Collapse—and His Fears Over What's Next." *Fortune*, March 15, 2023. https://fortune.com/2023/03/15/economist-douglas-diamond-silicon-valley-bank-collapse/?queryly=related_article.

U.S. Securities and Exchange Commission. "Holding Foreign Companies Accountable Act." n.d. 2007. https://www.sec.gov/hfcaa (accessed February 10, 2022).

Walter, Carl E., and Fraser J. T. Howie. *Red Capitalism: The Fragile Financial Foundation of China's Extraordinary Rise*. John Wiley & Sons, 2011.

Wang, Fei-Ling. "China's Household Registration (*Hukou*) System: Discrimination and Reform." Statement to the Congressional Executive Commission on China, September 2, 2005. https://www.cecc.gov/sites/chinacommission.house.gov/files/documents/roundtables/2005/CECC%20Roundtable%20Testimony%20-%20Fei-Ling%20Wang%20-%209.2.05.pdf.

Wei, Lingling. "Jack Ma Makes Ant Offer to Placate Chinese Regulators." *Wall Street Journal*, December 20, 2020. https://www.wsj.com/articles/jack-ma-makes-ant-offer-to-placate-chinese-regulators-11608479629.

Wong, Edward. "U.S. Diplomat's Same-Sex Marriage Causes Stir in China." *New York Times*, May 3, 2016. https://www.nytimes.com/2016/05/04/world/asia/us-diplomats-same-sex-marriage-causes-stir-in-china.html.

Wong, Young-tsu. *China's Conquest of Taiwan in the Seventeenth Century: Victory at Full Moon*. Springer, 2007.

Yuan, Li. "Why China Turned Against Jack Ma," *New York Times*, January 20, 2021. https://www.nytimes.com/2020/12/24/technology/china-jack-ma-alibaba.html.

Zhang, Cici. "What's Baijiu, and Where Does Its Unique Flavor Come From?" *Chemical and Engineering News*, August 7, 2018. https://cen.acs.org/environment/food-science/What-s-baijiu-and-where-does-its-unique-flavor-come-from/96/i33.

INDEX

Page numbers followed by *f* indicate figures

China Investment Corporation
(CIC), 22, 221
China Merchants Bank, 303
China's Civilian Army (Martin),
253–4, 310–11
China Securities Regulatory
Commission (CSRC), 108
Chinese Americans, 283
Chinese Banking Regulatory
Commission
(CBRC), 45–6, 107
Chinese Commercial Negotiating Style
(Pye), 251–2
Chinese Communist Party (CCP)
19th Party Congress of, 322
and banking joint ventures, 27
Central Committee of, 237, 242
and Chinese economy, 227–37
and contracts, 249–50
and control, 147, 207, 258–60
18th Party Congress of, 272
expectations of, from foreign
companies, 12, 242–3,
248–51, 307–8
fear of retaliation from, xxiii
founding of, 226
and history, 260–2
as Mafia, 38, 113–14
membership in, xxvi, 115–16, 150
nationalistic propaganda of,
xxiv, 239–40, 243, 262,
269–70, 280–1
and Nationalist Party, 20

and negotiation, 251–7
non-Chinese people in, 146
others' opinions about the, 40, 70,
75, 77, 113–14, 237–9, 241
Third Plenary of, 242
and Umbrella Revolution, 212–13
see also Organization Department;
Party Committees
Chinese Exclusion Act, 270
Chinese language, 31–2, 206, 213
Chinese medicine, 130–1
Chinese Venture Capital
Association, 9
the chops, 36, 210
Cigna Insurance, 118
Cisco Systems, 4
Citibank, 320
Citizen's Bank, 232
collateral, 5–6, 178
Collins, Jim, 165
Commission on the Theft of American
Intellectual Property, 95
Committee of 100, 283
Committee on Foreign Investment in
the United States (CFIUS), 210
company culture, 164–8
compensation, 26, 93, 112, 231
compliance, 61, 157, 178
compliments, 26, 180
conflicts of interest, 257
Confucius (Confucianism), 258–9, 318
contracts, 72, 179, 249–50
copying, 94